The Structural Insulated Panel Association is a non-profit trade association that supports all segments of the structural insulated panel industry, including design professionals, supplie[...] [...]ers who build with SIPs. SIPA was fo[...] [...]e and acceptance of SIPs through a[...] [...]ovides an industry forum for promoti[...] [...], education, research, and quality assurance.

By offering a unified industry-wide approach, SIPA reaches innovative builders and educated consumers interested in adding high performance building technologies to their homes. Structural insulated panels provide a high performance building envelope capable of significantly reducing the amount of energy needed to heat and cool a home. It is SIPA's mission to promote the widespread adoption of SIPs integrated with other high performance technologies that advance the world towards a sustainable future.

Quality control is also one of SIPA's core values. SIPA strives to establish quality standards for SIP manufacturing and installation that ensure high performance, energy savings and durability. Through an active builder outreach program, SIPA supplies resources and conducts educational seminars that enable builders to deliver the best possible SIP installation. Member manufacturers adhere to consistent quality control guidelines as well.

To further ensure quality SIP production and installation, as well as to streamline the design process, SIPA has undertaken several initiatives to develop generic product standards for structural insulated panels. These initiatives include ASTM standard development, ANSI standard development and prescriptive requirements listed in the International Residential Code.

Builders and design professionals make up a large component of SIPA's membership. Membership presents the opportunity for key industry groups to interact and explore the possibilities of the emerging technology of SIPs. Members of SIPA also have access to a wide range of educational resources, marketing materials and qualified leads to help them grow their own SIP business. To learn more about the Structural Insulated Panel Association, visit **www.sips.org**.

The History of SIPs

The concept of a structural insulated panel began in 1935 at the Forest Products Laboratory (FPL) in Madison, Wisconsin. FPL engineers speculated that plywood and hardboard sheathing could take a portion of the structural load in wall applications. Their prototype structural insulated panels (SIPs) were constructed using framing members within the panel combined with structural sheathing and insulation.

The panels were used to construct test homes that were continually monitored for over thirty years, then disassembled and reexamined. During this time, FPL engineers continued to experiment with new designs and materials.

Famed architect Frank Lloyd Wright used structural insulated panels in some of his affordable Usonian houses built throughout the 1930's and 1940's. SIPs took a major leap in technology when one of Wright's students, Alden B. Dow, son of the founder of The Dow Chemical Company, created the first foam core SIP in 1952.

By the 1960's rigid foam insulation products became readily available, resulting in the production of structural insulated panels as we know them today. The Structural Insulated Panel Association was founded in 1990 to provide support and visibility for those manufacturing and building with this emerging building technology.

In the 1990's SIPs saw the development of advanced computer aided manufacturing (CAM) technology. Using these systems, computerized architectural drawings (CAD drawings) can be converted to allow automated cutting machines to fabricate SIPs to the specific design of a building. CAD to CAM technology has streamlined the SIP manufacturing process, bringing further labor savings to builders.

Today, SIPs offer a high tech solution for residential and low rise nonresidential buildings. Advances in computer aided design and manufacturing allow SIPs to be produced with amazing accuracy to deliver flat, straight, and true walls. SIPs are now made with a variety of structural skin materials, including oriented strand board (OSB), treated plywood, fiber-cement board, and metal. SIPs are available in thicknesses ranging from 4-inch to 12 inches, depending on climate conditions and structural requirements. Many manufacturers also offer curved SIPs for curved roof applications. The design capabilities, exceptional strength and energy saving insulation make SIPs a twenty-first century building material for high performance buildings.

Builder's Guide

to Structural Insulated Panels (SIPs)

for all Climates

Written by: **Joseph Lstiburek, Ph.D. , P. Eng.**
Building Science Corporation
3 Lan Drive, Suite 102
Westford, MA 01886
(978) 589-5100
buildingscience.com

Comments and constructive criticism of this publication are welcomed by the author and all such comments will be considered in future revisions. Please contact the author directly at joe@buildingscience.com

This guide was significantly enhanced by the thoughtful review of the following individuals whose input is greatly appreciated:

Alex Lukachko, Building Science Corporation
Armin Rudd, Building Science Corporation
Bill Wachtler, Structural Insulated Panel
    Association (SIPA)
Chris Schwind, Structural Insulated Panel
    Association (SIPA)
Jim DeStefano, DeStefano Associates

SIPA Technical Committee Members
Todd Bergstrom, AFM R-Control
Tom Savoy, Premier Building Systems
Joe Pasma, Premier Building Systems
Jim Whalen, PFB Corporation
Frank Baker, PFB Corporation
Bo Foard, Foard Panel, Inc.
Paul Malko, Foard Panel, Inc.
Jack Armstrong, BASF–The Chemical Company
Dave Gauthier, Winter Panel Corp.
Neal Wilkinson, Better Building Products, LLC
Damian Pataluna, FischerSIPS, LLC

Book Design and Illustrations by: Stephanie Finegan
Building Science Corporation
Cover Photos: SIPA

About the Author

Joseph Lstiburek is principal of Building Science Corporation in Westford, Massachusetts. He is an ASHRAE Fellow and has been a licensed professional engineer since 1982.

He received an undergraduate degree in Mechanical Engineering from the University of Toronto, a master's degree in Civil Engineering from the University of Toronto and a doctorate in Building Science from the University of Toronto.

He used to be a contractor—and then he crossed to the "dark side."

When we build, let us think that we build forever. Let it not be for present delight nor for present use alone. Let it be such work as our descendants will thank us for; and let us think, as we lay stone on stone, that a time is to come when those stones will be held sacred because our hands have touched them, and that people will say, as they look upon the labor and wrought substance of them, "See! This our parents did for us."

John Ruskin

Contents

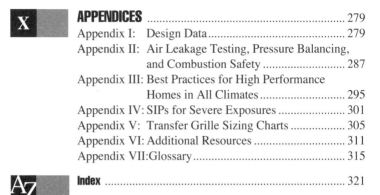

Firmness Commodity Delight

"These are properly designed, when due regard is had to the country and climate in which they are erected. For the method of building which is suited to Egypt would be very improper in Spain, and that in use in Pontus would be absurd at Rome: so in other parts of the world a style suitable to one climate, would be very unsuitable to another: for one part of the world is under the sun's course, another is distant from it, and another, between the two is temperate."

Marcus Vitruvius Pollio
Ten Books on Architecture
27 B.C.

About this Guide

Buildings should be suited to their environment. It is irrational to expect to construct the same manner of building in Montreal, Memphis, Mojave and Miami. It's cold in Montreal, it's humid in Memphis, it's hot and dry in Mojave and it's hot and wet in Miami. And that's just the outside environment. It is equally irrational to expect to construct the same manner of building to enclose a warehouse, a house or a health club with a swimming pool. The interior environment also clearly matters.

We have accepted that design and construction must be responsive to varying seismic regions, wind loads and snow loads. We also consider soil conditions and frost depth, orientation and solar radiation. Yet we typically ignore the variances in temperature, humidity, rain of the exterior climate and the variances in the interior climate.

Building enclosures and mechanical systems should be designed for a specific hygro-thermal region, rain exposure zone and interior climate class in addition to the previously mentioned external environmental loads. The following hygro-thermal regions, rain exposure zones and interior climate classes influence design:

Hygro-Thermal Regions (see pages xiv and xv)
    Arctic/subarctic
    Very cold
    Cold
    Marine
    Mixed-humid
    Hot-humid
    Hot-dry/Mixed-dry

Rain Exposure Zones (see page 70)
    Extreme (above 60 inches/1500 mm annual precipitation)
    High (40 to 60 inches/1000 mm to 1500 mm annual precipitation)
    Moderate (20 to 40 inches/500 mm to 1000 mm annual precipitation)
    Low (less than 20 inches/500 mm annual precipitation)

Interior Climate Classes
  I   Warehouses, Garages, Storage Rooms
      Temperature moderated
      Vapor pressure uncontrolled
      Air pressure uncontrolled

II Houses, Apartments, Condominiums, Offices, Schools
    Temperature controlled
    Vapor pressure moderated
    Air pressure moderated

III Hospitals, Museums, Swimming Pool Enclosures and
    Computer Facilities
    Temperature controlled
    Vapor pressure controlled
    Air pressure controlled

This builder's guide addresses construction in all hygro-thermal regions with extreme to low rain exposure zones for building enclosures and mechanical systems suited for a Class II interior climate — that is an interior climate that is temperature controlled, vapor pressure moderated and air pressure moderated. In other words houses, apartments, condominiums, townhouses, and manufactured housing. Information on specialized enclosures such as pools, spas and ski lodges in extreme climates can be found in the Appendices.

Hygro-Thermal Regions for this Guide

This guide contains information that is applicable to all climates. Figure A, Hygro-Thermal Regions, illustrates the eight major climate zones in North America used to distinguish the range of applicability of this guide. Each climate zone specified is broad and general for simplicity. The climate zones are generally based on Herbertson's Thermal Regions, a modified Koppen classification (see Goode's World Atlas, 19th Edition, Rand McNally & Company, New York, NY, 1990), the ASHRAE definition of warm humid climates (see ASHRAE Fundamentals, ASHRAE, Atlanta, GA, 1997), the International Energy Conservation Code (IECC) Climate Zones, and average annual precipitation obtained from the U.S. Department of Agriculture. For a specific climate zone, designers and builders should consider weather records, local experience, and the micro-climate around a building. Elevation, incident solar radiation, nearby water and wetlands, vegetation, and undergrowth can all affect the micro-climate.

Although this guide provides general recommendations with applicability based on Figure A, local experience and local building codes should also be considered. Where a conflict between local code and regulatory requirements and the recommendations in this guide occur, authorities having jurisdiction should be consulted or the local code and regulatory requirements should govern.

Precise specification of materials and products is not typically provided on the illustrations or in the text to provide maximum flexibility. It is the responsibility of the designer, builder, supplier and manufacturer to determine specific material compatibility and appropriateness of use. For example, there are a wide range of performance and cost issues dealing with sealants, adhesives, tapes and gaskets. Hot weather or cold weather construction and oily, damp or dusty surfaces affect performance along with substrate compatibility issues. Tapes must be matched to substrates. Similarly, sealants and adhesives must be matched to materials and joint geometry. In hot-humid and hot-dry climates, intense solar exposure typically results in damage to materials from ultraviolet radiation. Paints, sealants and coatings have greatly reduced service lives. Roofing materials and wood products are particularly sensitive.

Generally, several different tapes, sealants, adhesives or gaskets can be found to provide satisfactory performance when installed in the locations illustrated in this guide. Premium tapes, sealants, adhesives or gaskets typically (but not always) out perform budget tapes, sealants, adhesives or gaskets. It is always advisable to obtain samples and test compatibility and performance on actual material substrates prior to construction and over an extended period of time.

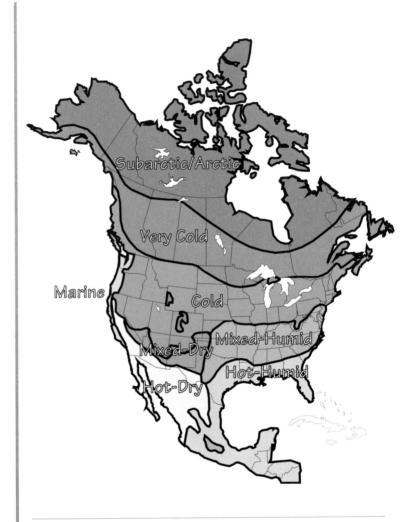

Figure A
Hygro-Thermal Regions
  • Based on Herbertson's Thermal Regions, a modified Koppen Classification, the
    ASHRAE definition of hot-humid climates, the International Energy Conservation
    Code (IECC) Climate Zones, and average annual precipitation from the U.S.
    Department of Agriculture and Environment Canada

1   Celsius: 7,000 heating degree days (18°C basis)
2   Celsius: 5,000 heating degree days (18°C basis)
3   Celsius: 3,000 heating degree days (18°C basis)
4   Celsius: 5,000 heating degree days (18°C basis)
5   Celsius: 3,000 heating degree days (18°C basis)

Legend

Subarctic/Arctic

A subarctic and arctic climate is defined as a region with approximately 12,600 heating degree days (65°F basis)[1] or greater

Very Cold

A very cold climate is defined as a region with approximately 9,000 heating degree days (65°F basis)[2] or greater and less than approximately 12,600 heating degree days (65°F basis)

Cold

A cold climate is defined as a region with approximately 5,400 heating degree days (65°F basis)[3] or greater and less than approximately 9,000 heating degree days (65°F basis)[4]

Mixed-Humid

A mixed-humid climate is defined as a region that receives more than 20 inches (50 cm) of annual precipitation, has approximately 5,400 heating degree days (65°F basis)[5] or less, and where the monthly average outdoor temperature drops below 45°F (7°C) during the winter months

Marine

A marine climate meets all of the following criteria:
- A mean temperature of the coldest month between 27°F (-3°C) and 65°F (18°C)
- A warmest month mean of less than 72°F (22°C)
- At least four months with mean temperatures over 50°F (10°C)
- A dry season in summer. The month with the heaviest precipitation in the cold season has at least three times as much precipitation as the month with the least precipitation in the rest of the year. The cold season is October through March in the Northern Hemisphere and April through September in the Southern Hemisphere.

Hot-Humid

A hot-humid climate is defined as a region that receives more than 20 inches (50 cm) of annual precipitation and where one or both of the following occur:*
- a 67°F (19.5°C) or higher wet bulb temperature for 3,000 or more hours during the warmest six consecutive months of the year; or

- a 73°F (23°C) or higher wet bulb temperature for 1,500 or more hours during the warmest six consecutive months of the year.

* These last two criteria are identical to those used in the ASHRAE definition of warm-humid climates and are very closely aligned with a region where monthly average outdoor temperature remains above 45°F (7°C) throughout the year.

Mixed-Dry

A mixed-dry climate is defined as a region that receives less than 20 inches (50 cm) of annual precipitation, has approximately 5,400 heating degree days (65°F basis) or less, and where the average monthly outdoor temperature drops below 45°F (7°C) during the winter months

Hot-Dry

A hot-dry climate is defined as a region that receives less than 20 inches (50 cm) of annual precipitation and where the monthly average outdoor temperature remains above 45°F (7° C) throughout the year

Approach

Reducing a builder's number one headache: warranty and callback expenses, should be considered a "payback" concept. Reducing warranty and callback expenses often involves increasing initial construction costs. The good news to the builder is that the up front cost to the builder results in subsequent cost savings also to the builder. It is logical to pay a little more up front to prevent warranty and callback expenses, rather than a great deal more down the road to deal with warranty and callback expenses.

Building energy-efficient homes can also be considered a "payback" concept. Energy-efficient construction usually involves upgrading materials or equipment to increase the energy efficiency of a home. These changes typically add to the initial cost of a home. Economically, the increased cost is often justified to the home owner based on subsequent cost savings from reduced energy bills. This is also a "pay more up front" and get savings "in the long term" approach. Unfortunately, for the builder, the up front cost is to the builder, but the subsequent cost savings are to the home owner. Builders have to pass on the up front costs to the home owner resulting in a more expensive home. Not all home owners recognize the long term savings from this approach and typically object to the higher up front costs.

The payback concept is not the only approach to reducing warranty and callback expenses or the only approach to energy-efficient construction. There are "break points" where the cost of the warranty and callback reduction strategies as well as the energy-efficient features are balanced by the reductions of other construction costs. These "break points" involve construction strategies or levels of energy efficiency that allow a specific component of a building to be downsized or deleted. For example, construction costs can be increased by changes and improvements to the building enclosure that reduce warranty and callback expenses as well as reduce heat gain and heat loss. The improved building enclosure performance allows the mechanical equipment to be downsized. The initial construction cost increases are offset by the reduced costs associated with the downsized mechanical system.

Electrical service has increased over the past couple of decades as power consumption has gone up. Residential electrical service has gone from 60 amp to 100 amp to 200 amp and beyond. As enclosure efficiency increases this trend can be reversed.

The construction cost savings that occur from applying a systems engineering approach to warranty and callback reduction, and energy conservation, are typically able to pay for the increased costs associated with "healthy housing" and resource efficiency. The end result becomes a home that is healthier, safer, more comfortable, durable and affordable, with no increased cost to the builder or home buyer.

This builder's guide addresses both warranty and callback expenses as well as energy-efficient construction using Structural Insulated Panels (SIPs). Strategies are presented to reduce paint and trim problems, dust marking of carpets and comfort complaints.

Introduction

This guide was developed specifically for Structural Insulated Panel (SIP) buildings. A SIP building has to meet the same requirements that all buildings meet. Hence these "building" requirements need to be understood. What will become obvious as these requirements are explored, is that SIP buildings meet many of these requirements more easily than typically constructed buildings.

The basic requirement for buildings is to create an indoor environment different from the outdoors. In this regard, buildings are environmental separators. They allow the regulation of temperature, air movement, humidity, rain, snow, light, dust, odors, noise, vibrations, insects and vermin. They must accomplish this in a safe, healthy and durable manner.

In the past, the design and construction of buildings had been based on building practices developed through an evolutionary process of trial and error. Since the end of the Second World War, the technology of construction has become exceedingly complex and there have been major developments in materials, products and systems. The evolutionary process of trial and error is no longer adequate.

Specialization and an abundance of specialists have been the consequences of the complexity of current construction. These specialists have tended to focus on their own disciplines. The list of specialists involved in house construction can be endless, from the financial consultant and interior designer to the soils engineer, truss designer, lighting consultant and environmental advisor. However, all of these disciplines are interrelated and have an effect on the durability and performance of a building.

Building design and construction have become fragmented as a consequence of the increasing specialization and sheer quantity of available information. Prior to the post-war building boom, the architectural profession and the "master builder" provided the understanding of the construction process. Architects and master builders were the generalists who knew all aspects of the construction process; they were the original "building scientists." Architects and master builders applied knowledge of traditional materials combined with aesthetic judgment to create magnificent and effective buildings. Tradition and past experience assisted in improving the understanding of a slowly evolving construction process. Architects and master builders provided the "systems view"; tradition and past experience provided a "system model."

During the post-war building boom, the emphasis on educating architects shifted to aesthetics and design theory relating to aesthetics and away from the fundamental aspects of construction and an understanding of materials, assemblies, building systems and subsystems. For builders, the focus became finance, land development and marketing. Accountants became kings. As in the case of architects, builders began to lose their understanding of the fundamental aspects of construction. Tradition and past experience remained dominant, but fundamental understanding waned.

At the same time, service conditions changed as well as materials. Slow, evolutionary changes in the construction process gave way to rapid changes. Buildings became more heavily insulated, building enclosures became tighter, forced air heating and cooling systems were introduced, countless new construction materials were introduced, and the post-war consumer revolution resulted in a plethora of interior surface finishes, furnishings and consumer amenities. Larger and more sophisticated kitchens and more and larger bathrooms became the norm. Rooflines became more complex, and overhangs became narrower or non-existent. Lifestyles changed resulting in more time spent within conditioned spaces and occupant comfort needs became preeminent. However, the construction process remained based on tradition.

As architects and builders focused more on aesthetics and finance and less on the construction process, gaps in the process began to be filled by specialists. Some specialists such as subcontractors have extensive training and experience in putting the pieces together efficiently. As a consequence, we typically get buildings constructed on time and on budget. However, the understanding of performance and predictability has become lost, so, although buildings are constructed on time and on budget, they often do not work.

The current process remains based on tradition and past experience without understanding. Tradition has a great weakness in that it deals only with a way of doing something but not with an understanding of why the traditional methods work.

In order to impose rationality on the current fragmented design/build process, a systems view and a system model are necessary. A systems view of buildings is necessary to provide predictability and understanding.

Changes in Construction

In the last fifty years there have been three important changes to the way we build homes:

- the introduction of thermal insulation
- development of tighter building enclosures
- the advent of forced air heating and cooling systems

Each of these changes has made homes more comfortable, but has also made the same houses less durable and more unpredictable in terms of performance.

Thermal Insulation

Thermal insulation was added to wall cavities and ceilings to keep the heat in the home during the winter, keep it out in the summer and make the home more comfortable. Wall cavities and attics became colder because the insulation did its job. As a result, two things happened; the walls got wetter because as they got colder the relative humidities went up and therefore so did moisture contents, and the ability of these assemblies to dry when they get wet from either interior or exterior sources was reduced because there was less energy available to dry them. How do you dry a material? You heat it. No heat, no drying. The addition of thermal insulation increased the "wetting potential" of the building enclosures while at the same time it reduced their "drying potential."

Tighter Building Enclosures and New Materials

Homes built today are much tighter than the homes of yesterday. This is particularly true for SIP building enclosures. SIP components are "straighter," "flatter" and more "true" than typical building components. The tolerances for SIP construction are more precise. The joints are fewer and "smaller." And there is more: we use prefabricated windows instead of site glazing; we put more caulk, glue and sealants on our houses than ever before; and, we can buy material that actually sticks and holds. The results are fewer holes and a lower air change. The lower the air change, the less the dilution of interior pollutants such as moisture (from people, soil and appliances), formaldehyde (from particle board, fiberglass insulation, furniture and kitchen and bathroom cabinets), volatile organic compounds (from carpets, paints, cleaners and adhesives), radon (from basements, slabs, crawlspaces and water supplies) and carbon dioxide (from people).

This trend to lower air change occurred simultaneously with the introduction of hundreds of thousands of new chemical compounds, materials and products which were developed to satisfy the growing consumer demand for household goods and furnishings. Interior pollutant sources have increased while the dilution of these pollutants has decreased. As a result, indoor air pollutant concentrations have increased.

Additionally, chimneys don't work well in tight homes. In tight homes, other exhaust fans compete with chimneys and flues for available air. The chimneys and flues typically lose in the competition for available air, resulting in spillage of combustion products, and backdrafting of furnaces and fireplaces.

As air change goes down, interior moisture levels rise causing condensation problems on windows where the surface is cold, mold on walls, dust mites in carpets and decay in wall cavities and attic spaces even in traditionally forgiving climates such as hot-dry and mixed-dry climates. Even though interior moisture levels are rising, builders continue to install central humidifiers rather than installing dilution ventilation or dehumidification and neglect to warm potential condensing surfaces such as window frames and glazing by installing thermally broken frames and insulating glass.

Traditional chimneys in many new homes have been replaced with power vented, sealed combustion furnaces. Many new homes have no chimneys or flues and rely on heat pumps or electric heating. Traditional chimneys ("active chimneys") acted as exhaust fans. They extracted great quantities of air from the conditioned space that resulted in frequent air changes and the subsequent dilution of interior pollutants. Eliminating the "chimney fan" has led to an increase in interior pollutant levels such as moisture.

Active chimneys also tended to depressurize conditioned spaces during heating periods. Depressurization led to a reduced wetting of building assemblies from interior air-transported moisture and therefore a more forgiving building enclosure.

Heating and Cooling Systems

Today, forced air systems (heating and air conditioning) move large quantities of air within building enclosures of increasing tightness. The tighter the building enclosure the easier it is to pressurize or depressurize. Improperly installed forced air systems can lead to serious health, safety, durability, and operating cost issues.

Supply duct systems are typically more extensive than return duct systems. There are usually supply registers in each room with common centralized returns. Centralized returns replaced distributed returns to reduce costs. Pressurization of rooms and depressurization of common areas is created by the combination of more extensive supply systems, leaky supply and return ductwork combined with interior door closure.

Typical ductwork leaks. Air handlers leak. When leaky supply ducts are run outside the building enclosure in garages, vented attics, roof and crawlspaces, depressurization of the building enclosure occurs. Similarly, locating air handlers outside the building enclosure leads to the same result. Depressurization can cause infiltration of radon, moisture, pesticides and soil gas into foundations as well as the probable spillage and backdrafting of combustion appliances and potential flame roll-out resulting in fire.

Leaky return ducts and chases connected to exterior spaces can lead to pressurization of the building enclosure. Pressurization in cold climates can lead to the exfiltration of warm moisture-laden air into wall and roof cavities which are at lower drying potentials because of higher levels of insulation.

Since SIP building enclosures are inherently "tighter" than typical building enclosures pressure effects are more "pronounced." Duct systems need to be "better" designed to function in SIP building enclosures. Combustion appliances need to be selected and installed more carefully. Having said that, "tighter" enclosures allow duct systems to "work" better. More efficient duct systems are now possible as compared to typical building enclosures.

Integration

The three important changes in the way we build homes today interact with each other. This is further complicated by the effects of climate and occupant lifestyle. The interrelationship of all of these factors has led to major warranty problems that include health, safety, durability, comfort and affordability concerns. Problems are occurring despite the use of good materials and good workmanship.

We cannot return to constructing drafty building enclosures without thermal insulation, without consumer amenities, and with less efficient heating and air conditioning systems. The marketplace demands sophisticated, high performance buildings operated and maintained intelligently. As such, buildings must be treated as integrated systems that address health, safety, durability, comfort and affordability.

Quality construction consists of more than good materials and good workmanship. If you do the wrong thing with good materials and good workmanship, it is still wrong. You must do the right thing with good materials and good workmanship. The purpose of this guide is to promote the use of good materials and good workmanship in a systematic way, so that all the parts work together and promote good performance, durability, comfort, health and safety in an environmentally responsible manner.

The House System

Functional Relationships

Residential construction is a complex operation including thousands of processes by dozens of industries, bringing together hundreds of components and sub-systems into a house. A house is a complex, interrelated system of people, the building itself and the environment (Figure HS.1).

A house consists of the building enclosure, the sub-systems contained within it and the fit and finish. The building enclosure is composed of assemblies. Assemblies are composed of elements. Sub-systems are

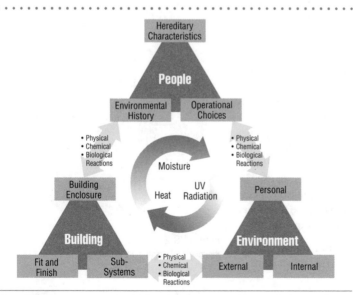

Figure HS.1
Analytical Model of the House System – Functional Relationships

composed of components. The fit and finish is composed of surfaces, appliances, trim, fixtures and the furnishings.

The building enclosure, assemblies, elements, sub-systems, components and the fit and finish are all interrelated. A change in an element can change the performance of an assembly, affect the building enclosure and subsequently change the characteristics of the house. Similarly, a change in a sub-system can influence the house, an assembly or an element of an assembly.

The house, in turn, interacts with the people who live in the house and with the local environment where the house is located. The functional relationships between the parameters are driven by physical, chemical and biological reactions. The basic factors controlling the physical, chemical and biological reactions are:

- heat flow
- moisture flow
- ultra-violet radiation

These basic factors are referred to as "damage functions."* Damage functions are responsible for the breakdown of materials via decay, corrosion, mold, spalling, efflorescence, etc.

Because large quantities of moisture can be transported by air — as well as the particulate and gaseous breakdown products of damage function action on building materials — air flow is also a significant factor affecting the functional relationships.

Controlling heat flow, moisture flow and ul-

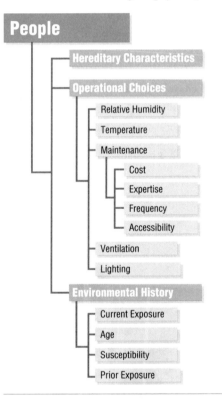

Figure HS.2
Hierarchical Relationships – People

---

tra-violet radiation (the "damage functions") along with air flow will control the interactions among the physical elements of the house, its occupants and the environment.

Building houses is really about the durability of people (health, safety and well being of people), the durability of buildings (the useful service life of a building is typically limited by its durability) and the durability of the planet (the well being of the local and global environment).

The relationships that define major elements of the residential construction process as well as continuing home operation are represented in Figures HS.2, HS.3, and HS.4.

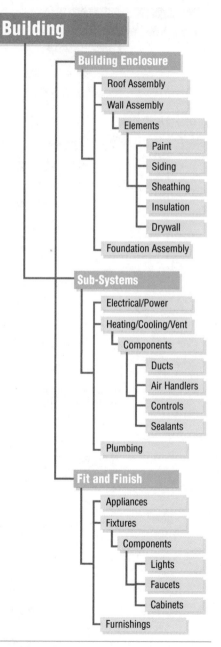

Figure HS.3
Hierarchical Relationships – Building

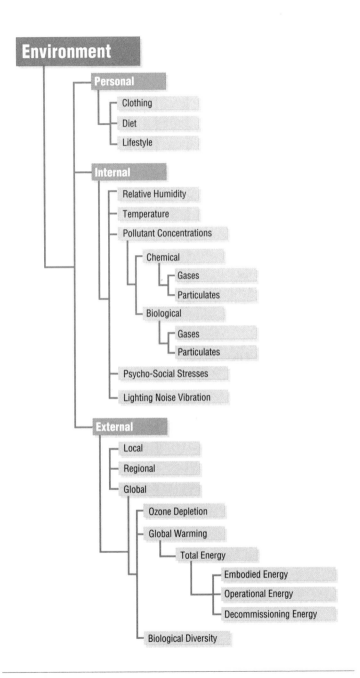

Prioritization

The construction process should minimize needs for energy, water and materials and satisfy these needs in the least disruptive manner possible (Figure HS.5).

The interior environment, or conditioned space, should be safe, healthy and comfortable. The building should be both durable and affordable in terms of purchase price and operating costs. And the building should be built in a manner that does the least harm to the local environment, including the construction site and the land around it. The impact of home production on the

> **Minimize Need for Energy, Water and Materials**
>
> ⬇ ⬇ ⬇ ⬇
>
> **Satisfy Need with Least Disruption. Reduce, Reuse, Recycle Managed Resource Extraction and Processing**

Figure HS.5
Minimization of Needs

global environment should also be considered. What resources will be used to build and operate the building? Are they renewable? What is the effect on the environment of extracting them?

The sometimes conflicting needs among people, buildings and the environment should be prioritized. For example, the needs of people should be considered before the needs of a building. The internal environment created by a building should be considered before the planetary environment. Short-term concerns should be considered before long-term concerns (Figure HS.6). But all should be considered.

Applying prioritization to the construction process would identify the immediate health risk from carbon monoxide poisoning as a result of

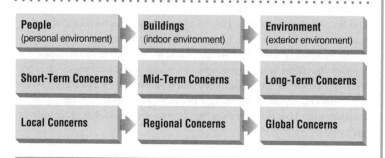

Figure HS.6
Priorities

11

improper installation of combustion appliances as more significant than long-term health concerns from the infiltration of radon gas.

Extending the prioritization process further shows that job-site recycling and reducing construction waste should have precedence over a global concern such as ozone depletion in the upper atmosphere. Finally, ozone depletion — a global short-term risk — should have precedence over global warming — a global long-term risk.

People Priorities

Houses should be safe, healthy, comfortable and affordable. A safe, healthy home is one in which concerns about clean water, fire and smoke spread, structural adequacy, indoor air quality, and security have been addressed. Comfort involves satisfying people's sensory perception. Comfort is addressed by dealing with thermal comfort, interior relative humidity, odors, natural light, sound and vibrations. Affordability means the designer, the builder and the various subcontractors and suppliers should be able to make a profit, and the occupant, for whom the home is built, should be able to purchase it and afford the operating and maintenance costs (Figure HS.7).

Building Priorities

Houses should be durable and capable of being maintained. The single most important factor affecting durability is deterioration of materials by moisture. Houses should be protected from wetting during construction and operation, and be designed to dry should they get wet. Buildings are going to get wet; after all, we build "outside." And accidents do happen during the useful service life of a building. Layering the enclosure with materials that dry both outwards and inwards is more than a good idea—it's a necessity.

Homeowners and occupants should be instructed on how to maintain and operate their buildings. Houses should be able to be renewed and renovated as new technologies, materials and products emerge. The house built today will likely be renovated at some point in the future. Houses should be able to be adapted as families and occupancy change. Finally, houses should be designed and constructed with decommissioning at the end of the useful service life in mind. This means taking into consideration how the materials that go into the house will ultimately be disposed of (Figure HS.7).

The House System

Environmental Priorities

Houses should be constructed in a manner that reduces materials in general and construction waste in particular. Furthermore, they should be operated in a manner that reduces occupancy waste. Recycling of construction and operating waste should be encouraged. Use of construction water, domestic water and irrigation water should be minimized. Erosion of soil during site preparation and the construction process should be controlled. Storm water should be infiltrated back into the site.

Activities that contribute to air pollution during construction, such as construction dust, painting and burning of trash, should be minimized.

People Priorities	Building Priorities	Environmental Priorities
Health & Safety	**Durability**	**Local Environment**
• potable water and sewage • fire and smoke spread • structure • indoor environment (air quality) • security • accessibility	• deterioration due to physical, chemical and biological reactions • operation, housekeeping and maintenance	• construction waste • operating waste • construction water • operating water • rain water run-off and local hydrology • erosion of soil
Comfort	**Renewal, Reuse and Renovation**	**Regional Environment**
• temperature • moisture (relative humidity) • odors • sound/vibrations • light • aesthetics	• future sub-system upgrading, such as communications, space conditioning and power • adaptability	• contamination of groundwater, streams and lakes (acid rainfall and acidification of lakes) • regional air pollution • regional recycled materials and waste disposal
Affordability	**Decommissioning/ Disassembly**	**Global Environment**
• capital cost, financing • operating cost from energy, water and maintenance	• benign materials • disposable and further recyclable materials	• ozone depletion affected by CFC-containing materials and systems • global warming affected by operating and embodied energy • biological diversity affected by utilizing materials from non-sustainable sources

Figure HS.7
People, Building and Environmental Priorities

Materials and systems that contribute to ozone depletion by releasing chlorofluorocarbons (CFCs) into the air should be avoided.

Biological diversity of plant and animal species should be protected by using materials from managed forests and managed mineral extraction processes. Finally, the use of energy to operate the building and to make and transport building products (embodied energy) should be minimized to reduce the production of greenhouse gases (e.g., carbon dioxide) that contribute to global warming (Figure HS.7).

Part I

1

Design

During the design phase, the designer makes fundamental decisions with respect to the siting, massing, layout and design of the house. The designer is often the general contractor but can be an architect or the home buyer. In many cases, design decisions are shared among the designer, general contractor, and home buyer. The designer must understand and be aware of the limitations of the project budget, the needs of the home buyer and the requirements of the general contractor. The designer must understand the local climate and the specific limitations of the proposed site. Furthermore, the designer must understand the project time, labor, construction sequence, material characteristics, the process of construction and the intended durability or expected lifespan of the structure (Figure 1.1).

During the design phase, fundamental decisions relating to foundation design, wall design, roof design and the design of the heating, ventilation and air conditioning (HVAC) system also occur. In order to make these decisions, the designer must be familiar with site and climate related issues such as the thermal and humidity conditions, annual rainfall, wind intensity and seismic zone.

Site Planning and Building Form

The ideal site is seemingly never available and there never is enough money. However, where flexibility exists, sites facing southeast, south, or southwest provide the best opportunities for optimizing a building's orientation with respect to daylighting and passive solar gain (Figure 1.2 and Figure 1.3). Sites sheltered from winter winds and open to summer breezes are warmer in winter and cooler in summer. Bodies of water and areas of vegetation moderate air temperature. Sites shaded by deciduous trees are cooler in summer. Sites that are well drained reduce the stress on drainage systems and water management. Building in a swamp is always more difficult than building on the top of a hill.

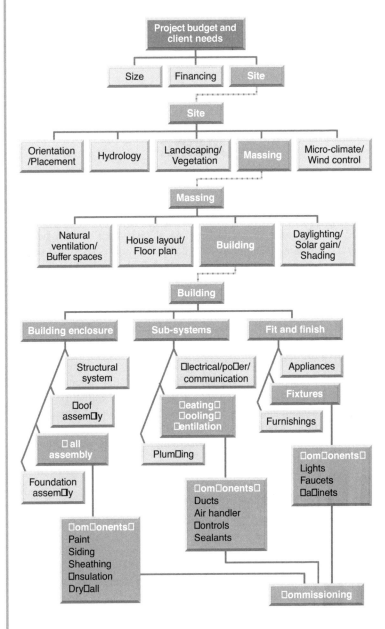

Figure 1.1
Process of House Construction

Summer vs. Winter Sun Angle and Overhang Sizing for Winter Gain and Summer Shade

Design

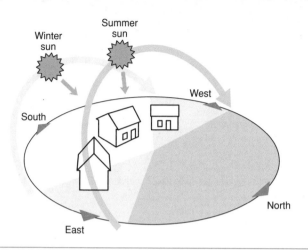

Figure 1.2
Summer vs. Winter Sun Angle

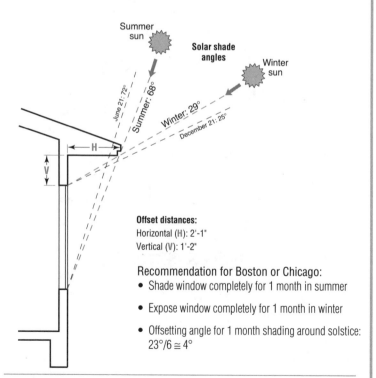

Figure 1.3
Overhang Sizing for Winter Gain and Summer Shade

Figure 1.4
Landscaping

- Deciduous trees, trellises or other features placed on the east and west sides of a house may be used to shade windows from summer solar gain but also permit solar gain in winter
- Ground cover can be used to decrease heat absorption
- Evergreens and other plantings may be used as wind breaks or be used to direct wind towards or away from buildings

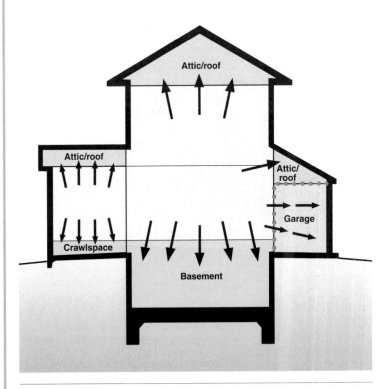

Figure 1.5
Expansion of Conditioned Space

- Conditioned space boundaries moving towards exterior surfaces of building
- Garage isolated from house by air barrier/pressure boundary
- Garage ventilated and conditioned independently of rest of conditioned spaces

The site access, site clearing, excavations, site manipulation and shaping, construction process, site development and landscaping all need to be considered with respect to soil erosion, and the existing hydrology. Sculpting the ground to permit a slab-on-grade rather than a walkout basement or elevated crawlspace can save thousands of dollars, but may also create severe environmental stress from the loss of topsoil and damage to vegetation.

Landscaping should be used to buffer the house from winter winds, allow winter solar gain and daylighting, and provide summer shading and cooling (Figure 1.4). Vegetation, walls, fences and other buildings can be utilized as wind breaks. Wind breaks and the building form can be used to channel breezes into buildings and outdoor spaces (Figure 1.6). Overhead structures can be used to provide shade for exterior walls and outdoor use areas (Figure 1.7). West and southwest facades, that provide the greatest potential for summer overheating, should be shaded from low-angled sun. Light colored walls or fences can be used to facilitate daylighting by reflecting sunlight into north windows. Paving should be minimized and shaded from the sun. Understory vegetation should be cleared and maintained to admit summer breezes. Air can be cooled by directing it through and under vegetation (Figure 1.8).

Site hydrology and the management of storm water have a major environmental impact. Under natural conditions most rainfall percolates into the ground upon which it falls, whereas almost all the rain that falls on a built-up area contributes to surface run-off. The principal advantage of vegetation is that it controls soil erosion from run-off water. Grass encourages percolation into the water table and is an effective vegetation for erosion control. In fact, many grasses work to reduce the impact of pollutants by breaking them down before they reach the water table. Turf grass requires considerably more water than other ground covers. Xeriscaping (vegetation or amenities which require little or no water) should be considered.

An ideal situation would be one in which no increase in run-off occurs as a result of development, so that problems are localized rather than passed on to others. This concept can be promoted by reducing the amount of paving and other impervious surfaces or using porous pavement in order to permit a greater portion of the storm water to seep into the ground. Vegetation can be increased and/or retained in order to maximize the amount of storm water consumed and stored by plants. Storm water can be drained to temporary or permanent storage areas by means of surface collection and low volume underground systems. It's okay to have puddles of water after a rain. Just don't have those puddles right next to the house. The most important area is the first ten feet from the house. If the puddles are kept at least ten feet from the house it is much less likely that water ends up in your house.

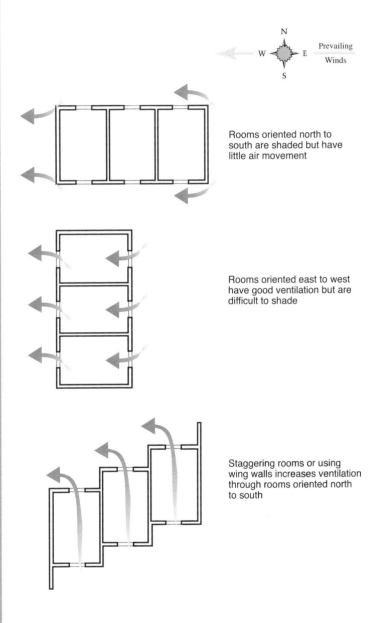

Rooms oriented north to south are shaded but have little air movement

Rooms oriented east to west have good ventilation but are difficult to shade

Staggering rooms or using wing walls increases ventilation through rooms oriented north to south

Figure 1.6
Solar and Wind Orientation

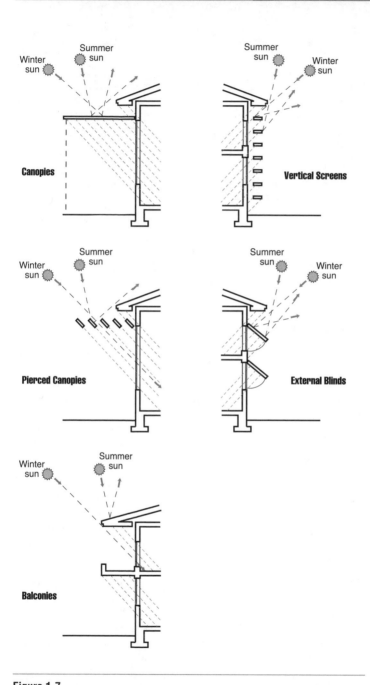

Figure 1.7
Shade for Exterior Walls for Both Summer and Winter

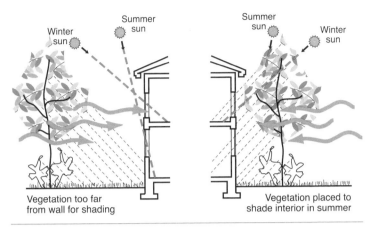

Figure 1.8
Shading Air Using Vegetation

House Layout

The building layout is a major factor influencing cost and performance. Heat gain and heat loss occur across building surfaces. Maximizing volume while minimizing surface area will increase operating efficiencies and will minimize the use of materials. Building layouts that are compact are typically more resource and energy efficient than those which are spread out. The trend to move into finished basements and finished attics is an example of this logic (Figure 5). Unused attics, crawlspaces and basements are a waste of resources.

In terms of floor plans, locating the most actively used spaces where they will most benefit from daylighting makes the most sense. Kitchens, living rooms and family rooms should be located to the south side. Buffer spaces should be utilized both within a building (vestibules) and external to a building (porches, sunspaces, sheltered patios) to temper weather extremes.

Outdoor use areas used primarily during winter months should be located adjacent to south side of buildings and southern exposures should be free from obstructions except with respect to shading from the summer sun. The opposite is true for outdoor use areas used primarily during summer months. Large paved surfaces should be avoided on windward sides of buildings. Such surfaces, if necessary, should be located to the lee side of use areas with respect to summer breezes so as to minimize summer thermal mass effects.

Open floor plans allow for air flow and ventilation efficiencies, increased daylighting, and summer cross ventilation. During heating, heat is more evenly distributed.

Windows should be sized and positioned so as to decrease heat loss during the winter and decrease heat gain in the summer while providing daylighting year round. In hot-humid climates, north-facing glazing is preferred. East/west glazing should be minimized — particularly west-facing glazing due to potential overheating. Moderate amounts of southern glazing with appropriate shading can provide improved comfort during heating (sun tempering) while providing views without an energy penalty. Substantial south- and west-facing glass can lead to overheating in summer as well as winter and should be avoided.

In designing for cooling load, east- and west-facing windows typically cause the most summertime overheating. Spectrally selective glazing should be used throughout, but is essential for extensive east- and west-facing glazing. These types of window systems reduce solar gain, while still providing daylighting. They are sometimes referred to as "southern Low E glass." These types of windows have low solar heat gain coefficients, high visible light transmittance and low U-values.

Yes, you read that correctly, "southern Low E glass" in cold climate buildings. Bottom line, if you install air conditioning, you need to use "southern Low E glass," period.

Large areas of glazing overhead (large skylights) should be avoided. Vegetation such as deciduous trees should be considered to shade windows during the summertime while leaving windows unshaded in winter time. Fencing or a trellis can also be used to shade glazing, particularly on east and west exposures.

Light colored walls, floors and ceilings should be used to reflect incoming light deep into rooms. A small skylight can be used to get light to the back of the rooms. Light ground colors should be avoided in front of south facing windows to minimize reflected summer heat gain, but should be considered for walls and fences on north exposures to reflect sunlight into north windows for improved daylighting.

The design challenge has always been to distribute operable windows and glazing in such a manner as to provide flow through ventilation without the penalties associated with excessive solar thermal gains during the summer while still providing sun tempering during the winter. Local practice and historical experience can often provide examples of elegant climatic optimization (Figure 1.8) in this regard.

With the advent of spectrally selective glazing, the introduction of new construction materials, coupled with traditional experience and the application of building science analysis it is possible to displace significant cooling loads and allow glazing where traditionally it would have contributed to excessive solar gain.

Basic Structure and Dimensions

The house layout and massing define the basic structure. The type of foundation system (crawlspace, slab or basement), roof system (attic, cathedral ceiling or flat), floor system (joist, truss, SIP, or slab) and structural system (SIP, timber frame, steel frame, concrete, masonry, insulated concrete forms (ICF), etc.) are selected by the designer based on costs, availability of materials, regional practices and preferences, site conditions and micro-climate, environmental impact and availability of experienced trades.

The type of structural system chosen affects building dimensions. SIPs can be ordered from the supplier in a wide variety of widths and lengths but other materials in the building may directly influence the building layout. For example, plywood, oriented strand board (OSB), and gypsum board typically come in 4-foot wide sheets. It makes sense to design dimensions to reduce sheet good waste. Similarly, concrete block, concrete formwork and ICF dimensions should be considered when dimensioning floor plans and foundations to minimize waste and labor.

Mechanical Systems

Mechanical equipment and ductwork should not be located outside of a home's thermal barrier and air pressure boundary. The building's thermal barrier and pressure boundary enclose the conditioned space. The pressure boundary is typically defined by the air barrier. Therefore, mechanical equipment and ductwork should not be located in exterior walls, vented attics, vented crawlspaces, garages or at any location exterior to a building's air barrier and thermal insulation. All air distribution systems should be located within the conditioned space. Additionally, ductwork should never be installed in or under floor slabs due to soil gas, radon, moisture condensation issues, and flooding of ductwork.

With SIPs it is easy to construct unvented, conditioned attics ("conditioned spaces") that become ideal locations for air handlers and ductwork (Figure 1.9).

The cold air portion of most air conditioning equipment is internally insulated with 1-inch of fiberglass insulation. This insulation thickness is not sufficient to prevent sweating of the exterior metal cabinet when it is located outside in vented attics, vented (unconditioned) crawlspaces or garages.

Similar comments can be made about insulated cold supply ducts. Although these ducts can be insulated with additional insulation, it is virtually impossible to install a 100% effective vapor barrier around these ducts. This means that water vapor finds its way past the vapor barrier and easily passes through the fiberglass insulation to the cold supply duct where it condenses. It is not recommended that ductwork be located outside in vented attics, vented (unconditioned) crawlspaces or garages in any climate zone.

The result is condensation, rust and mold. Units can rust-through in less than five years. Air handling units are not fit or suitable for installation in these locations.

Although it is not recommended that air handlers and ductwork be located in vented attics, vented crawlspaces or garages, this often occurs. The consequences of this often lead to major problems with thermal comfort, operating costs, durability, health and safety. If ductwork and air handlers located in vented attics are not installed in a leak-free manner, significant negative air pressures can occur within the occupied spaces (Figures 1.10 and 1.11) that can result in the uncontrolled ingress of exterior air, moisture, radon, soil gas and pollutants as well as lead to backdrafting of combustion appliances such as fireplaces. Leaky air handlers and leaky ductwork located in vented attics typically result in a 20 percent to 40 percent energy penalty to the overall performance of the building and significant humidity control problems. Even if installed in a leak-free manner, an approximate 5 percent energy penalty to the overall performance to the building results.

Even worse, the heat loss associated with locating ductwork and air handlers in vented attics is the single largest cause of ice dams. It is just plain dumb to install mechanical systems outside of conditioned spaces.

Techniques have been developed that allow ductwork and air handlers to be installed in a leak-free manner (see Chapter 11). Leak-free ductwork and air handler installation is absolutely critical if ductwork and air handlers are installed outside of a building's thermal barrier and air pressure boundary such as in a vented attic. Recall that it is dumb to install them here — you've been warned. Leak-free ductwork and air handler installation is a good idea even if ductwork and air handlers are installed within building thermal barriers and air pressure boundaries. Leakage of ductwork within interior building interstitial cavities can result in carpet dust marking and pollutant transfer as well as affecting thermal performance and comfort.

Negative air pressures in common areas often occurs in conjunction with pressurization of bedrooms even with tight ductwork and leak-free air handlers due to insufficient return air paths (Figure 1.12). These air pressure differences can significantly increase uncontrolled air change and thereby increase energy costs, adversely affect comfort as well as result in carpet dust marking, spillage and backdrafting of combustion appliances. Clear return air paths must be provided via ducted returns, transfer grilles, jump ducts or a combination of all of the above.

Locating air handlers within closets and mechanical rooms also needs to be done in a leak-free manner, with adequate provision for return air in order to avoid depressurization (Figures 1.13 and 1.14).

Interior chases must be considered and provided during the schematic design phase to make it easy to install services within conditioned spaces. A designer must think about stair locations and openings while allowing ductwork and plumbing to get by them as they go from one side of the house to the other.

Complaints on how plumbers and HVAC installers butcher framing during rough-in are often heard. However, if the designer does not leave them space, or make it easy for them to install equipment, piping and ductwork, it is often the only way to install services. The designer almost never talks to the plumber or HVAC contractor during the design phase about locating soil stacks, ductwork layouts and equipment locations. It's time we start the dialog, or stop complaining about cut floor framing, having to pad-out walls to hide plumbing and paying for tortured ductwork layouts that deliver only a fraction of the air that they should.

Unvented Crawlspaces

Vented crawlspaces are not recommended in any climate for that matter. Crawlspaces should be sealed and enclosed like any other conditioned space such as a bedroom or a living room. They should be heated during the winter and cooled during the summer. They should be insulated around the perimeter and not between the crawlspace and the main floor. Good drainage is required. More discussion on crawlspaces can be found in Chapter 6.

Fireplaces

Fireplaces should not be located on exterior walls, they should be totally contained within the conditioned space. A warm chimney drafts much better than a cold one. In addition, masonry chimneys that are located within the conditioned space have thermal mass that stores the heat created by a fire and continues to warm the space even after the fire has gone out. Fireplaces should always be provided with ducted exterior combustion and make-up air.

Building Enclosure

The building enclosure should exclude rain, control rain water absorption, control air flow and vapor diffusion. Additionally, the building enclosure should be forgiving so that if it does get wet it can dry to the interior or exterior. Interior vapor barriers such as polyethylene should be avoided in all climates. SIP assemblies due to the nature of their panel construction and the materials used do not need any additional vapor control in any climate.

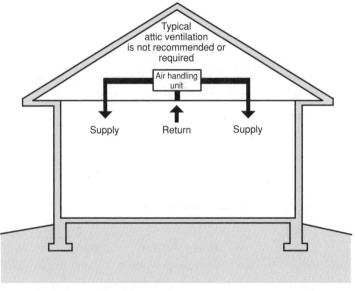

Note: Colored shading depicts the building's thermal enclosure and pressure boundary. The thermal barrier and pressure boundary enclose the conditioned space.

Figure 1.9
Slab-on-Grade
Unvented, Conditioned Attic ("Conditioned Space")
- The "attic" is inside the thermal enclosure
- Typical attic ventilation is not recommended or required
- The air handling unit is located in an unvented, conditioned attic ("conditioned space")
- Low efficiency gas appliances that are prone to spillage or backdrafting are not recommended in this type of application; heat pumps, heat pump water heaters or sealed combustion furnaces and water heaters should be used
- A hot water-to-air coil in an air handling unit can be used to replace the gas furnace/heat exchanger. The coil can be connected to a sealed combustion (or power vented) water heater located within the conditioned space

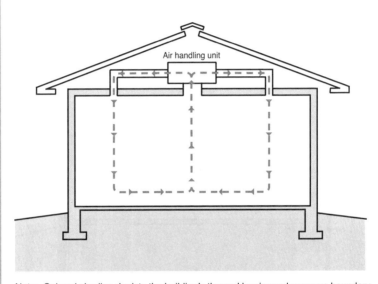

This Approach is Not Recommended:
Without SIPs roof assemblies, this situation could exist

Air handling unit

Note: Colored shading depicts the building's thermal barrier and pressure boundary. The thermal barrier and pressure boundary enclose the conditioned space.

Figure 1.10
Ductwork and Air Handlers in Vented Attics
- No air pressure differences result in a house with an air handler and ductwork located in a vented attic if there are no leaks in the supply ducts, the return ducts or the air handler and if the amount of air delivered to each room equals the amount removed
- If no air leakage occurs in the ductwork and air handler, locating the ductwork and air handler in a vented attic typically results in an approximate 5% to 10% energy penalty to the overall performance of the building due to conductive gains and losses across the ductwork and air handler
- This approach is prone to ice dams and should be avoided
- If this approach is used, duct leakage testing should be used to assure leak-free installation

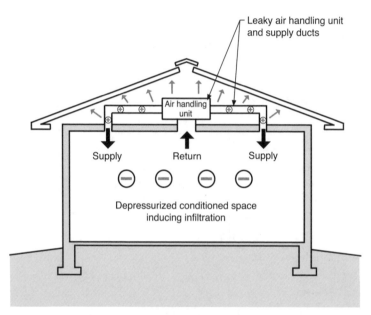

This Approach is Not Recommended:
Without SIPs roof assemblies, this situation could exist

Leaky air handling unit
and supply ducts

Air handling unit

Supply   Return   Supply

Depressurized conditioned space
inducing infiltration

Note: Colored shading depicts the building's thermal barrier and pressure boundary.
The thermal barrier and pressure boundary enclose the conditioned space.

Figure 1.11
Ductwork and Air Handlers in Vented Attics

- Supply ductwork and air handler leakage is typically 20% or more of the flow through the system; in a 5 ton A/C system there is approximately 400 cfm of leakage, or almost the equivalent to 2 tons of capacity
- Leakage out of the supply system into the vented attic results in an equal quantity of infiltration; in other words, 400 cfm of leakage out of the supply system into the attic results in 400 cfm of infiltration (typically $2/3$ or more) through the attic ceiling. This guarantees ice dam creation.
- Air leakage in ductwork and air handlers located in vented attics typically results in an approximate 20% to 40% thermal penalty to the overall performance of the building

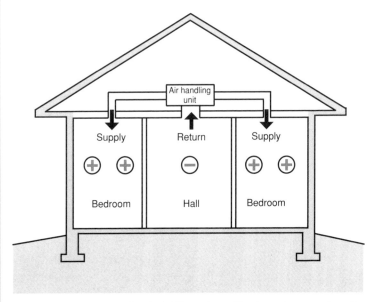

Note: Colored shading depicts the building's thermal barrier and pressure boundary. The thermal barrier and pressure boundary enclose the conditioned space.

Figure 1.12
Insufficient Return Air Paths

- Pressurization of bedrooms occurs if insufficient return air pathways are provided; undercutting bedroom doors is usually insufficient; transfer grilles (see Figure 11.25), jump ducts or fully ducted returns may be necessary to prevent pressurization of bedrooms
- Master bedroom suites are often the most pressurized as they typically receive the most supply air; a fully ducted return in the master bedroom suite is generally recommended
- When bedrooms pressurize, common areas depressurize; this can have serious consequences when fireplaces are located in common areas and subsequently backdraft

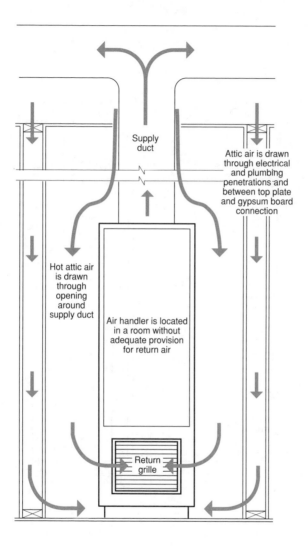

Figure 1.13
Air Handler Closet Depressurization
- Air handler typically located in closet with louvered door

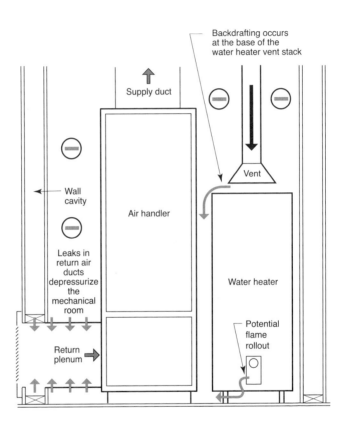

Backdrafting occurs
at the base of the
water heater vent stack

Supply duct

Vent

Wall
cavity

Air handler

Leaks in
return air
ducts
depressurize
the
mechanical
room

Water heater

Potential
flame
rollout

Return
plenum

Figure 1.14
Backdrafting in Mechanical Room/Utility Room
- Mechanical room depressurized by return system leakage of ductwork and air handling unit cabinet
- **Must** have power-vented sealed combustion appliances

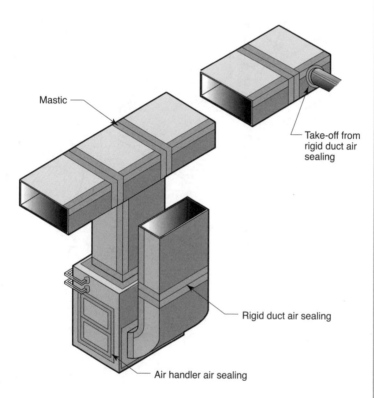

Mastic

Take-off from rigid duct air sealing

Rigid duct air sealing

Air handler air sealing

Figure 1.15
HVAC Air Sealing to Eliminate Backdrafting
- Air sealing of return plenum prevents depressurization of the mechanical room
- Must have power-vented sealed combustion appliances

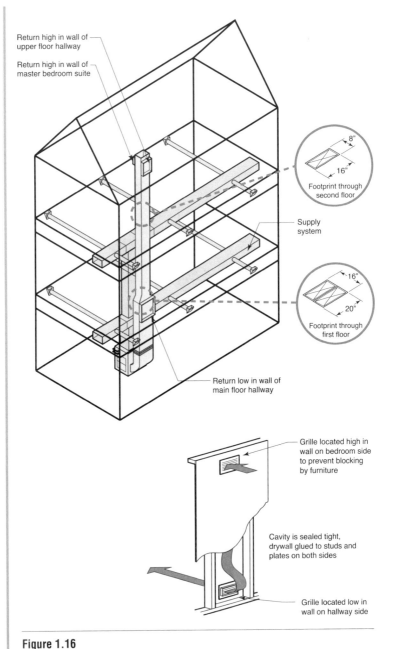

Return high in wall of upper floor hallway

Return high in wall of master bedroom suite

8"
16"
Footprint through second floor

Supply system

16"
20"
Footprint through first floor

Return low in wall of main floor hallway

Grille located high in wall on bedroom side to prevent blocking by furniture

Cavity is sealed tight, drywall glued to studs and plates on both sides

Grille located low in wall on hallway side

Figure 1.16
New Construction Air Distribution Systems
- Use fully ducted returns or transfer grilles for return airflow paths. Do not use panned floor joists or other building cavities as returns.

Specifically, the building enclosure must:

- hold the building up
- keep the rain water out
- keep the ground water out
- keep the wind out
- keep the water vapor out
- let the water and vapor out if they get in
- keep the soil gas out
- keep the heat in during the winter
- keep the heat out during the summer
- keep the noise out

The designer has to choose materials, equipment and systems to make all this work. Will building papers or housewraps be used? What will the thermal resistance of the building enclosure be? Chapter 4 discusses building papers and housewraps.

A key concept should be used at this point in the design approach—the concept of "break points." A break point denotes the situation where an increase in cost in one area is balanced by a reduction in cost in another area.

For example, increasing thermal resistance of the building enclosure will result in an increased cost. However, the heating and cooling system can be made much smaller and operate more efficiently with lower operating costs with a resulting decrease in the size and cost of ductwork and equipment.

Decisions relating to "keeping the rain water out" should reflect the local conditions. Zones that see a great deal of rain (some coastal or mountain areas) will likely need a more "robust" approach to rain control than other zones. Specific wall assembly details for rain control can be found in Chapter 2—Rain, Drainage Planes and Flashings.

Controlled Ventilation and Equipment Selection

All buildings require controlled mechanical ventilation. Building intentionally leaky buildings and installing operable windows does not provide sufficient outside air in a consistent manner. Building enclosures must be "built tight and then ventilated right." Why? Because before you can control air you must enclose it. Once you eliminate big holes it becomes easy to control air exchange between the inside and the outside. Controlled mechanical ventilation can be provided in many forms such as HRV's and ERV's (see Chapter 11), but what is important at this stage is that the designer recognize that a controlled mechanical ventilation system is necessary and that controlled mechanical ventilation works best in a tight building enclosure. You can't control anything in a leaky building.

Selecting a fuel source is usually based on availability, regional practices and customer preference. Electric heat pumps and natural gas are the most common choice for space and domestic water heating. If gas heating or a gas water heater is selected, the appliances must be power vented, sealed combustion or installed external to the conditioned space (i.e. installed in a garage — except in cold or very cold climates). Gas appliances should not interact aerodynamically with the building (i.e. affected by interior air pressures or other air consuming devices). If a gas cook top or gas oven is installed, it must be installed in combination with a kitchen range hood directly ducted to the exterior (exhaust fan). Unvented gas fireplaces should never be installed.

Air change through mechanical ventilation should be used to control interior moisture levels year round. Dehumidification through the use of mechanical cooling (air conditioning) and supplemental dehumidification may also be necessary during cooling periods and part load conditions. Mechanical ventilation strategies are described in Chapter 11.

The need for mechanical cooling (air conditioning) should be reduced by displacing the cooling load as much as possible through the use of architectural design, spectrally selective glazing, and the use of low heat producing appliances and lighting. Comfort levels can be enhanced at higher interior temperatures by inducing air movement through the use of ceiling fans thereby reducing the need for mechanical cooling.

Air conditioners, furnaces, air handlers and ductwork should be located within the conditioned space and provided with easy access to accommodate servicing, filter replacement, cooling coil and drain pan cleaning, future upgrading or replacement as technology improves. Hostile locations (extreme temperatures and moisture levels) such as vented attics and unconditioned (vented) crawlspaces or garages should be avoided.

Material Selection

There are only a few inherently bad materials, but there are many bad ways to use materials. The use of a material should be put into the context of a system. In general, the system is more important than the material. Once the system is selected, you must determine if the material can perform its intended function as part of that system for the desired life of the system. What is the risk of using the material to the occupants, the building and to the local and global environment when used in that system (Figure 1.16)?

Extending the argument further, there are no truly benign materials, only degrees of impact. Nothing is completely risk free. However, risk can be managed. There may be no alternative to a particularly toxic material in a specific system, but the use of that material may pose little risk when used properly and provide significant benefits to that system. For example, bituminous dampproofing is a toxic material, but if it is installed on the exterior of a concrete foundation wall, there is little risk to the occupants, but there are substantial moisture control benefits to the foundation assembly.

The risk to occupants of a particular synthetic or natural agent in a building product, system or assembly is generally low where that agent is not inhaled or touched. In any case, building products and materials that do not off-gas are preferable to those that do. Less toxic alternatives should be used in place of more toxic materials (Figure 1.17). Remember that these material choices need to be placed in the context of the system or assembly of which it is a part. Is the toxic material being used in roofing? If so, it may pose little hazard to the occupants.

In addition to the specific concerns about material and product use on the interior environment of a building and the occupants, are the concerns relating to the local and global environment. Is it more appropriate to use a recycled, refurbished or remanufactured product or material in place of a new material or product? Is the new material or product obtained or manufactured in a non-disruptive or the least-disruptive manner to the environment? Can the cost of a product justify its use? How far was the material transported? How much energy was used to make it?

Appliances

The designer is typically responsible for the selection of appliances, typically with home owner input. If home owners assume the responsibility of selecting some or all of the appliances, it is the responsibility of the designer to provide the necessary information to the home owner so that an informed decision be made within the context of the house system.

Appliances should be selected and installed in such a manner that they do not adversely affect the building enclosure or building sub-systems. For example, gas cook tops and ovens should provide for their own exhaust of combustion products by installing vented range hoods or exhaust fans. They also need to be installed in a manner which prevents excessive depressurization (i.e. make-up air for indoor barbecues).

Material Selection

1 **Requirements**
What should materials do?

2 **Suitability**
Can material do it?

3 **Impact**
What is the risk?

**Figure 1.17
Material Selection**

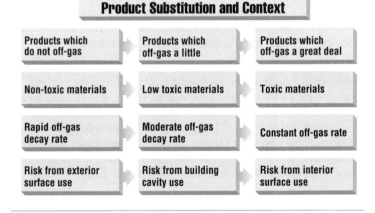

Product Substitution and Context

Products which do not off-gas	Products which off-gas a little	Products which off-gas a great deal
Non-toxic materials	Low toxic materials	Toxic materials
Rapid off-gas decay rate	Moderate off-gas decay rate	Constant off-gas rate
Risk from exterior surface use	Risk from building cavity use	Risk from interior surface use

**Figure 1.18
Product Substitution and Context**

Fireplaces and wood stoves should be considered appliances. They
should be provided with their own air supply independent of the other
air requirements of the building enclosure. The location of combustion
appliances should take into consideration air pressure differentials that
may occur due to the stack effect or competition for air from other combustion appliances. Indoor barbecues should be considered similarly.
Air supply, air pressure differentials and combustion product venting
need to be addressed.

Energy consumption should be a prime consideration in the selection of refrigerators, freezers, light fixtures, washers and dryers. The yellow D.O.E. Energy Guide label should be consulted. Dryers should be vented directly to the exterior and should not adversely affect the air pressure dynamics of the building enclosure when they are operating.

Commissioning

The home designer must ensure that of the home occurs so that the home functions as intended by the design. Commissioning allows problems to be spotted through testing and then immediately remedied ("fix and tune"). The commissioning can be done by the designer, the contractor or some other competent person. At minimum, commissioning should include:

- testing of building enclosure leakage area
- testing of the leakage of duct systems
- testing of the air pressure relationships under all operating conditions
- testing for proper venting of all combustion appliances under all operating conditions
- testing of the carbon monoxide output of all combustion appliances (gas oven, range, water heater, gas fireplace)
- confirmation of air flow and refrigerant charge in HVAC systems

As part of the commissioning process, the home owner or occupants should be educated and informed as to the correct operation, maintenance and housekeeping requirements of the building and equipment. What are appropriate temperature, relative humidity and ventilation ranges for the building? How do owners or occupants identify a system failure or the improper operation of a system? How do owners or occupants monitor the building conditions (temperature sensors, humidity sensors, ventilation sensors)? How often should filters be changed?

A system data sheet listing equipment, models, sizes and serial numbers should be placed in a permanent plastic documentation envelope along with equipment manuals, filter sizes and a copy of commissioning documentation.

There is information relating to air leakage testing of building enclosure leakage areas, testing of the leakage of duct systems, air pressure differentials and combustion safety in Appendix II.

2

Rain, Drainage Planes and Flashings

Rain is the single most important factor to control in order to construct a durable structure. Although controlling rain has preoccupied builders for thousands of years, significant insight into the physics of rain and its control was not developed until the middle of this century by the Norwegians and the Canadians. Both peoples are blessed by countries with miserable climates which no doubt made the issue pressing.

Experience from tradition-based practices combined with the physics of rain developed by the Norwegians and Canadians has provided us with effective strategies to control rain entry. The strategies are varied based on the frequency and severity of rain.

The amount of rain determines the amount of rain control needed. No rain, no rain control needed. Little rain, little rain control needed. Lots of rain, lots of rain control needed. Although this should be obvious, it is often overlooked by codes, designers, and builders. Strategies which work in Las Vegas do not necessarily work in Seattle. In simple terms, the amount of rain water deposited on a surface determines the type of approach necessary to control rain.

The susceptibility of the building system to water damage also impacts the type of approach necessary to control rain. Buildings constructed from moisture-sensitive materials such as wood, gypsum, OSB or plywood sheathings and fiberglass or cellulose cavity insulation require a different approach than masonry or concrete structures insulated with foam plastics. The more moisture sensitive the materials, the more rain control required.

Wind strength, wind direction, and rainfall intensity determine in a general way the amount of wind-driven rain deposited. These are factors governed by climate, not by design and construction. The actual distribution of rain on a building is determined by the pattern of wind flow around buildings. This, to a limited extent, can be influenced by design and construction.

Physics of Rain

Once rain is deposited on a building surface, its flow over the building surface will be determined by gravity, wind flow over the surface, and wall-surface features such as overhangs, flashings, sills, copings, and mullions. Gravity cannot be influenced by design and construction, and wind flow over building surfaces can only be influenced marginally. However, wall-surface features are completely within the control of the designer and builder. Tradition-based practice has a legacy of developing architectural detailing features that have been used to direct water along particular paths or to cause it to drip free of the wall. Overhangs were developed for a reason. Flashings with rigid drip edges protruding from building faces were specified for a reason. Extended window sills were installed for a reason.

Rain penetration into and through building surfaces is governed by capillarity, momentum, surface tension, gravity, and wind (air pressure) forces. Capillary forces draw rain water into pores and tiny cracks, while the remaining forces direct rain water into larger openings.

In practice, capillarity can be controlled by capillary breaks, capillary resistant materials or by providing a receptor for capillary moisture. Momentum can be controlled by eliminating openings that go straight through the wall assembly. Rain entry by surface tension can be controlled by the use of drip edges and kerfs. Flashings and layering the wall assembly elements to drain water to the exterior (providing a "drainage plane") can be used to control rain water from entering by gravity flow, along with simultaneously satisfying the requirements for control of momentum and surface tension forces. Sufficiently overlapping the wall assembly elements or layers comprising the drainage plane can also control entry of rain water by air pressure differences. Finally, locating a ventilated or pressure moderated air space immediately behind the exterior cladding can be used to control entry of rain water by air pressure differences by reducing those air pressure differences and providing moisture removal. This approach is called the "Rain Screen" approach.

The more susceptible or vulnerable to moisture damage the materials comprising an assembly are, the more "robust" the rain control strategy required. Additionally, assemblies have different drying characteristics based on material characteristics, insulation levels, interior and exterior climatic conditions and cross-assembly or inter-assembly air flows. In general, vulnerable assemblies with low drying characteristics require greater rain control than moisture insensitive assemblies with high drying potentials.

Coupling a ventilated or pressure moderated air space with a capillary resistant drainage plane ("Rain Screen") in an assembly constructed

2

from moisture insensitive materials with a high drying potential represents the state-of-the-art for Norwegian and Canadian rain control practices. This approach addresses all of the driving forces responsible for rain penetration into and through building surfaces under the severest exposures.

This understanding of the physics of rain leads to the following general approach to rain control:
- reduce the amount of rain water deposited and flowing on building surfaces
- control rain water deposited and flowing on building surfaces

Water Management Approaches

The first part of the general approach to rain control involves locating buildings so that they are sheltered from prevailing winds, providing roof overhangs and massing features to shelter exterior walls and reduce wind flow over building surfaces, and finally, providing architectural detailing to shed rain water from building faces.

The second part of the general approach to rain control involves dealing with capillarity, momentum, surface tension, gravity and air pressure forces acting on rain water deposited on building surfaces.

The second part of the general approach to rain control employs two general design principles:

- Face Sealed/Barrier Approach
    Storage/Reservoir Systems/Durable Materials
        (all rain exposures)
    Non-Storage/Non-Reservoir Systems/Durable Materials
        (less than 20 inches average annual precipitation)

- Water Managed Approach
    Drain Screen Systems
        (less than 40 inches average annual precipitation)
    Rain Screen Systems
        (40 inches or greater average annual precipitation)

Rain is expected to enter through the cladding skin in the water managed systems: drain screen and rain screen systems. "Drain the rain" is the cornerstone of water managed systems. In the water managed systems, drainage of water is provided by a capillary resistant drainage plane or a capillary resistant drainage plane coupled with a ventilated air space behind the cladding.

In the face-sealed barrier approach, the exterior face is the only means to control rain entry. In storage/reservoir systems, some rain is also expected to enter and is stored in the mass of the wall assembly until drying occurs to either the exterior or interior. In non-storage/non-reservoir systems, no or negligible quantities of rain can be permitted to enter.

The performance of a specific system is determined by frequency of rain, severity of rain, system design, selection of materials, workmanship, and maintenance. In general, water managed systems outperform face-sealed/barrier systems due to their more forgiving nature. However, face-sealed/barrier systems constructed from water resistant materials that employ significant storage have a long historical track-record of exemplary performance even in the most severe rain exposures. These "massive" wall assemblies constructed out of masonry, limestone, granite and concrete, many of which are 18 inches or more thick, were typically used in public buildings such as courthouses, libraries, schools and hospitals.

The least forgiving and least water resistant assembly is a face-sealed/ barrier wall constructed from water sensitive materials that does not have storage capacity. Some external insulation finish systems (EIFS) are of this type and are not generally recommended. Water managed EIFS do not have this problem and are excellent claddings.

The most forgiving and most water resistant assembly is a ventilated rain screen wall constructed from water resistant materials. These types of assemblies perform well in the most severe rain exposures.

Water managed strategies are recommended in all climate regions. Drain-screen systems (drainage planes without ventilated air spaces) should be limited to regions where average annual rainfall is less than 40 inches and rain-screen systems (drainage planes with ventilated air spaces) are recommended everywhere and are essential wherever average annual rainfall is greater than 40 inches.

Face-sealed/barrier strategies should be carefully considered. Non-storage/non-reservoir systems constructed out of water sensitive materials are not generally recommended. Storage/reservoir systems constructed with water resistant materials can be built anywhere. However, their performance is design, workmanship, and materials dependent. In general, these systems should be limited to regions or to designs with high drying potentials to the exterior, interior or, better still, to both.

Drainage Planes/Water Resistive Barriers

Drainage planes are water repellent materials (building paper, housewrap, foam insulation, etc.), which are located behind the cladding and are designed and constructed to drain water that passes through the cladding. They are interconnected with flashings, window and door openings, and other penetrations of the building enclosure to provide drainage of water to the exterior of the building. The materials that form the drainage plane overlap each other shingle fashion or are sealed so that water drains down and out of the wall.

The most common drainage plane is "tar paper" or building paper. More recently, the term "housewrap" has been introduced to describe building papers that are not asphalt impregnated felts or coated papers. Drainage planes can also be created by sealing or layering water resistant sheathings such as a rigid insulation or a coated structural sheathing.

There have been problems with housewraps that are "perforated" and other problems with housewraps associated with "surfactants" such as wood sugars. Problems with housewraps can be avoided by installing cladding over a drained and ventilated space; in other words, providing an airspace between the housewrap and the back of the cladding.

In general "perforated" housewraps should be avoided. A simple test can be used to determine if a housewrap is perforated. Place a sample of housewrap over a paper towel. Place several teaspoons of water over the housewrap. If the water penetrates the housewrap and wets the paper towel it is perforated. If the sample passes this test, repeat the test, but this time put your finger in the droplet of water and leave it there for a couple minutes. If the paper towel gets wet, don't use the housewrap.

With respect to "surfactants," the best approach is to back-ventilate cladding so that liquid phase water does not accumulate in the cladding or sheathing in sufficient quantity to "leach" extractives.

Wood siding is best installed over furring (i.e. "spacer strips"). The furring can be as thin as $1/4$-inch (6 mm). A cost-effective way to do this is by cutting $1/4$-inch (6 mm) thick "fan-fold" siding backer into 2-inch (50 mm) wide strips. It is a fast, economical method of back-venting and draining wood siding. Fiber cement siding can be installed in a similar way.

Cedar shingles, traditional stucco, and manufactured stone veneers should be installed over drainage mats. The most common drainage mat is a polypropylene mesh that comes in a roll—it resembles a "plastic Brillo® pad" in a sheet. This "plastic mesh" is approximately $3/8$-inch to $3/4$-inch thick and is installed over the drainage plane to create the "drainage space."

Cedar shingles are installed directly over drainage mats. However, with traditional stucco and manufactured stone veneers, a layer of "tar paper" or asphalt impregnated felt is installed over the top of the drainage mat to keep it from getting clogged with mortar or stucco.

2

Only vinyl and aluminum siding should be directly applied to house-wraps as they are inherently "back-ventilated" due to their profile.

The drainage plane is also referred to as the "water resistive barrier" or WRB.

All exterior claddings pass some rain water. Siding leaks, brick leaks, stucco leaks, stone leaks, etc. As such, some control of this penetrating rain water is required. In most walls, this penetrating rain water is controlled by the drainage plane that directs the penetrating rain water downwards and outwards.

Since all exterior claddings "leak," all wood frame wall assemblies require a drainage plane coupled with a drainage space - where it rains. "Where it rains" is defined as all locations in North America—even deserts. It doesn't rain much in a desert, but when it does, it really does. Traditionally, drainage planes consisted of tar paper installed shingle fashion behind exterior claddings coupled with a flashing at the base of each wall to direct rain water that penetrated the cladding systems to the exterior. It was important that some form of air space or drainage space was also provided between the cladding system and the drainage plane to allow drainage (as noted above).

With wood siding, the drainage space is typically intermittent and depends largely on the profile of the siding. Wood siding should therefore be installed over furring creating a drained (and vented) air space between the drainage plane and wood siding. With vinyl and aluminum siding, the drainage space is more pronounced and furring is not necessary.

With stucco claddings, the drainage space was traditionally provided by using two layers of asphalt impregnated felt paper. The water absorbed by the felt papers from the base coat of stucco caused the papers to swell and expand. When the assembly dried, the papers would shrink, wrinkle, and de-bond providing a tortuous, but reasonably effective drainage space. This drainage space was typically between $1/16$-inch and $1/8$-inch wide. With more modern building papers this gap no longer occurs since these materials are more dimensionally stable—as such two layers of building paper with a drainage mat between are necessary.

With brick veneers, the width of the drainage space has been based more on tradition rather than physics. A 1-inch airspace is more-or-less the width of a mason's fingers, hence, the typical requirement for a 1-inch airspace. However, from our experience with stucco and other cladding systems, spaces as small as $1/16$-inch drain. However large the space it must be coupled with a functional drainage plane.

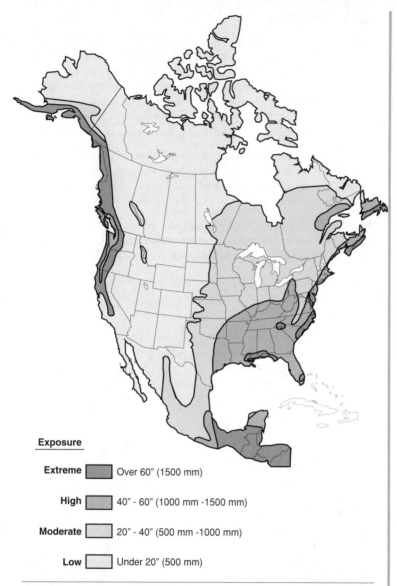

Exposure

Extreme		Over 60" (1500 mm)
High		40" - 60" (1000 mm -1500 mm)
Moderate		20" - 40" (500 mm -1000 mm)
Low		Under 20" (500 mm)

Figure 2.1
Annual Rainfall Map
• Based on information from the U.S. Department of Agriculture and Environment Canada

2

Rain Water Control

The fundamental principle of rain water control is to shed water by layering materials in such a way that water is directed downwards and outwards from the building or away from the building. It applies to assemblies such as walls, roofs and foundations, as well as to the components that can be found in walls, roofs and foundations such as windows, doors and skylights. It also applies to assemblies that connect to walls, roofs and foundations such as balconies, decks, railings and dormers.

Layering materials to shed water applies to the building as a whole (see Figure 2.2). Overhangs can be used to keep water away from walls. Canopies can be used to keep water away from windows, and site grading can be used to keep water away from foundation perimeters.

When selecting building materials, take into account that building materials may be exposed to rain or other elements during construction. For example, walls without roofs on them will get wet. It is not a good idea

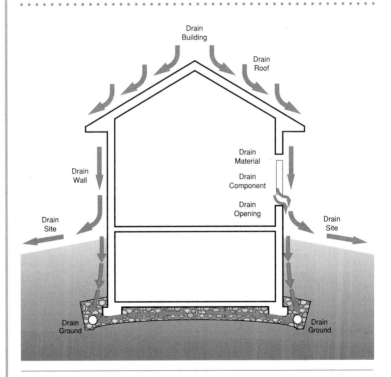

Figure 2.2
Layering Materials to Shed Water
- Applies to whole building

to build these walls with exterior gypsum board that is paper-faced since they hold water. This is a major concern with party walls or fire walls in multifamily buildings. Glass-faced gypsum board or other water-resistant alternatives should be used.

Drainage is the key to rain water control:

- Drain the site (see Figure 2.2)
- Drain the ground
- Drain the building (see Figure 2.3)
- Drain the assembly
- Drain the opening (see Figure 2.4)
- Drain the component
- Drain the material

Reservoirs on the outside of homes are a problem. What are reservoirs? Materials that store rain water – sponges that get wet when it rains.

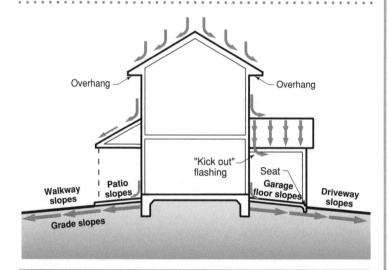

Figure 2.3
Drain the Building

- Patios and decks lower than floors and slope away from building
- Garage floor lower than main floor and slope away from building
- Driveway lower than garage floor and slope away from building
- Grade lower than main floor and slope away from building
- Stoops and walkways lower than main floor and slope away from building
- Kick-out flashings or diverters direct water away from walls at roof/wall intersections
- Overhangs protect walls

Once the reservoirs get wet, the stored water can migrate elsewhere and cause problems (see Figure 2.6). Common reservoirs are brick veneers, stuccos, wood siding, wood trim and fiber cement cladding.

How to handle reservoirs? Easy. Get rid of them or disconnect them from the building (see Figure 2.7). Back priming (painting all surfaces, back, front, edges and ends of wood siding, cement siding and all wood trim) gets rid of the moisture storage issue with these materials. No reservoir, no problem.

Back-venting brick veneers disconnects the brick veneer moisture reservoir from the home (see Figure 2.8). Installing stucco over two layers of building paper or over an appropriate capillary break, such as foam sheathing, similarly addresses stucco reservoirs.

Roofs should be designed to shed rain water away from the building. Steep pitches are better than shallow pitches. Crickets should be used to divert water away from chimneys and architectural features.

Roofs should also be designed to protect walls. Large overhangs are better than small overhangs or no overhangs.

Ideally, roofs should have simple geometry. The more complex the roof, the more dormers, ridges and valleys, the more likely a roof will leak. Penetrations should also be minimized or avoided.

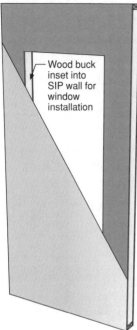

Wood buck inset into SIP wall for window installation

Step 1
SIP with housewrap

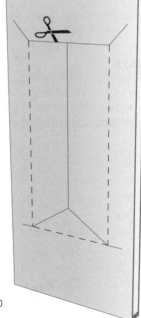

Step 2
Modified "I" cut in housewrap

Figure 2.4
Installing a Window with Housewrap Over a SIP Wall in Twelve Steps

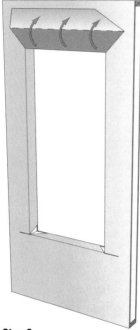

Step 3
- Housewrap folded in at jambs and sill and secure tightly
- Head flap folded outward; alternately, tuck head flap under

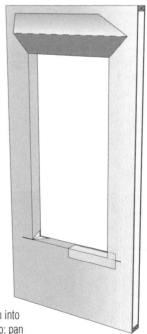

Step 4
- Install first piece of sill pan into horizontal slit in housewrap; pan must fit tightly
- Mechanically fasten at exterior vertical face only

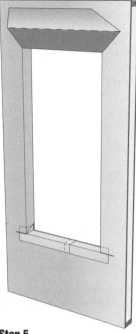

Step 5
- Slip second piece of sill pan into horizontal slit in housewrap; pan must fit tightly
- Mechanically fasten at exterior vertical face only
- Ensure a minimum 3-inch over-lap at sill

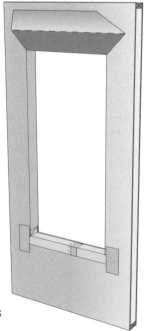

Step 6
Tape or flash sill pan at jambs and sill joint

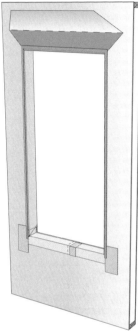

Step 7
- Back-caulk window
- Apply sealant at jambs and head; do not apply to sill
- Alternatively, caulk can be applied to window nailing flange prior to installation

Step 8
Install window plumb, level and square per manufacturer's instructions

Step 9
Install jamb flashing; extend minimum 1-inch above head nailing flange and a minimum 3-inches below sill nailing flange

Step 10
Install head flashing; extend minimum 2-inches past edge of jamb flashing

Step 11
- Fold housewrap down at head
- Ensure head flap has not been
  damaged during the installation
  process

Step 12
- Apply corner patches at head;
  extend minimum 1-inch beyond
  cut in housewrap
- Air seal window around entire
  perimeter on the interior with
  sealant or non-expanding foam
- For air sealing inside of window,
  see Figure 3.7

Step 1
• Drainage gap created by furring
(shown) or drainage mat

Figure 2.5
Installing Window Trim and Flashings Over a Drainage Gap in Seven Steps
- Wood siding and fiber cement siding should be back-ventilated and drained where annual rainfall exceeds 20 inches (500 mm)
- Furring (i.e. "spacer strip") can be as thin as $1/_4$-inch (6 mm). A cost effective way to do this is by cutting $1/_4$-inch (6 mm) thick "fan-fold" siding backer into 2-inch (50 mm) wide strips. It is a fast, economical method of back-ventilating and draining siding.
- Cedar shingles, traditional stucco and manufactured stone veneers should be installed over drainage mats where annual rainfall exceeds 20 inches (500 mm)

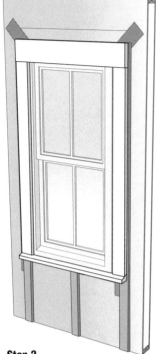

Step 2
- Trim installed at head and jambs; sloped cap flashing (shown) or sill over lower trim

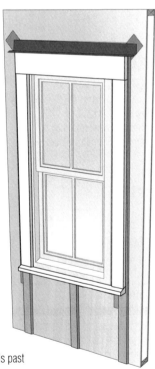

Step 3
- Head cap flashing extends past window trim

Step 4
- Adhesive membrane strip extends past cap flashing

Step 5
- Sheathing tape applied over adhesive membrane strip

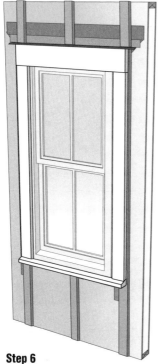

Step 6
- Drainage gap created by furring (shown) or drainage mat
- Do not fasten furring through head cap flashing

Step 7
- Install wood or fiber cement siding

Exterior Conditions

Temperature: 80°F
Relative humidity: 75%
Vapor pressure: 2.49 kPa

Conditions within Cavity:

Temperature: 100°F
Relative humidity: 100%
Vapor pressure: 6.45 kPa

Interior Conditions

Temperature: 75°F
Relative humidity: 60%
Vapor pressure: 1.82 kPa

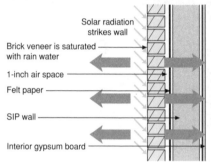

Solar radiation strikes wall

Brick veneer is saturated with rain water

1-inch air space

Felt paper

SIP wall

Interior gypsum board

Vapor is driven both inward and outward by a high vapor pressure differential between the brick and the interior and the brick and the exterior.

Figure 2.6
Problems with Inward Moisture Movement Due to Solar Radiation
- Moisture is driven inward due to solar radiation from reservoir claddings
- Other reservoir claddings are stucco, wood and fiber cement; these claddings should be "back-ventilated"

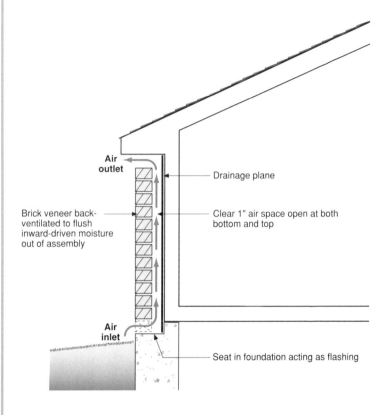

Figure 2.7
Ventilated Cavity
- To effectively uncouple a brick veneer reservoir cladding from a wall system by using back ventilation, a clear cavity must be provided along with both air inlets at the bottom and air outlets at the top

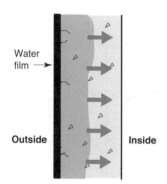

Capillary suction draws
water into porous material
and tiny cracks

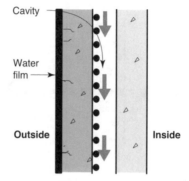

Cavity acts as capillary
break and receptor for
capillary water interrupting flow

Figure 2.8
Capillarity as a Driving Force for Rain Entry
- Capillary suction draws water into porous material and tiny cracks
- Cavity acts as capillary break and receptor for capillary water interrupting flow

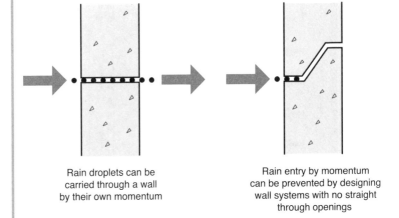

Rain droplets can be
carried through a wall
by their own momentum

Rain entry by momentum
can be prevented by designing
wall systems with no straight
through openings

Figure 2.9
Momentum as a Driving Force for Rain Entry
- Rain droplets can be carried through a wall by their own momentum
- Rain entry by momentum can be prevented by designing wall systems with no straight through openings
- Condition example: window sill

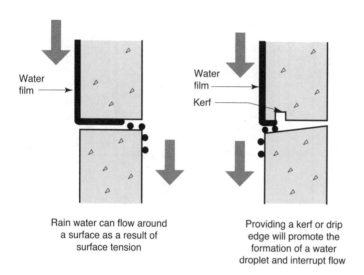

Rain water can flow around
a surface as a result of
surface tension

Providing a kerf or drip
edge will promote the
formation of a water
droplet and interrupt flow

Figure 2.10
Surface Tension as a Driving Force for Rain Entry
- Rain water can flow around a surface as a result of surface tension
- Providing a kerf or drip edge will promote the formation of a water droplet and interrupt flow
- Condition example: window head

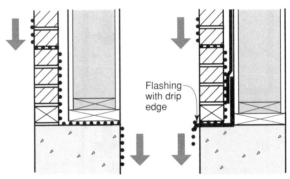

Rain water can flow down
surfaces and enter through
openings and cavities

Flashing with drip edge

Flashings direct gravity
flow rain water back toward
the exterior

Figure 2.11
Gravity as a Driving Force for Rain Entry
- Rain water can flow down surfaces and enter through openings and cavities
- Flashings direct gravity flow rain water back to the exterior

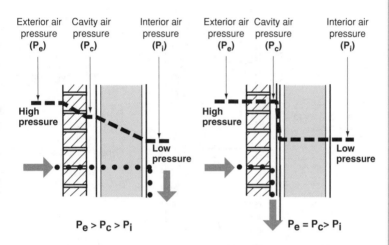

$P_e > P_c > P_i$

Driven by air pressure differences,
rain droplets are drawn through
wall openings from the exterior
to the interior

$P_e = P_c > P_i$

By using pressure moderation
between the exterior and cavity air,
air pressure is diminished as a
driving force for rain entry

Figure 2.12
Air Pressure Difference as a Driving Force for Rain Entry
- Driven by air pressure differences, rain droplets are drawn through wall openings
  from the exterior to the interior
- By using pressure moderation between the exterior and cavity air, air pressure is
  diminished as a driving force for rain entry

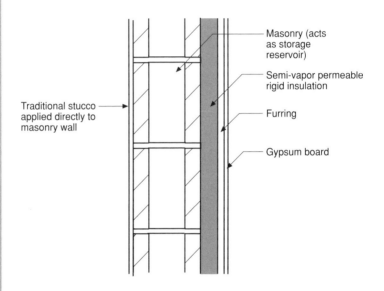

Masonry (acts as storage reservoir)

Semi-vapor permeable rigid insulation

Traditional stucco applied directly to masonry wall

Furring

Gypsum board

Figure 2.13
Face-Sealed Barrier Wall
Storage Reservoir System
- Some rain entry past exterior face permitted
- Penetrating rain stored in mass of wall until drying occurs to interior or exterior
- Can be used in all rain exposure regions

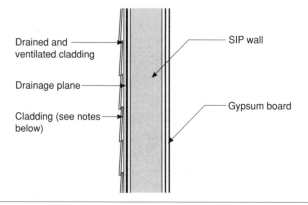

Figure 2.14a
Water Managed Wall—Drained and Ventilated Cladding
- All claddings should be drained
- Claddings should be both drained and back-ventilated where **annual rainfall exceeds 20 inches (500 mm)**
- Wood siding and fiber cement siding can be back-ventilated and drained by installing them over a $1/4$-inch (6 mm) spacer strip over a water resistive barrier
- Cedar shingles, traditional stucco, and manufactured stone veneer can be back-ventilated and drained by installing them over $3/8$-inch (9 mm) drainage mat over a water resistive barrier
- Vinyl or aluminum siding is inherently back-ventilated

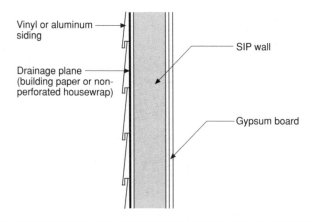

Figure 2.14b
Water Managed Wall—Drained and Ventilated Vinyl or Aluminum Siding Cladding
- Can be used in all regions

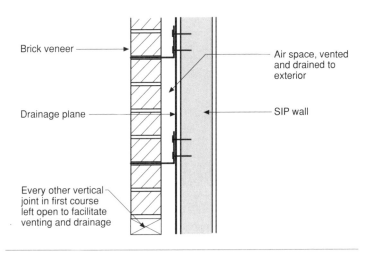

Figure 2.15a
Water Managed Wall—Brick Veneer
- Brick installed over a 1-inch (25 mm) air space with vent openings top and bottom

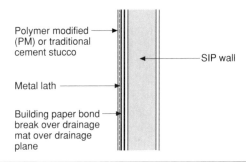

Figure 2.15b
Water Managed Wall—Drained and Ventilated Stucco Cladding

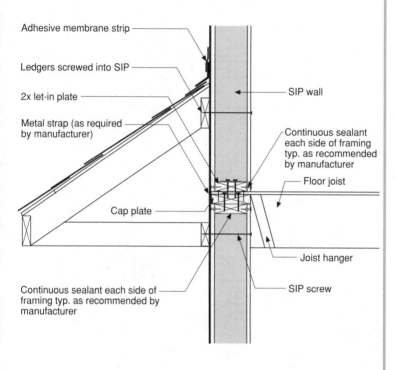

Adhesive membrane strip

Ledgers screwed into SIP

2x let-in plate

Metal strap (as required by manufacturer)

SIP wall

Continuous sealant each side of framing typ. as recommended by manufacturer

Floor joist

Cap plate

Joist hanger

Continuous sealant each side of framing typ. as recommended by manufacturer

SIP screw

Figure 2.16
Flashing Above Shed Roof

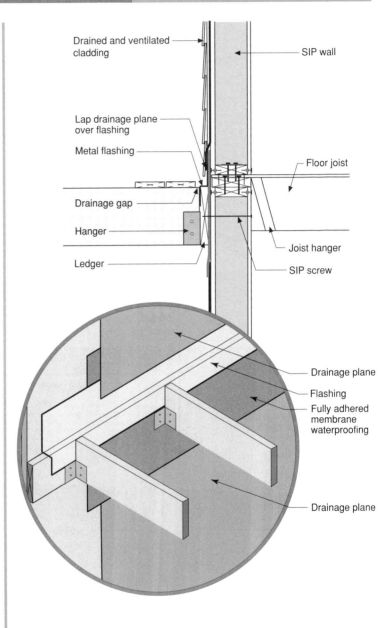

Drained and ventilated cladding

SIP wall

Lap drainage plane over flashing

Metal flashing

Floor joist

Drainage gap

Hanger

Joist hanger

Ledger

SIP screw

Drainage plane

Flashing

Fully adhered membrane waterproofing

Drainage plane

Figure 2.17
Flashing Over Deck Ledger

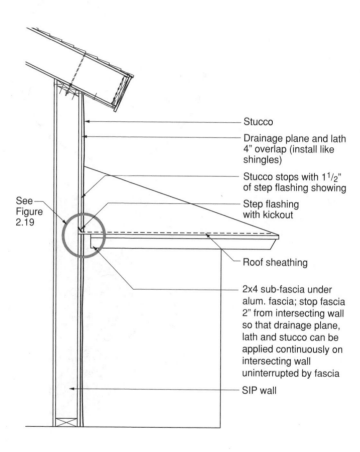

Stucco

Drainage plane and lath 4" overlap (install like shingles)

Stucco stops with 1 1/2" of step flashing showing

Step flashing with kickout

See Figure 2.19

Roof sheathing

2x4 sub-fascia under alum. fascia; stop fascia 2" from intersecting wall so that drainage plane, lath and stucco can be applied continuously on intersecting wall uninterrupted by fascia

SIP wall

Figure 2.18
Roof Encroaching Wall Detail
• Prevents leaks into wall behind stucco

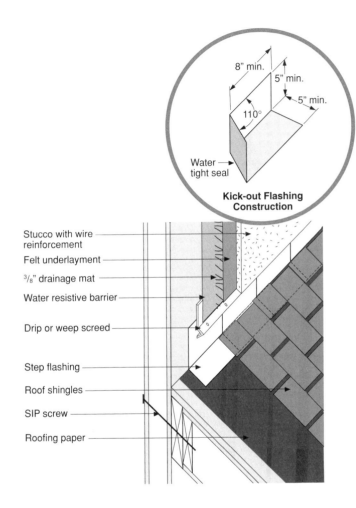

8" min.

5" min.

5" min.

110°

Water
tight seal

**Kick-out Flashing
Construction**

Stucco with wire reinforcement

Felt underlayment

$^{3}/_{8}$" drainage mat

Water resistive barrier

Drip or weep screed

Step flashing

Roof shingles

SIP screw

Roofing paper

Figure 2.19
Stucco at Step Flashing
• Kick-out flashing installed at bottom of intersecting roof

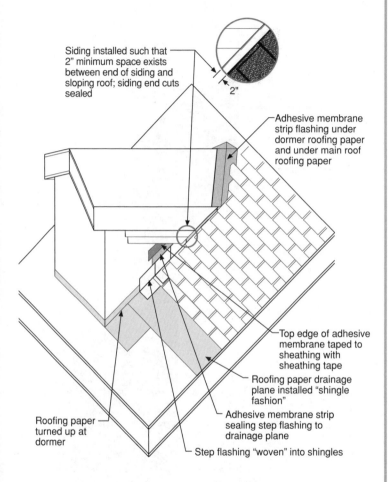

Siding installed such that 2" minimum space exists between end of siding and sloping roof; siding end cuts sealed

2"

Adhesive membrane strip flashing under dormer roofing paper and under main roof roofing paper

Top edge of adhesive membrane taped to sheathing with sheathing tape

Roofing paper drainage plane installed "shingle fashion"

Adhesive membrane strip sealing step flashing to drainage plane

Step flashing "woven" into shingles

Roofing paper turned up at dormer

Note: Layering cut away in this figure shown for clarity, not as recommendation for installation sequencing

Figure 2.20
SIP Dormer Flashing

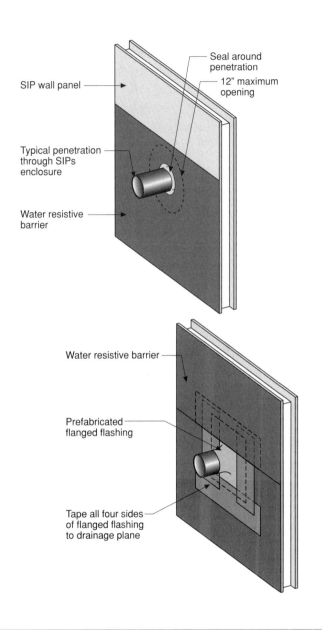

Figure 2.21
Wall Penetration Maximum Size and Flashing Details

Air Barriers

Air barriers are systems of materials designed and constructed to control airflow between a conditioned space and an unconditioned space. The air barrier system is the primary air enclosure boundary that separates indoor (conditioned) air and outdoor (unconditioned) air. In multi-unit/townhouse/apartment construction the air barrier system also separates the conditioned air from any given unit and adjacent units. Air barrier systems also typically define the location of the pressure boundary of the building enclosure.

In multi-unit/townhouse/apartment construction the air barrier system is also the fire barrier and smoke barrier in inter-unit separations. In such assemblies the air barrier system must also meet the specific fire resistance rating requirement for the given separation.

The air barrier system also separates garages from conditioned spaces. In this regard the air barrier system is also the "gas barrier" and provides the gas-tight separation between a garage and the remainder of the house or building.

Air barriers are intended to resist the air pressure differences that act on them. Rigid materials such as gypsum board, exterior sheathing materials like plywood or OSB, and supported flexible barriers are typically effective air barrier systems if joints and seams are sealed. Spray foam systems can also act as effective air barrier systems either externally applied over structural elements or internally applied within cavity systems.

Air barrier systems keep outside air out of the building enclosure or inside air out of the building enclosure depending on climate or configuration. Sometimes, air barrier systems do both.

Air barrier systems can be located anywhere in the building enclosure — at the exterior surface, the interior surface, or at any location in between. In cold climates, interior air barrier systems control the exfiltration of interior, often moisture-laden air. Whereas exterior air barrier

3

systems control the infiltration of exterior air and prevent wind-washing through cavity insulation systems.

Air barrier systems should be:
- impermeable to airflow
- continuous over the entire building enclosure or continuous over the enclosure of any given unit
- able to withstand the forces that may act on them during and after construction
- durable over the expected lifetime of the building

Performance Requirements

Air barrier systems typically are assembled from **materials** incorporated in **assemblies** that are interconnected to create **enclosures**. Each of these three elements has measurable resistance to airflow. The recommended minimum resistances or air permeances for the three components are listed as follows:
- Material   0.02 l/(s-m^2)@75 Pa
- Assembly   0.20 l/(s-m^2)@75 Pa
- Enclosure   2.00 l/(s-m^2)@75 Pa

Materials and assemblies that meet these performance requirements are said to be air barrier materials and air barrier assemblies. Air barrier materials incorporated in air barrier assemblies that in turn are interconnected to create enclosures are called air barrier systems.

Materials and assemblies that do not meet these performance requirements, but are nevertheless designed and constructed to control airflow are said to be air retarders.

The recommended minimum resistances are based on experience and current practice:
- gypsum board is a common air barrier material and it readily meets the material air permeance recommendation (0.0196 l/(s-m^2)@75 Pa as tested by NRCC, 1997)
- The National Building Code of Canada specifies that the principal air barrier material must meet a minimum resistance or air permeance of 0.02 l/(s-m^2)@75 Pa
- The U.S. Department of Energy Building America project sets an airtightness requirement of 1.65 l/(s-m^2)@75 Pa for residences (see Appendix II)

Approaches

In SIP buildings, the SIP themselves are the air barrier system. Each panel meets both the air barrier material requirement and the air barrier assembly requirement.

The key with SIPs are the connections between panels in order to meet the air barrier enclosure requirement—as well as to control air flow within the panel joints themselves.

Almost any joint sealing approach can be used and SIPs easily meet the air barrier enclosure requirement. However, extremely careful and specific joint sealing approaches are necessary to control airflow within the panel joints themselves. This is a critical requirement in roof assemblies in mixed-cold, cold, very cold and subarctic/arctic climate, where an almost "perfect" air seal must be located to the interior of each panel joint. It is not critical in wall assemblies as they can be designed to "dry" outwards by ventilating the cladding. This approach is not typically practical for roof assemblies.

Sealing SIPs at their joints is necessary; in fact, most SIP manufacturers will void their warranties if proper sealing is not executed. SIPs themselves are good vapor barriers. The OSB facingss, two glue-lines, and a core of either urethane or polystyrene foam typically results in a perm rating of under 1.0. While these large monolithic components are very effective at limiting vapor born moisture transmission, air flow through joints can completely dominate moisture flow in a SIP structure if joints are not properly sealed.

Joint Sealing Conditions

There are three different sealing conditions with SIPs; foam-to-foam, foam-to-wood, and wood-to-wood. "Wood" in this case may be blocking, spline connection materials, plates, or supplementary structural members. "Wood" is also taken to be solid-sawn dimensional lumber of any species or grade, or engineered lumber such as LVL, PSL, OSB rim joist material and similar, plywood, or any other "solid" material such as sheet metal or structural steel or the like.

In all cases, the main function is to provide an air seal that is expected to last the life of the structure and withstand movement due to humidity and temperature swings and wood shrinkage.

For foam-to-foam conditions, an expanding foam sealant is preferable. Other "mastic" or "gummy" type materials are not designed to span the large gaps typical in this application. In fact, this is the crucial issue with all sealant applications; that is, that if the gap to be sealed is too wide and the modulus of elasticity of the cured and aged sealant is too high, the sealant itself won't remain a "flexible bridge" and either the adhesive connection will fail, or more likely, the material will yield and fail immediately past the line of adhesion.

For foam-to-wood joints or wood-to-wood joints a "mastic" or "gummy" type sealant may work well but again, expanding foam sealant will also work well. What is important is that the sealant material is selected for its ability to bridge gaps. The larger the gap, the lower the required modulus of elasticity of the sealant. For relatively tight joints of wood-to-wood materials, a "mastic" or "gummy" type sealant is appropriate. This would be typical of plates or the edges of blocking inserts against the SIP OSB facings. If the application system is for sealant applied to the back face of blocking that is against a foam core, a foam sealant should be utilized.

Materials

Foam sealants are recommended to be of the expanding urethane type, either of the one or two component variety. The rate and amount of expansion varies with temperature and humidity. Follow the manufacturer's recommendations to insure that adequate expansion takes place so that sealing is occurring with no breeches or gaps. Other sealants or adhesives may be utilized in accordance with the manufacturer's recommendations of their ability to bridge the required gap once cured and aged. Many sealants or adhesives lose their flexibility over time. Accordingly, low modulus, non-hardening materials will perform best over time, and are recommended.

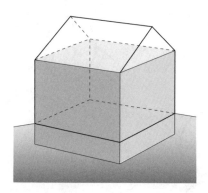

Figure 3.1
Air Barrier System — Single Family Detached
- Separates indoor (conditioned) and outdoor (unconditioned) air
- Separates garages from the conditioned spaces; acts as the "gas barrier"

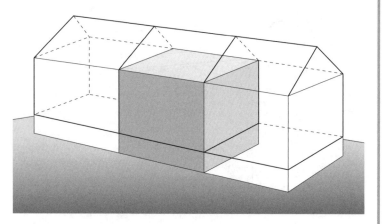

Figure 3.2
Air Barrier System — Multi-Family
- Separates indoor (conditioned) and outdoor (unconditioned) air
- Separates the conditioned air from any given unit and adjacent units

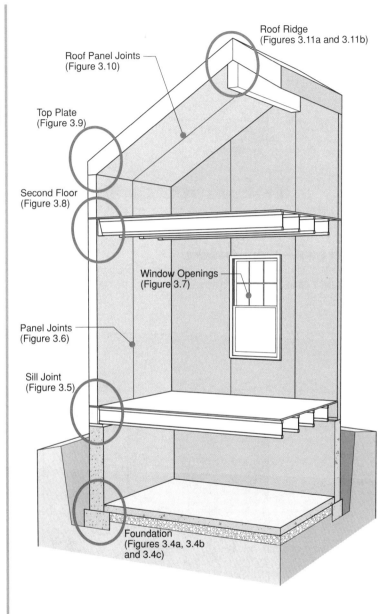

Roof Ridge
(Figures 3.11a and 3.11b)

Roof Panel Joints
(Figure 3.10)

Top Plate
(Figure 3.9)

Second Floor
(Figure 3.8)

Window Openings
(Figure 3.7)

Panel Joints
(Figure 3.6)

Sill Joint
(Figure 3.5)

Foundation
(Figures 3.4a, 3.4b
and 3.4c)

Figure 3.3
Air Sealing Detail Locations
• See following pages for details

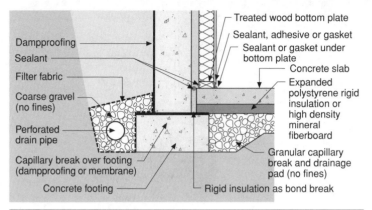

Dampproofing
Sealant
Filter fabric
Coarse gravel (no fines)
Perforated drain pipe
Capillary break over footing (dampproofing or membrane)
Concrete footing

Treated wood bottom plate
Sealant, adhesive or gasket
Sealant or gasket under bottom plate
Concrete slab
Expanded polystyrene rigid insulation or high density mineral fiberboard
Granular capillary break and drainage pad (no fines)
Rigid insulation as bond break

Figure 3.4a
Air Sealing at Concrete Foundation Wall

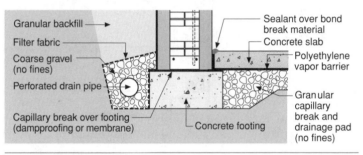

Granular backfill
Filter fabric
Coarse gravel (no fines)
Perforated drain pipe
Capillary break over footing (dampproofing or membrane)
Concrete footing

Sealant over bond break material
Concrete slab
Polyethylene vapor barrier
Granular capillary break and drainage pad (no fines)

Figure 3.4b
Air Sealing at ICF Foundation Wall

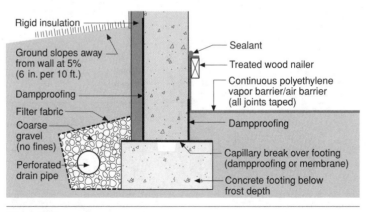

Rigid insulation
Ground slopes away from wall at 5% (6 in. per 10 ft.)
Dampproofing
Filter fabric
Coarse gravel (no fines)
Perforated drain pipe

Sealant
Treated wood nailer
Continuous polyethylene vapor barrier/air barrier (all joints taped)
Dampproofing
Capillary break over footing (dampproofing or membrane)
Concrete footing below frost depth

Figure 3.4c
Air Sealing at Crawlspace without Slab

3

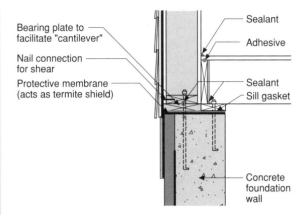

Bearing plate to facilitate "cantilever"
Nail connection for shear
Protective membrane (acts as termite shield)
Sealant
Adhesive
Sealant
Sill gasket
Concrete foundation wall

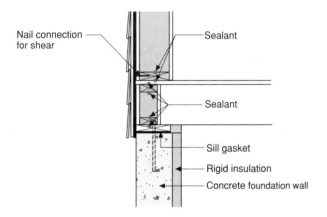

Nail connection for shear
Sealant
Sealant
Sill gasket
Rigid insulation
Concrete foundation wall

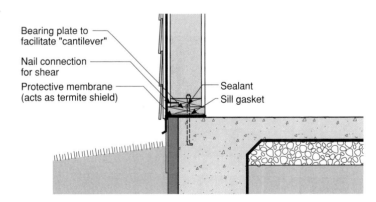

Bearing plate to facilitate "cantilever"
Nail connection for shear
Protective membrane (acts as termite shield)
Sealant
Sill gasket

Figure 3.5
Air Sealing at Sill Joint
- Close-up of the sill area with a floor to panel joint

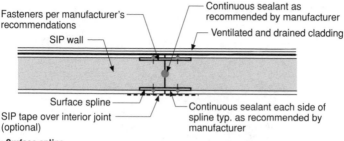

A: Surface spline

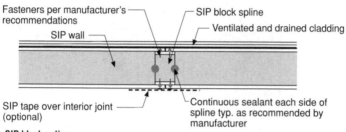

B: SIP block spline

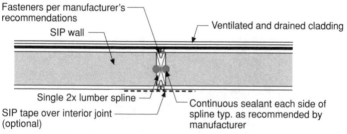

C: Single 2x lumber spline

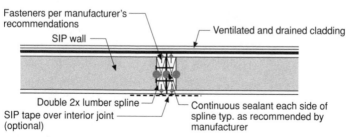

D: Double 2x lumber spline

Figure 3.6
SIPs Air Sealing at Wall Panel Joints
- Close-up of the wall panel joint area

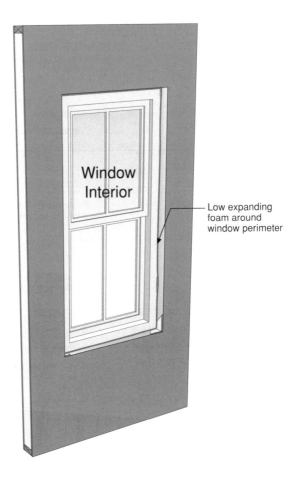

Low expanding
foam around
window perimeter

Figure 3.7
Air Sealing Window from Inside
- For window flashing details and installation sequence see Figure 2.5a through Figure 2.5g

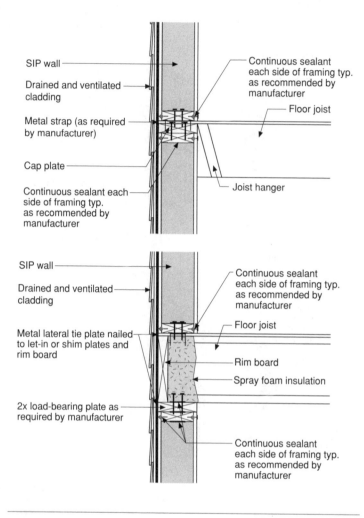

- SIP wall
- Drained and ventilated cladding
- Metal strap (as required by manufacturer)
- Cap plate
- Continuous sealant each side of framing typ. as recommended by manufacturer
- Continuous sealant each side of framing typ. as recommended by manufacturer
- Floor joist
- Joist hanger

- SIP wall
- Drained and ventilated cladding
- Metal lateral tie plate nailed to let-in or shim plates and rim board
- 2x load-bearing plate as required by manufacturer
- Continuous sealant each side of framing typ. as recommended by manufacturer
- Floor joist
- Rim board
- Spray foam insulation
- Continuous sealant each side of framing typ. as recommended by manufacturer

Figure 3.8
Second Floor Connection Details—Hanging Floor and Rim Board
- Vinyl and aluminum siding can be directly applied to housewraps as they are inherently "back-ventilated" due to their profile
- Drained and ventilated cladding such as vinyl siding installed directly over a water resistive barrier, wood siding or cement siding installed over a $1/4$-inch (6 mm) spacer strip over a water resistive barrier, cedar shingles installed over $3/8$-inch (9 mm) drainage mat over a water resistive barrier
- Spacer strip (i.e. "furring") can be as thin as $1/4$-inch (6 mm); cutting foam $1/4$-inch (6 mm) thick "fan-fold" siding backer into 2-inch (50 mm) wide strips is a fast, economical method of back-ventilating and draining siding

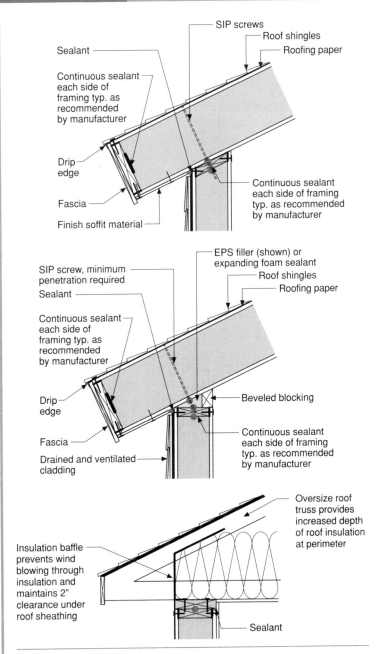

Figure 3.9
SIPs Air Sealing at Top Plate
- Close-up of the top plate area
- Shingles shown for illustrative purposes only; other roof claddings can be used

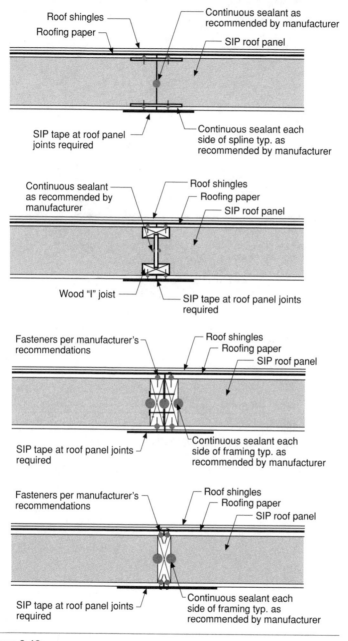

Figure 3.10a
SIPs Air Sealing at Roof Panel Joints

- Close-up of the roof panel joint area
- Shingles shown for illustrative purposes only; other roof claddings can be used

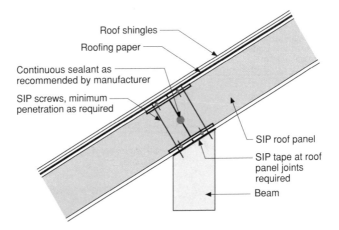

Roof shingles

Roofing paper

Continuous sealant as
recommended by manufacturer

SIP screws, minimum
penetration as required

SIP roof panel

SIP tape at roof
panel joints
required

Beam

Figure 3.10b
SIPs Air Sealing at Roof Panel Joint Over a Beam
- Close-up of the roof panel joint area
- Shingles shown for illustrative purposes only; other roof claddings can be used

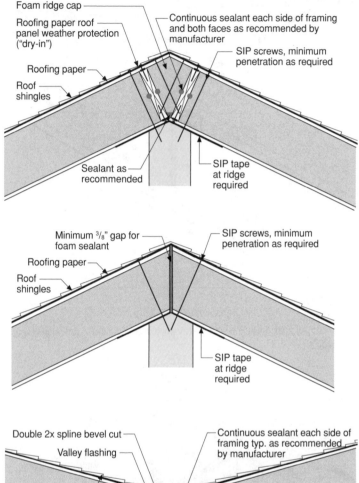

Foam ridge cap

Roofing paper roof panel weather protection ("dry-in")

Roofing paper

Roof shingles

Continuous sealant each side of framing and both faces as recommended by manufacturer

SIP screws, minimum penetration as required

Sealant as recommended

SIP tape at ridge required

3

Minimum ³/₈" gap for foam sealant

Roofing paper

Roof shingles

SIP screws, minimum penetration as required

SIP tape at ridge required

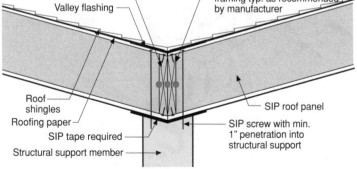

Double 2x spline bevel cut

Valley flashing

Continuous sealant each side of framing typ. as recommended by manufacturer

Roof shingles

Roofing paper

SIP tape required

Structural support member

SIP roof panel

SIP screw with min. 1" penetration into structural support

Figure 3.11
SIPs Air Sealing at Roof Ridge and Roof Valley
- Close-up of the roof ridge and roof valley
- Shingles shown for illustrative purposes only; other roof claddings can be used

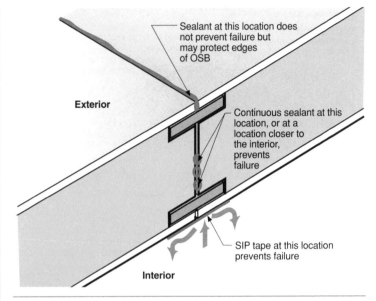

Figure 3.12
Seal Locations
- Air transported moisture leads to decay when interior surface of panel joints is not sealed

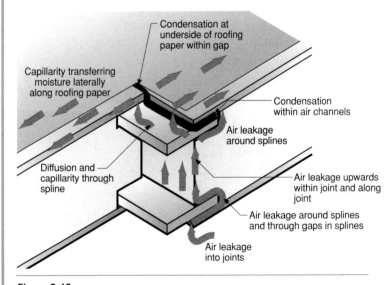

Figure 3.13
SIP "Ridge Rot"—Air Leakage Pathway within Panel Joint
- Air transported moisture leads to decay when interior surface of panel joints is not sealed

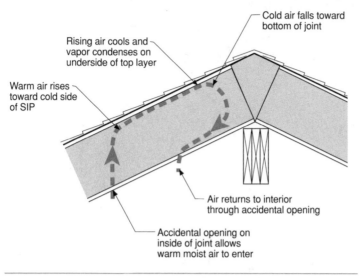

Cold air falls toward bottom of joint

Rising air cools and vapor condenses on underside of top layer

Warm air rises toward cold side of SIP

Air returns to interior through accidental opening

Accidental opening on inside of joint allows warm moist air to enter

Figure 3.14
SIP "Ridge Rot"—Air Leakage Pathway within Panel Joint
• Air transported moisture leads to decay when interior surface of panel joints is not sealed

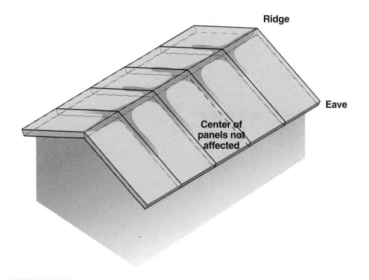

Ridge

Eave

Center of panels not affected

Figure 3.15
SIP "Ridge Rot"
• Air transported moisture leads to decay when interior surface of panel joints is not sealed

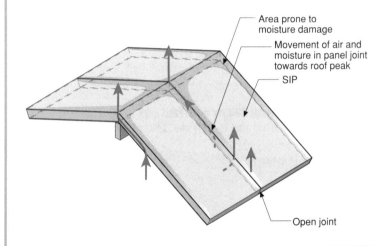

Area prone to
moisture damage

Movement of air and
moisture in panel joint
towards roof peak

SIP

Open joint

Figure 3.16
SIP "Ridge Rot"—Air Leakage Pathway

Wall Design

Ideally, building assemblies would always be built with dry materials under dry conditions, and would never get wet from imperfect design, poor workmanship or occupants. Unfortunately, these conditions do not exist.

It has been accepted by the building industry that many building assemblies become wet during service, and in many cases start out wet. Furthermore, the industry has recognized that in many circumstances it may be impractical to design and build building assemblies which never get wet. This has given rise to the concept of acceptable performance. Acceptable performance implies the design and construction of building assemblies which may periodically get wet, or start out wet yet are still durable and provide a long, useful service life. Repeated wetting followed by repeated drying can provide acceptable performance if during the wet period, materials do not stay wet long enough under adverse conditions to deteriorate.

Good design and practice involve controlling the wetting of building assemblies from both the exterior and interior. They also involve the drying of building assemblies should they become wet during service or as a result of building with wet materials or under wet conditions.

Moisture Balance

Moisture accumulates when the rate of moisture entry into an assembly exceeds the rate of moisture removal. When moisture accumulation exceeds the ability of the assembly materials to store the moisture without degrading performance or long term service life, moisture problems result.

Building assemblies can get wet from the building interior or exterior, or they can start out wet as a result of the construction process due to wet building materials or construction under wet conditions. Good design and practice address these wetting mechanisms.

Various strategies can be implemented to minimize the risk of moisture damage. The strategies fall into the following three groups:
- control of moisture entry
- control of moisture accumulation
- removal of moisture

Strategies in the three groupings can be utilized in combination and have been proven to be most effective in that manner. Strategies effective in the control of moisture entry, however, are often not effective if building assemblies start out wet, and in fact can be detrimental. If a technique is effective at preventing moisture from entering an assembly, it is also likely to be effective at preventing moisture from leaving an assembly. Conversely, a technique effective at removing moisture may also allow moisture to enter. Balance between entry and removal is the key in many assemblies.

Historically successful approaches to moisture control have typically been based on the following strategy: prevent building assemblies and surfaces from getting wet from the exterior, prevent building assemblies and surfaces from getting wet from the interior, and should building assemblies or surfaces get wet, or start out wet, allow them to dry the exterior, the interior or both.

Approach

Water can come in several phases: liquid, solid, vapor and adsorbed. The liquid phase as rain and ground water has driven everyone crazy for hundreds of years but can be readily understood — drain everything and remember the humble flashing. The solid phase also drives everyone crazy when we have to shovel it or melt it, but at least most professionals understand the related building problems (ice damming, frost heave, freeze-thaw damage). But the vapor phase is in a class of craziness all by itself. We will conveniently ignore the adsorbed phase and leave it for someone else to deal with. Note that adsorbed water is different than absorbed water. Adsorbed water sticks to the surface of materials whereas absorbed water is held within materials.

The fundamental principle of control of water in the liquid form is to drain it out if it gets in — and let us make it perfectly clear it will get in if you build where it rains or if you put your building in the ground where there is water in the ground. This is easy to understand, logical, with a long historical basis.

The fundamental principle of control of water in the solid form is to not let it get solid; and, if it does, give it space; or, if it is solid not let it get liquid; and, if it does drain it away before it can get solid again. This is a little more difficult to understand, but logical and based on solid research. Examples of this principle include the use of air entrained concrete to control freeze-thaw damage and the use of attic venting to provide cold roof decks to control ice damming.

The fundamental principle of control of water in the vapor form is to keep it out and to let it out if it gets in. Simple, right? No chance. It gets complicated because sometimes the best strategies to keep water vapor out also trap water vapor in. This can be a real problem if the assemblies start our wet because of the use of wet materials or get wet via a liquid form like rain.

It gets even more complicated because of climate. In general water vapor moves from the warm side of building assemblies to the cold side of building assemblies. This is simple to understand, except we have trouble deciding what side of a wall is the cold or warm side. Logically, this means we need different strategies for different climates. We also have to take into account differences between summer and winter.

Finally, complications arise when materials can store water. This can be both good and bad. A cladding system such as a brick veneer can act as a reservoir after a rainstorm and significantly complicate wall design. Alternatively, wood framing or masonry can act as a hygric buffer absorbing water lessening moisture shocks.

Building assemblies can be designed to dry to either the outside or the inside or to both sides. In general, assemblies should be designed to both sides in all climates.

Wall Assembly Design Recommendations

The recommendations apply to residential occupancies. The recommendations do not apply to business, assembly, educational and mercantile occupancies and to special use enclosures such as spas, pool buildings, museums, hospitals, data processing centers or other engineered enclosures such as factory, storage or utility enclosures.

The recommendations are based on the following principles:
- Avoidance of using vapor barriers where vapor retarders will provide satisfactory performance. Avoidance of using vapor retarders where vapor permeable materials will provide satisfactory performance. Thereby encouraging drying mechanisms over wetting prevention mechanisms.
- Avoidance of the installation of vapor barriers on both sides of assemblies — i.e. "double vapor barriers" in order to facilitate assembly drying in at least one direction.
- Avoidance of the installation of vapor barriers such as polyethylene vapor barriers, foil-faced batt insulation and reflective radiant barri-

er foil insulation on the interior of air-conditioned assemblies — a practice that has been linked with moldy buildings.

- Avoidance of the installation of vinyl wall coverings on the inside of air conditioned assemblies — a practice that has been linked with moldy buildings.

Design Approach

The design approach focuses on controlling rain first, air second, vapor third and heat fourth.

Rain

The best method of rain water control is to provide a drained and ventilated airspace behind a cladding. Installing wood siding on furring strips over a housewrap is one excellent example of this approach. Installing cedar shingles/shakes over a polypropylene mesh (or "Brillo®" pad) and housewrap is another.

Vinyl siding, with its "inherent" leakiness and cross-sectional profile provides its own drainage space and "back-ventilation" without any additional spacing system — just install it over a housewrap and "presto" you have a drained and ventilated cladding.

The key element is the air space between the cladding and the rest of the wall. It allows the wall assembly to dry outwards into it without water being "trapped" in the system by the exterior cladding. The airspace also allows the cladding to dry inwards into the airspace thereby improving cladding and coating durability. Finally, the airpsace acts as a capillary break. The wall just works "better" with an airspace.

Air and Vapor

In general, water vapor moves from the warm side of building assemblies to the cold side of building assemblies.

The good news is that water vapor moves only two ways — vapor diffusion and air transport. If we understand the two ways, we can solve the problem.

The bad news is that techniques that are effective at controlling vapor diffusion can be ineffective at controlling air transported moisture, and vice versa.

Building assemblies need to control the migration of moisture as a result of both vapor diffusion and air transport.

Vapor diffusion is the movement of moisture in the vapor state through a material as a result of a vapor pressure difference (concentration gradient) or a temperature difference (thermal gradient). It is often confused with the movement of moisture in the vapor state into building assemblies as a result of air movement. Vapor diffusion moves moisture from an area of higher vapor pressure to an area of lower vapor pressure as well as from the warm side of an assembly to the cold side. Air transport of moisture will move moisture from an area of higher air pressure to an area of lower air pressure if moisture is contained in the moving air (Figure 4.1).

Vapor pressure is directly related to the concentration of moisture at a specific location. It also refers to the density of water molecules in air. For example, a cubic foot of air containing 2 trillion molecules of water in the vapor state has a higher vapor pressure (or higher water vapor density) than a cubic foot of air containing 1 trillion molecules of water in the vapor state. Moisture will migrate by diffusion from where there is more moisture to where there is less. Hence, moisture in the vapor state migrates by diffusion from areas of higher vapor pressure to areas of lower vapor pressure.

Moisture in the vapor state also moves from the warm side of an assembly to the cold side of an assembly. This type of moisture transport is called thermally driven diffusion.

The second law of thermodynamics governs the exchange of energy and can be used to explain the concept of both vapor pressure driven diffusion and thermally driven diffusion. The movement of moisture from an area of higher vapor pressure to an area of lower vapor pressure as well as from the warm side of an assembly to the cold side of an assembly is a minimization of available "system" energy (or an increase in entropy).

When temperature differences become large, water vapor can condense on cold surfaces. When condensation occurs, water vapor is removed from the air and converted to liquid moisture on the surface resulting in a reduction in water vapor density in the air near the cold surface (i.e. a lower vapor pressure). These cold surfaces now act as "dehumidifiers" pulling more moisture towards them.

Vapor diffusion and air transport of water vapor act independently of one another. Vapor diffusion will transport moisture through materials and assemblies in the absence of an air pressure difference if a vapor pressure or temperature difference exists. Furthermore, vapor diffusion will transport moisture in the opposite direction of small air pressure differences, if an opposing vapor pressure or temperature difference exists. For example, in a hot-humid climate, the exterior is typically at a high vapor pressure and high temperature during the summer. In addition, it is common for an interior air conditioned space to be maintained at a cool temperature and at a low vapor pressure through the dehumidification characteristics of the air conditioning system. This causes vapor diffusion to move water vapor from the exterior towards the interior. This will occur even if the interior conditioned space is maintained at a higher air pressure (a pressurized enclosure) relative to the exterior (Figure 4.2).

Vapor Retarders

The function of a vapor retarder is to control the entry of water vapor into building assemblies by the mechanism of vapor diffusion. The vapor retarder may be required to control the diffusion entry of water vapor into building assemblies from the interior of a building, from the exterior of a building or from both the interior and exterior.

Vapor retarders should not be confused with air barriers whose function is to control the movement of air through building assemblies. In some instances, air barrier systems may also have specific material properties which also allow them to perform as vapor retarders. For example, a rubber membrane on the exterior of a masonry wall installed in a continuous manner is a very effective air barrier. The physical properties of rubber also give it the characteristics of a vapor retarder; in fact, it can

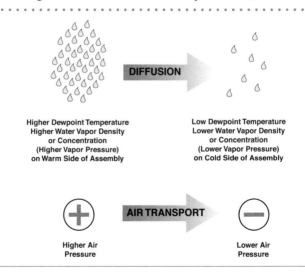

Figure 4.1
Water Vapor Movement
- Vapor diffusion is the movement of moisture in the vapor state as a result of a vapor pressure difference (concentration gradient) or a temperature difference (thermal gradient)
- Air transport is the movement of moisture in the vapor state as a result of an air pressure difference

be considered a vapor "barrier." Similarly, a continuous, sealed polyethylene ground cover installed in an unvented, conditioned crawlspace acts as both an air barrier and a vapor retarder; and, in this case, it is also a vapor "barrier." The opposite situation is also common. For example, a building paper or a housewrap installed in a continuous manner can be a very effective air barrier. However, the physical properties of most building papers and housewraps (they are vapor permeable - they "breathe") do not allow them to act as effective vapor retarders.

4

Water Vapor Permeability

The key physical property which distinguishes vapor retarders from other materials, is permeability to water vapor. Materials which retard water vapor flow are said to be impermeable. Materials which allow water vapor to pass through them are said to be permeable. However, there are degrees of impermeability and permeability and the classification of materials typically is quite arbitrary. Furthermore, under changing conditions, some materials that initially are "impermeable," can become "permeable." Hygroscopic materials change their permeability characteristics as relative humidity increases. For example, plywood sheathing

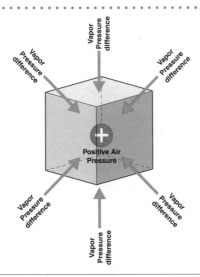

Figure 4.2
Opposing Air and Vapor Pressure Differences
- The atmosphere within the cube is under higher air pressure but lower vapor pressure relative to surroundings
- Vapor pressure acts inward in this example
- Air pressure acts outward in this example

under typical conditions is relatively impermeable. However, once plywood becomes wet, it can become relatively permeable. As a result we tend to refer to plywood as a vapor semi-permeable material.

Non-hygroscopic materials such as polyethylene or plastic housewraps do not change their permeability as a function of relative humidity.

The unit of measurement typically used in characterizing permeability is a "perm." Many building codes define a vapor retarder as a material that has a permeability of one perm or less as tested under dry-cup test method.

4

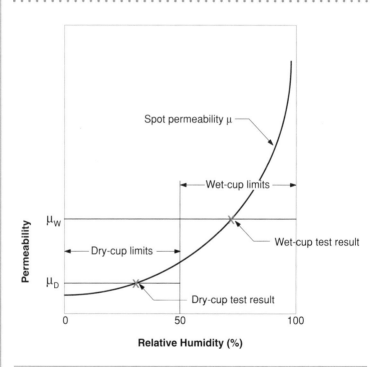

Figure 4.3
Permeability vs. Relative Humidity
- Typical relationship between dry- and wet-cup methods and spot permeability for many hygroscopic building materials such as asphalt impregnated felt building papers, plywood, OSB and kraft facings on insulation batts
- $\mu_w \cong 2$ to 5 times greater than μ_D
- Wet-cup testing occurs with 50% RH on one side of test specimen and 100% RH on other side
- Dry-cup testing occurs with 0% RH on one side of test specimen and 50% RH on other side

Materials are typically tested in two ways to determine permeability: dry-cup testing and wet-cup testing. Some confusion occurs when considering the difference between wet-cup perm ratings and dry-cup perm ratings. A wet-cup test is conducted with 50 percent relative humidity maintained on one side of the test sample and 100 percent relative humidity maintained on the other side of the test sample. A dry-cup test is conducted with 0 percent relative humidity maintained on one side of the test sample and 50 percent relative humidity maintained on the other side of the test sample.

Different values are typical between the two tests for materials that absorb and adsorb water — materials that are hygroscopic. As the quantity of adsorbed water on the surface of hygroscopic materials increases, the vapor permeability of the materials also increases. In other words, for hygroscopic materials, the vapor permeability goes up as the relative humidity goes up (Figure 4.3).

In general, for hygroscopic materials, the wet-cup test provides perm ratings many times the dry-cup test values. For non-hygroscopic materials, materials that are hydrophobic, there is typically no difference between wet-cup and dry-cup test results. For OSB, a hygroscopic material, a dry-cup permeability of 0.5 perms is common. However, as the OSB gets wet, it "breathes" and wet-cup permeabilities of 3 perms or higher are common.

Materials can be separated into four general classes based on their permeance:

- vapor impermeable   0.1 perm or less
- vapor semi-impermeable   1.0 perms or less and greater than 0.1 perm
- vapor semi-permeable   10 perms or less and greater than 1.0 perm
- vapor permeable   greater than 10 perms

Materials that are generally classed as impermeable to water vapor are:

- rubber membranes
- polyethylene film
- glass
- aluminum foil
- sheet metal
- foil-faced insulating sheathings
- foil-faced non-insulating sheathings

Materials that are generally classed as semi-impermeable to water vapor are:

- SIPs
- oil-based paints
- most vinyl wall coverings
- unfaced extruded polystyrene (XPS) greater than 1-inch thick
- traditional hard-coat stucco applied over building paper and OSB sheathing

Materials that are generally classed as semi-permeable to water vapor are:

- plywood
- bitumen impregnated kraft paper
- OSB
- unfaced expanded polystyrene (EPS-Type I*); $3^{1}/_{2}$-inch thick or less
- unfaced extruded polystyrene (XPS); 1-inch thick or less
- fiber-faced isocyanurate; $3^{1}/_{2}$-inch thick or less
- heavy asphalt impregnated building papers (#30 building paper)
- most latex-based paints

Depending on the specific assembly design, construction and climate, all of these materials may or may not be considered to act as vapor retarders. Typically, these materials are considered to be more vapor permeable than vapor impermeable. Again, however, the classifications tend to be quite arbitrary.

Materials that are generally classed as permeable to water vapor are:

- unpainted gypsum board and plaster
- unfaced fiberglass insulation
- cellulose insulation
- synthetic stucco
- some latex-based paints
- lightweight asphalt impregnated building papers (#15 building paper)
- asphalt impregnated fiberboard sheathings
- "housewraps"

---

* EPS-Type I has a vapor resistance of approximately 3.5 perms per inch.

Part of the problem is that we struggle with names and terms. We use the terms vapor retarder and vapor barrier interchangeably. This can get us into serious trouble. Defining these terms is important.

A vapor retarder is the element that is designed and installed in an assembly to retard the movement of water by vapor diffusion. There are several classes of vapor retarders:

Class I vapor retarder	0.1 perm (6 ng/Pa-s-m^2) or less
Class II vapor retarder	1.0 perm (60 ng/Pa-s-m^2) or less and greater than 0.1 perm (6 ng/Pa-s-m^2)
Class III vapor retarder	10 perms (600 ng/Pa-s-m^2) or less and greater than 1.0 perm (60 ng/Pa-s-m^2)

(Test procedure for vapor retarders: ASTM E-96 Test Method A — the desiccant or dry-cup method.)

Finally, a vapor barrier is defined as:

Vapor barrier	A Class I vapor retarder

The current International Building Code (and its derivative codes) defines a vapor retarder as 1.0 perms (60 ng/Pa-s-m^2) or less using the same test procedure. In other words, the current code definition of a vapor retarder is equivalent to the definition of a Class II vapor retarder used here. The National Building Code of Canada defines a vapor control layer as having a permeability of under 60 ng/Pa-s-m^2 (1.0 perm), i.e. a "Class II vapor retarder" as defined in this guide.

Air Barriers

The key physical properties which distinguish air barriers from other materials are continuity and the ability to resist air pressure differences. Continuity refers to holes, openings and penetrations. Large quantities of moisture can be transported through relatively small openings by air transport if the moving air contains moisture and if an air pressure difference also exists. For this reason, air barriers must be installed in such a manner that even small holes, openings and penetrations are eliminated.

Air barriers must also resist the air pressure differences that act across them. These air pressure differences occur as a combination of wind, stack and mechanical system effects. Rigid materials such as interior gypsum board, exterior sheathing and rigid draftstopping materials are effective air barriers due to their ability to resist air pressure differences.

Magnitude of Vapor Diffusion and Air Transport of Vapor

The differences in the significance and magnitude vapor diffusion and air transported moisture are typically misunderstood. Air movement as a moisture transport mechanism is typically far more important than vapor diffusion in many (but not all) conditions. The movement of water vapor through a 1-inch square hole as a result of a 10 Pascal air pressure differential is 100 times greater than the movement of water vapor as a result of vapor diffusion through a 32-square-foot sheet of gypsum board under normal heating or cooling conditions (see Figure 4.4).

In most climates, if the movement of moisture-laden air into a wall or building assembly is eliminated, movement of moisture by vapor diffusion is not likely to be significant. The notable exceptions are rain wetted walls experiencing solar heating or assemblies where no reverse vapor drive occurs such as in subarctic/arctic climate zones or "freezer" room assemblies.

Furthermore, the amount of vapor which diffuses through a building component is a direct function of area. That is, if 90 percent of the building enclosure surface area is covered with a vapor retarder, then that vapor retarder is 90 percent effective. In other words, continuity of the vapor retarder is not as significant as the continuity of the air barrier.

SIP Wall Properties

SIP assemblies have several unique properties. One of them is that they are "air tight" because their cores are "solid" and "homogenous." The foam cores do not make them prone to "convection" and "condensation" due to air leakage. Since SIP cores are "air impermeable," convective air flows and condensation due to air leakage are not possible[*] (see Figure 4.5).

Another of the unique properties of SIP assemblies are the panel permeance characteristics. The three distinct layers in a SIP (inner layer, outer layer and the core) are typically of equal vapor resistance. For example, if OSB is used as both the inner and outer layers, the permeance of each OSB layer is approximately 1.0 perm. If the core is EPS-Type I and is 3.5 inches thick, the permeance of the core is also approximately 1.0 perm (EPS-Type I has a vapor resistance of approximately 3.5 perms per inch – therefore 3.5 inches yields approximately 1.0 perm).

The typical, almost ubiquitous, 4.5 inch thick standard SIP, is therefore "uniformly" vapor semi-impermeable. The overall vapor resistance is about 0. 33 perms (1 perm plus 1 perm plus 1 perm; see Figure 4.6). However, the resistance to vapor flow inward and outward is the same

---

[*] Except at panel joints—air sealing at panel joints is necessary and important.

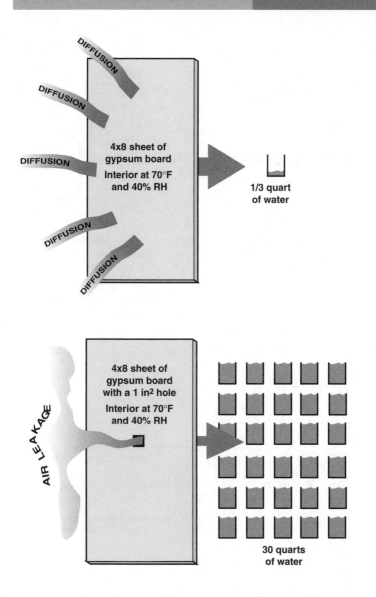

Figure 4.4
Diffusion vs. Air Leakage
- In most cold climates over an entire heating season, $1/3$ of a quart of water can be collected by diffusion through gypsum board without a vapor retarder; 30 quarts of water can be collected through air leakage

Design

Frame Wall vs. SIP Wall and Calculating Vapor Resistance

4

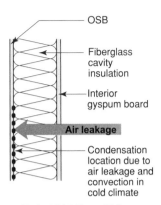
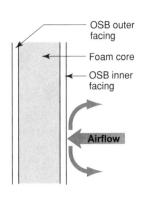

- OSB
- Fiberglass cavity insulation
- Interior gyspum board
- Air leakage
- Condensation location due to air leakage and convection in cold climate

- OSB outer facing
- Foam core
- OSB inner facing
- Airflow

Typical Stick Frame Wall
- Cavity within typical frame wall is prone to airflow and convection
- Condensation can occur at exterior sheathing in cold climates

SIP Wall
- Core is "solid" and "homogenous" and "air impermeable"
- Convection and air leakage is not possible within SIP
- Condensation due to convection and air leakage within SIP is not possible

Figure 4.5
Frame Wall vs. SIP Wall

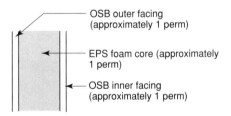

- OSB outer facing (approximately 1 perm)
- EPS foam core (approximately 1 perm)
- OSB inner facing (approximately 1 perm)

The resistance of a SIP to water vapor flow by diffusion is the sum of the individual resistances of the layers. This sum is determined by adding the reciprocals of the permeance of the individual layers. The sum is then inverted (i.e. we take the reciprocal of the sum of the reciprocals to convert it back to perms).

$$1/1 \text{ OSB} + 1/1 \text{ EPS} + 1/1 \text{ OSB} = 3 \text{ reps}$$

$$1/3 \text{ reps} = 0.33 \text{ perms}$$

Figure 4.6
Calculating Vapor Resistance

irrespective of which side of the panel you are considering. This is one of those "duh" moments. The typical panel is "bi-laterally" symmetrical – the resistance to vapor flow is identical from one side of the panel centerline to the next. Under dry-cup conditions it is also identical between the inner and outer layers and the core if the panel is OSB faced. What does this mean? Well, the panel, if it has a core at least 3.5 inches thick (or thicker) and if the core has a vapor resistance of 3.5 perms or less per inch, then the panel can be used in any climate zone on the planet.[*] It is a "universal" assembly (Figure 4.7).

The 4.5 inch thick standard SIP with OSB linings also meets the typical building code requirements for vapor retarders (US-IBC-1.0 perms) and vapor control layers (CDN-NBCC-60 ng/Pa-s-m^2) by virtue of the vapor permeability characteristics of the OSB inner lining. No additional interior plastic polyethylene vapor barrier is required—or desirable (exception: subarctic and arctic climates).

Now, keep in mind a couple of key points, the core should not be more "vapor open" than the inner and outer layers or moisture could accumulate within the panel. So increasing the thickness of the core thereby providing a "lower" vapor permeance than both exterior layers is a good thing. Or, increasing the permeance of the outer layers, by going to plywood, or fiber cement is also a good thing.

Note the words "under dry-cup conditions." That is under conditions where there is no moisture in the OSB facings. When there is moisture in the OSB facings, the OSB permeability increases (i.e. "under wet-cup conditions"). So, SIPs are forgiving if they get wet – assuming that they are not covered internally or externally with layers that do not "breathe" – such as vinyl wall coverings and fully adhered impermeable membranes.

What if I want a panel less than 4.5 inches thick? Okay, don't use EPS Type I, use XPS (but not less than 1 inch thick – since XPS has a vapor resistance of 1.0 perms per inch). You can't use polyurethane foam since its vapor resistance is similar to EPS Type I – or approximately 3 perms per inch. Of, course this is assuming you are sticking with OSB as both the inner and outer layers. If you go to plywood, not a problem, since plywood is significantly more vapor open than OSB (but only after it gets damp – i.e. under "wet-cup" conditions. Or go to fiber cement or to gypsum board.

What about all these sheet metal faced SIPs? Well, they are always somewhat of a risk as they rely on "perfect" joints and no penetrations since they can never "dry" outwards or inwards. They are pretty good for freezers if you don't perforate them with holes – so they would be

[*] In subarctic/arctic climates it may be necessary to install a fully adhered impermeable membrane over the inner layer.

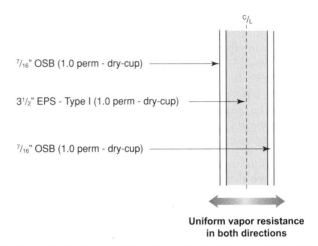

$^{7}/_{16}$" OSB (1.0 perm - dry-cup)

$3^{1}/_{2}$" EPS - Type I (1.0 perm - dry-cup)

$^{7}/_{16}$" OSB (1.0 perm - dry-cup)

**Uniform vapor resistance
in both directions**

Figure 4.7
Bilateral Symmetry
- Vapor resistance of each of the three distinct layers is approximately equal
- It does not matter which side is cold or which side is warm as characteristics do not change based on season; panels therefore work in all climates*
- Key to assembly performance is the linings on both sides of panel (exterior cladding and interior finish)

* Except north of the Arctic circle and south of the Antarctic circle.

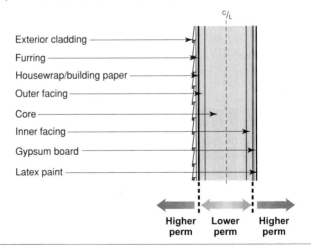

Exterior cladding

Furring

Housewrap/building paper

Outer facing

Core

Inner facing

Gypsum board

Latex paint

Higher perm **Lower perm** **Higher perm**

Figure 4.8
Outward and Inward Drying
- Vapor resistance of housewrap/building paper/cladding should be lower (more "breathable") than SIP thereby permitting outward drying
- Vapor resistance of interior gypsum board/latex paint layer should be lower (more "breathable") than SIP thereby permitting inward drying

a dumb idea as an exterior wall system with cladding attached with screws, but would be a pretty good idea if they were painted or had a direct applied stucco.

The vapor profile of a given wall assembly is important to the performance of the wall assembly. If the "basic rule" of low core vapor permeance is not followed, careful analysis and experimentation is likely necessary.

The general rule, if you could actually call it a general rule, is for the core to have an equal or lower vapor permeance (or equal or higher vapor resistance) than inner or outer layers. You can therefore manipulate the material characteristics by increasing the permeability of the inner or outer layers, or you could decrease the permeability of the core by increasing its thickness or by going to a lower permeability core material.

This same general rule should also be extended to whatever is placed over the exterior and interior surfaces of the SIP.

So, if I were to install a cladding over the exterior surface of the SIP, it would make sense to "back" ventilate the cladding by installing it over an airspace and to install a housewrap that has a higher vapor permeability than the exterior surface of the SIP. This is not typically an issue as the minimum permeability of housewraps is around 5 perms – and the permeability of OSB is around 1 perm. Similarly on the interior. Installing gypsum board and painting with latex paint allows the SIP to dry towards the interior since latex painted gypsum board has a vapor permeability typically greater than 10 perms (Figures 4.8 and 4.9).

The back-ventilation of claddings is an important necessity for durability where annual rainfall exceeds 20 inches (500 mm). See Figure 2.1 in Chapter 2. Unlike stick-built wall assemblies with vapor open cavity insulations, the exterior layer of OSB on a SIP cannot "dry" inwards into the core—it can only dry outwards—hence the necessity for the airspace between the exterior cladding and the SIP. Note that local exposure conditions dominate—overhangs matter, wind direction matters, etc. (see Figure A on page xiv).

What about those fully-adhered peel and stick impermeable membranes? In general, you should only use them when you absolutely have to use them due to elevated risk associated with rain. Most wall assemblies work best with ventilated claddings installed over vapor open drainage planes (housewraps). If the SIP outer layer gets wet it can dry through the vapor open drainage plane into the airspace between the cladding and the drainage plane. A fully-adhered peel and stick membrane prevents this drying—but it does "kick butt" in terms of wind-driven rain. So, the trade-off is excellent rain control versus lower drying.

4

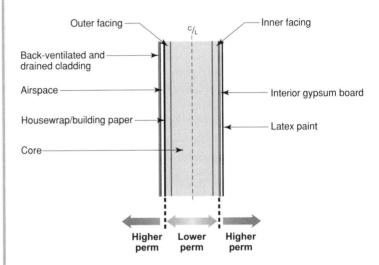

Outer facing — Inner facing

Back-ventilated and drained cladding

Airspace — Interior gypsum board

Housewrap/building paper — Latex paint

Core

Higher perm | Lower perm | Higher perm

Outer Layer Towards Cladding
- Outer layer should be more vapor permeable than core
- Housewrap/building paper should be more permeable than outer layer
- Back-ventilating and draining exterior cladding makes exterior cladding more permeable than housewrap/building paper

Inner Layer Towards Interior Gypsum Board
- Inner layer should be more vapor permeable than core
- Painted interior gypsum board should be more vapor permeable than inner layer

Figure 4.9
Outward and Inward Drying
- Back-ventilated and drained exterior claddings are necessary where annual rainfall exceeds 20 inches (500 mm) or in subarctic/arctic climates
- Wood and fiber cement siding are back-ventilated and drained by installing them over furring (i.e. spacer strips). The furring can be as thin as $1/4$-inch (6mm); cutting foam "fan-fold" siding backer into 2-inch (50 mm) wide strips works well.
- Cedar shingles, traditional stucco, and manufactured stone veneers are back-ventilated and drained by installing them over a $3/8$-inch (9 mm) drainage mat
- Vinyl and aluminum siding are inherently back-ventilated and drained

It can get rather complicated when climate factors are also considered. In the south, where the vapor drive is predominately inward, installing an impermeable membrane on the exterior is not a problem. In the north, this is a problem, since the vapor drive is predominately outward. But what does "south" mean? What does "north" mean? What if you are on the north side of south, or the south side of north? Arggah!

The general rule for fully adhered impermeable membranes applied to the **exterior** of a typical SIP is that in hot-humid climates you can use them without restriction. In all other climates, you are going to have to do some hygro-thermal analysis. In residential occupancies, without humidification (i.e. controlled ventilation and interior relative humidity controlled to 35 percent RH or lower during the winter months), fully adhered impermeable membranes will work in mixed humid climates, but not in marine climates and not in cold and very cold climates. They are definitely a no-no in subarctic and arctic climates unless an interior layer of equal or greater vapor resistance is also installed. This general rule also applies to roof SIP assemblies.

4

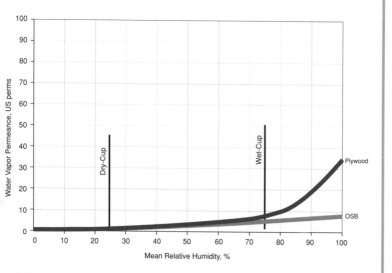

Figure 4.10
Water Vapor Resistance of OSB and Plywood
- The permeability of OSB and plywood goes up as the relative humidity goes up

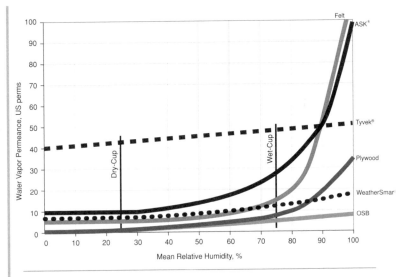

Figure 4.11
Housewraps and Building Papers
• The permeability of all housewraps and building papers is greater than OSB

* Asphalt saturated kraft paper

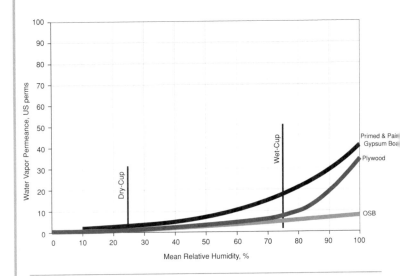

Figure 4.12
Painted Gypsum Board
• The permeability of painted gypsum board is greater than OSB

Roof Design

Roofs can be designed and constructed to be either vented ("cold roof") or unvented ("hot roof") in any hygro-thermal zone. The choice of venting or not venting is a design and construction choice not a requirement determined by the physics or by the building code. The model codes allow both vented ("cold roof") and unvented ("hot roof") roof assemblies. The applicable physics impacts the design of attic or roof systems as does the applicable building code but neither limit the choice.

In cold climates, the primary purpose of attic or roof ventilation is to maintain a cold roof temperature (hence the term "cold roof") to control ice dams created by melting snow, and to vent moisture that moves from the conditioned space to the attic. Melted snow, in this case, is caused by heat loss from the conditioned space. The heat loss is typically a combination of air leakage and conductive losses. The air leakage is due to exfiltration from the conditioned space (often because ductwork located in attic is not sealed) and from penetrations like non-airtight recessed lights. The conductive losses are usually from supply ductwork and equipment located in attic spaces above ceiling insulation (ductwork is typically insulated only to R-6; whereas ceiling insulation levels are above R-30). Conductive losses also occur directly through insulation, or where insulation is missing or thin. Unvented roof construction using SIPs avoids all of these problems.

In hot climates, the primary purpose of attic or roof ventilation is to expel solar heated hot air from the attic to lessen the building cooling load.

As the complexity of attic and roof assemblies increases, the difficulty to construct vented assemblies also increases. The more complex a roof geometry, the easier it is to construct the assembly in an unvented conditioned manner. With complex roof designs, multiple dormers, valleys, hips, skylights combined with cathedral construction with interior soffits, trey ceilings and multiple service penetrations it is often not practical to construct a vented roof assembly with an airtight interior air barrier at the ceiling plane. Again, unvented roof construction using SIPs avoids these problems.

Additionally, it is more common to locate mechanical systems and ductwork in attic spaces. When such ductwork is leaky significant problems can occur. There are significant energy advantages and durability advantages to move the thermal boundary and pressure boundary (air barrier) to the underside of the roof deck thereby locating these mechanical systems and ductwork within the building conditioned spaces.

In high wind regions – particularly in coastal areas, wind driven rain is a problem with vented roof assemblies. Additionally, during high wind events, vented soffit collapse leads to building pressurization and window blowout and roof loss due to increased uplift. Unvented roofs – principally due to the robustness of their soffit construction - outperform vented roofs during hurricanes – they are safer.

In coastal areas salt spray and corrosion are a major concern with steel frames, metal roof trusses and truss plate connectors in vented attics.

Finally, in wildfire zones, unvented roofs and attics have significant benefits in terms of fire safety over vented roof assemblies.

Effect on Shingle Life

Temperature and ultra-violet (UV) radiation affect the life of shingles. The greater the temperature of the shingle, the shorter the life of the shingle. The greater the UV exposure the shorter the life of the shingle.

In general, shingles installed on unvented attic assemblies ("hot roof") operate at a slightly higher temperature. This has impacts on the durability of roof assemblies. A 2 or 3 degree F (1 degree C) rise in average temperature is typical for asphalt shingles and a corresponding 10 degree F (6 degree C) rise in average temperature for sheathing.

All other things being equal, applying the Arrhenius equation, a 10 percent reduction in shingle useful service life should be expected when installed over an unvented roof deck. This is comparable to the effect of the installation of radiant barriers. What is more significant to note is that the color of shingles, roof orientation and geographic location have a more profound effect on the durability of shingles than the choice of venting or not venting – double or triple the effect of venting/non-venting.

A vented shingle roof in Houston, TX "warrantied for 15 years" lasts about 10 years and a vented shingle roof in Minneapolis, MN "warrantied for 15 years" last about 20 years. The solar and UV exposure in Houston is about twice that of Minneapolis. Note that the warranty guarantee has nothing to do with the prediction of shingle service life — it is strictly a marketing tool.

A light colored roof in Houston or Minneapolis lasts about twice as long as a dark colored roof in either location—all other things being equal.

Installing asphalt shingles on unvented SIP roof assemblies typically results in a reduction in shingle life of between 1 and 2 years—depending on location, color and orientation. Dark colored shingles in southern locations facing west are the most affected—light colored shingles in northern locations on north exposures are the least affected.

Telegraphing of Panel Joints

Changing moisture contents in the outer layers of SIP roof assemblies can result in the "telegraphing" of panel joints through asphalt shingle roofs (Figure 5.1). This can also happen with stick frame truss or rafter assemblies. It is principally an aesthetic issue. This is not a problem with wood shingles, wood shakes, standing seam metal roofs due to the "slippage" and "give" of these roof claddings relative to asphalt shingles. However, it can be annoying with asphalt shingles.

One way to prevent "telegraphing" in asphalt shingle SIP roofs is to "over-clad"—add another layer of roof sheathing on purlins on the top of SIP roofs (Figure 5.2). Another way is to add an additional layer of OSB over the top of a SIP roof—i.e. "over-sheath" the SIP to provide some slippage and movement between the SIPs and the asphalt shingles.

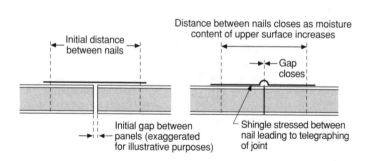

Figure 5.1
Telegraphing of Panel Joints
- Telegraphing can occur due to panel movement driven by temperature and relative humidity

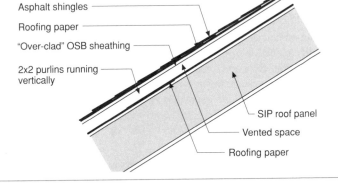

Figure 5.2
Over-Cladding of SIP Roof
- Additional layer of roof sheathing installed over vented air space on top of SIP roof
- Roofing paper installed at two locations—under shingles and under purlins on top of SIP roof
- Roofing paper under asphalt shingles can be replaced with a fully adhered impermeable membrane; however, roofing paper under purlins should always remain "vapor permeable" or "breathable"
- A "cold roof" is installed over top of "hot roof"

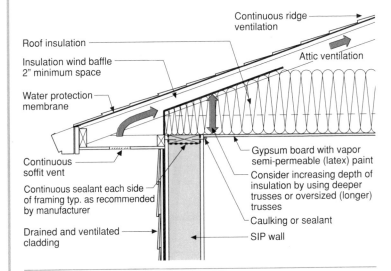

Figure 5.3
Vented Roof
- Roof insulation at perimeter should be equal to or greater than the thermal resistance of the wall
- 1:300 roof ventilation recommended

Vented Roofs

It is possible to construct stick-framed vented attics over SIP buildings. When constructing vented attics the vented attic should not communicate with the conditioned space. An air barrier at the ceiling line – such as sealed gypsum board - should be present to isolate the attic space from the conditioned space (Figure 5.3). Ideally, no services such as HVAC distribution ducts, air handlers, plumbing or fire sprinkler systems should be located external to the ceiling air barrier.

The recommended ventilation ratio to provide for vented attic assemblies when an air barrier is present, is the 1:300 ratio (as specified by most building codes). This is based principally on good historical experience.

In vented cathedral ceiling assemblies a minimum 2-inch clear airspace is recommended between the underside of the roof deck and the top of the cavity insulation.

In addition to an air barrier at the ceiling line, a Class II vapor retarder should be installed in Climate Zones 6 or higher.

Class I vapor retarders (i.e. vapor barriers) can be installed in vented attic assemblies in Climate Zones 6 or higher but should be avoided in other climate zones as top side condensation can occur in summer months during air conditioning periods.

No interior attic assembly side vapor control is required or recommended in climate zones other than Climate Zones 6 or higher for vented attic assemblies. With vented attic assemblies moisture that diffuses into the attic space from the conditioned space is vented to the exterior by attic ventilation.

Ice Damming

Ice damming occurs when the temperature of the roof cladding is above freezing and when the outside temperature is below freezing with snow present on the roof.

In traditional vented roof construction ice damming failures occur principally due to heat loss from the house via air leakage. Since most SIP roof assemblies are inherently more airtight than stick-framed vented roofs, most SIP roof assemblies perform better than stick-framed vented roofs from an ice dam perspective. However, in extreme snow regions this may not always be the case – unless two additional causal factors are addressed.

First: snow has a demonstrable thermal resistance – it varies between R-1 and R-2 per inch. Ten inches of snow has a thermal resistance of between R-10 and R-20. The more snow on a roof, the greater the thermal resistance of the snow. With enough snow depth even airtight well-insulated roofs will experience ice damming simply due to the thermal resistance of the snow blanket.

Second: solar radiation heats wall claddings during sunny days sufficiently to create a "wall stack effect" causing heated air to rise up and be trapped by overhangs. When exterior air temperatures are below freezing, wall cladding temperatures can be in the 40's or higher. The darker the cladding the higher the temperature (Figure 5.4).

In extreme snow regions it is necessary to add a vented air space between the roof cladding (shingles) and the SIP roof assembly to flush heat away trapped due to the insulating value of the snow (the snow becomes an insulating "blanket") – and it is necessary to construct insulated "overhangs" to address the solar heating of wall assemblies (which are easy to create with SIP roof construction; see Figure 5.5). This approach creates a vented-unvented hybrid roof assembly ideal for ice dam control in extreme snow regions. Think of this approach as adding a "cold roof" over the top of a "hot roof."

Roof Cladding

Shingles can be installed directly on roofing underlayment over SIP assemblies. However, shingles work best when installed on "over-clad" SIP assemblies.

Wood shingles and wood shakes should always be installed over a vented drainage space such as drainage mats (i.e. "Cedar Breather®") or batten and counter-batten wood assemblies.

Slate roofs should also be installed over a vented drainage space similar to wood shingles and wood shakes. An additional layer of OSB or more robust wood battens and counter-battens are typically necessary for attachment purposes.

Metal roofs should also be installed such that they are on batten and counter-batten systems.

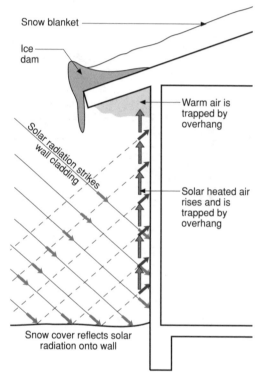

5

Figure 5.4
Solar Heated Wall
- Ice damming caused by solar heated wall warming air
- Warm air rises and is trapped by overhang leading to ice dam
- Vented attics perform worse as heat enters attic

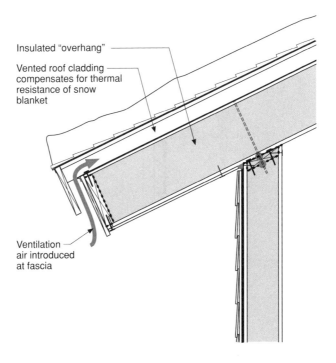

Insulated "overhang"

Vented roof cladding compensates for thermal resistance of snow blanket

Ventilation air introduced at fascia

Figure 5.5
Vented-Unvented Hybrid
- Note insulation of overhang
- Venting of roof cladding compensates for thermal resistance of snow blanket
- A "cold roof" is added over top of a "hot roof"

Foundation Design

The three foundation approaches common to residential construction are crawlspaces, slabs and basements. Each can be built with concrete, masonry or wood. Each can be insulated on the inside, the outside, the middle or on both sides. However, they all have to:

- hold the building up
- keep the groundwater out
- keep the soil gas out
- keep the water vapor out
- let the water vapor out if it gets inside
- keep the heat in during the winter
- keep the heat out during the summer

Water Managed Foundations

Water managed foundation systems rely on two fundamental principles (see Figure 6.1, Figure 6.2 and Figure 6.3):

- keep rain water away from the foundation wall perimeter
- drain groundwater with sub-grade perimeter footing drains before it gets to the foundation wall

Water managed foundation systems are different from waterproofing systems. Waterproofing relies on creating a watertight barrier without holes. It can't be done. Even boats need pumps. Water managed foundation systems prevent the buildup of water against foundation walls, thereby eliminating hydrostatic pressure. No pressure, no force to push water through a hole. Remember, we know the foundation wall will have holes.

Mixing control joints with water management is a fundamental requirement for functional foundation systems that provide an extended useful service life.

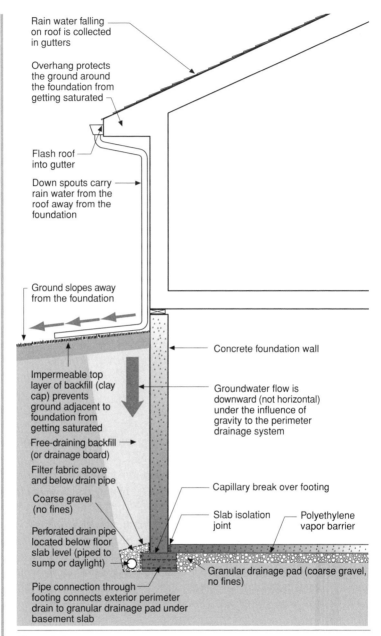

Rain water falling on roof is collected in gutters

Overhang protects the ground around the foundation from getting saturated

Flash roof into gutter

Down spouts carry rain water from the roof away from the foundation

Ground slopes away from the foundation

Impermeable top layer of backfill (clay cap) prevents ground adjacent to foundation from getting saturated

Free-draining backfill (or drainage board)

Filter fabric above and below drain pipe

Coarse gravel (no fines)

Perforated drain pipe located below floor slab level (piped to sump or daylight)

Pipe connection through footing connects exterior perimeter drain to granular drainage pad under basement slab

Concrete foundation wall

Groundwater flow is downward (not horizontal) under the influence of gravity to the perimeter drainage system

Capillary break over footing

Slab isolation joint

Polyethylene vapor barrier

Granular drainage pad (coarse gravel, no fines)

Figure 6.1
Groundwater Control with Basements

- Keep rain water away from the foundation perimeter
- Drain groundwater away in sub-grade perimeter footing drains before it gets to the foundation wall

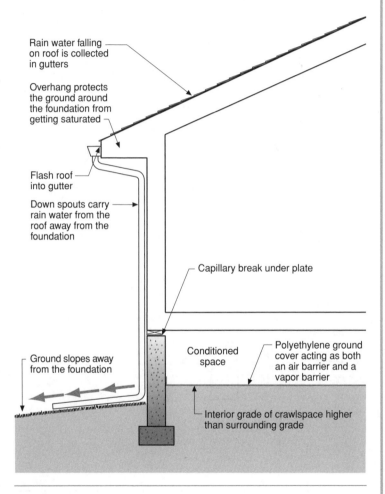

Rain water falling on roof is collected in gutters

Overhang protects the ground around the foundation from getting saturated

Flash roof into gutter

Down spouts carry rain water from the roof away from the foundation

Capillary break under plate

Ground slopes away from the foundation

Conditioned space

Polyethylene ground cover acting as both an air barrier and a vapor barrier

Interior grade of crawlspace higher than surrounding grade

Figure 6.2
Groundwater Control with Crawlspaces

- Keep rain water away from the foundation perimeter
- If the interior crawlspace is lower than the exterior grade, a sub-grade perimeter footing drain is necessary as in a basement foundation
- The crawlspace in this configuration is conditioned space; it is part of the "interior" of the building and should be heated, cooled and ventilated as part of the building's heating, cooling and ventilating strategy

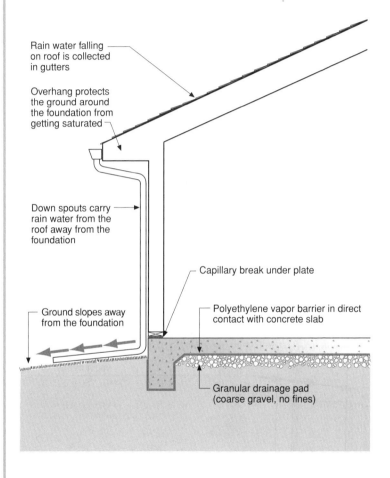

Rain water falling on roof is collected in gutters

Overhang protects the ground around the foundation from getting saturated

Down spouts carry rain water from the roof away from the foundation

Capillary break under plate

Ground slopes away from the foundation

Polyethylene vapor barrier in direct contact with concrete slab

Granular drainage pad (coarse gravel, no fines)

Figure 6.3
Groundwater Control with Slabs
- Keep rain water away from the foundation perimeter
- Do not place sand layer over polyethylene vapor barrier under concrete slab

Dampproofing should not be confused with waterproofing. Dampproofing protects foundation materials from absorbing ground moisture by capillarity. Dampproofing is not intended to resist groundwater forces (hydrostatic pressure). If water management is used, waterproofing is not necessary. However, control of capillary water is still required (dampproofing). Dampproofing is typically provided by coating the exterior of a concrete foundation wall with a tar or bituminous paint or coating.

Draining groundwater away from foundation wall perimeters is typically done with free-draining backfill such as sand, gravel or other water-permeable material, or drainage boards or exterior foundation insulations with drainage properties.

Soil Gas

Keeping soil gas (radon, water vapor, herbicides, termiticides, methane, etc.) out of foundations cannot be done by building hole-free foundations because hole-free foundations cannot be built. Soil gas moves through holes due to a pressure difference. Since we cannot eliminate the holes, the only thing we can do is control the pressure.

The granular drainage pad located under concrete slabs can be integrated into a sub-slab ventilation system to control soil gas migration by creating a zone of negative pressure under the slab. A vent pipe connects the sub-slab gravel layer to the exterior through the roof (Figures 6.4, 6.5 and 6.6). An exhaust fan can be added later, if necessary.

Moisture

Controlling water vapor in foundations relies first on keeping it out, and second, on letting it out when it gets in. Make no mistake, it will get in. The issue is complicated by the use of concrete and masonry because there are thousands of pounds of water stored in freshly cast concrete and freshly laid masonry to begin with. This moisture of construction has to dry to somewhere, and it usually (but not always) dries to the inside.

For example, we put coarse gravel (no fines) and a polyethylene vapor retarder under a concrete slab to keep the water vapor and water in the ground from getting into the slab from underneath. The gravel and polyethylene do nothing for the water already in the slab. This water can only dry into the building. Installing flooring, carpets or tile over this concrete before it has dried sufficiently and in a manner that does not permit drying, is a common mistake that leads to mold, buckled flooring and lifted tile, even in hot-dry and mixed-dry climates.

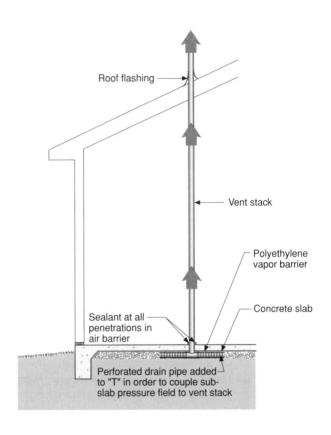

Roof flashing

Vent stack

Polyethylene
vapor barrier

Concrete slab

Sealant at all
penetrations in
air barrier

Perforated drain pipe added
to "T" in order to couple sub-
slab pressure field to vent stack

Figure 6.4
Soil Gas Ventilation System — Slab Construction
- Granular drainage pad depressurized by active fan located in attic or by passive stack action of warm vent stack located inside conditioned space or garage
- Communication to all sub-slab areas is required. Where slabs are divided by a thickened section to support a bearing wall, pipe connections through the thickened section will be necessary. Multiple connection points or interconnection piping may be required between multi-level slabs similar to those found in split level homes.

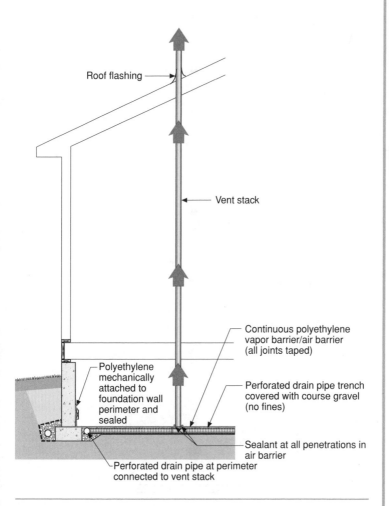

Roof flashing

Vent stack

Continuous polyethylene
vapor barrier/air barrier
(all joints taped)

Polyethylene
mechanically
attached to
foundation wall
perimeter and
sealed

Perforated drain pipe trench
covered with course gravel
(no fines)

Sealant at all penetrations in
air barrier

Perforated drain pipe at perimeter
connected to vent stack

Figure 6.5
Soil Gas Ventilation System — Crawlspace Construction
- Perforated drain pipe in trenches covered with coarse gravel create depressurized zones under air barrier due to active fan located in attic or by passive stack action of warm vent stack located inside heated space
- Crawlspace is conditioned (heated during the winter, cooled during the summer) by a supply HVAC system duct
- Perforated drain pipe may not be necessary with tightly sealed polyethylene and coarse gravel
- Perimeter trench connected to centrally located vent stack

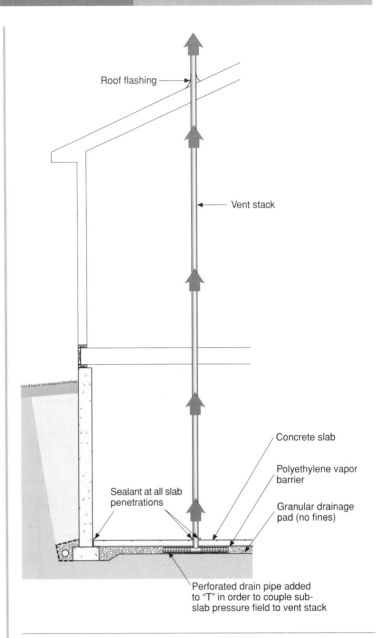

Roof flashing

Vent stack

Concrete slab

Polyethylene vapor barrier

Granular drainage pad (no fines)

Sealant at all slab penetrations

Perforated drain pipe added to "T" in order to couple sub-slab pressure field to vent stack

Figure 6.6
Soil Gas Ventilation System — Basement Construction

- Granular drainage pad depressurized by active fan located in attic or by passive stack action of warm vent stack located inside heated space
- Avoid offsets or elbows in vent stack to maximize air flow

Similarly, we install dampproofing on the exterior of concrete foundation walls and provide a water managed foundation system to keep water vapor and water in the ground from getting into the foundation from the exterior. Again, this does nothing for the water already in the foundation wall. When we then install interior insulation and finishes on the interior of a foundation wall in a manner that does not permit drying to the interior, mold will grow.

Foundation wall and slab assemblies must be constructed so that they resist water vapor and water from getting in them, but they also must be constructed so that it is easy for water vapor to get out when it gets in or if the assembly was built wet to begin with (as they typically are).

Insulating under a concrete slab with vapor permeable or semi-vapor permeable rigid insulation will cause the concrete slab to dry into the ground as well as into the building. By insulating under the slab, the slab becomes much warmer than the ground. Water vapor flows from warm to cold. If the sub-slab insulation is not a major vapor retarder, the slab will be able to dry into the ground, even if the ground is saturated. A polyethylene vapor retarder under a concrete slab is unnecessary when sub-slab insulation is used. You should use either a polyethylene vapor retarder or sub-slab insulation. It is not necessary to use both. If you use both, put the polyethylene over the top of the insulation directly in contact with the concrete slab.

This approach can also be applied to foundation walls that are insulated on the exterior. By warming the foundation walls relative to the ground, the moisture moves outwards into the ground. Again, the exterior insulation must not be a major vapor retarder, and dampproofing cannot be installed. The exterior insulation used must also be a capillary break and provide drainage. Only rigid fiberglass, rock and slag wool insulation have these two properties. All other rigid insulations used on the exterior of foundation walls should be used with dampproofing.

Drying a foundation wall assembly or floor slab after it is insulated and after surface finishes have been installed should only be done using diffusion ("letting them breathe"), not air flow ("ventilation"). Allowing interior air (that is usually full of moisture, especially in the humid summer months) to touch cold foundation surfaces will cause condensation and wetting, rather than the desired drying. It is important that interior insulation assemblies and finishes be constructed as airtight as possible but vapor permeable. This will prevent interior moisture-laden air from accessing cold surfaces during both the winter and summer and still allow the assemblies to dry. It is extremely important not to have a vapor retarder on the interior of internally insulated basement assemblies.

Capillary Break

Concrete and masonry are sponges – they can absorb or "wick" water due to capillarity (see Figure 6.7). This is the main reason that damp-proofing (the black tar-like coating) is applied to exterior basement walls. The dampproofing fills in the pores in the concrete and masonry to reduce ground water absorption. The dampproofing is a capillary break. Under concrete floor slabs, the stone layer combined with poly-ethylene serves a similar function (they act as capillary breaks). Unfortunately, the capillary rise through footings is typically ignored. This can be a major problem if foundation perimeter walls are finished or insulated.

In new construction a capillary break should be installed on the top of the footing between the footing and the perimeter foundation wall (see Figure 6.8). This can be done by dampproofing the top of the footing or by installing a membrane at this location.

Interior Basement Insulation

In new construction, and particularly in renovations, the interior insula-tion and finishing approach must take into account the moisture migrat-ing up through the footing. This is best accomplished by installing va-

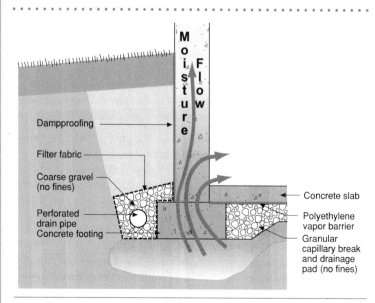

Figure 6.7
Capillary Rise Through Basement Footing

por semi-permeable rigid foam insulation on the interior of the assembly to protect the interior finishes and to release the capillary water to the interior in a controlled manner— at a rate that does not damage interior finishes or lead to mold.

The best foams to use have a perm rating of greater than 1 perm for the thickness used. This means limiting extruded polystyrene insulation to less than 1-inch thickness for walls (when they are more than 1-inch thick they do not breathe sufficiently) and making sure that the rigid insulation is not faced with polypropylene skins or foil facings. Additionally, since foams need to be protected from fire, and this is often done with gypsum board, only latex paint should be used on interior gypsum finishes (since latex breathes). This breathability requirement for rigid foams limits the thickness and therefore the thermal resistance of the wall. If higher insulation levels are required, an interior insulated frame wall can be added.

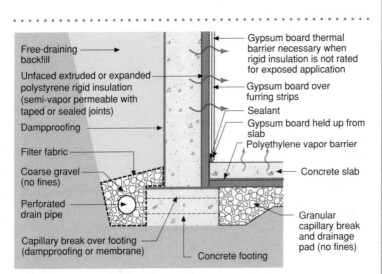

Figure 6.8
Capillary Break Over Footing

- Concrete wall cold, can only dry to the interior if interior assemblies are vapor semi-permeable (permeance greater than 1 perm — i.e. unfaced extruded polystyrene less than 1-inch thick); mold possible if interior assemblies do not permit drying
- Cold concrete wall must be protected from interior moisture-laden air in winter and in summer
- Basement floor slab can dry to the interior
- Thicker foam can be used if drainage is provided between the foam and the foundation wall (see Figure 6.11)

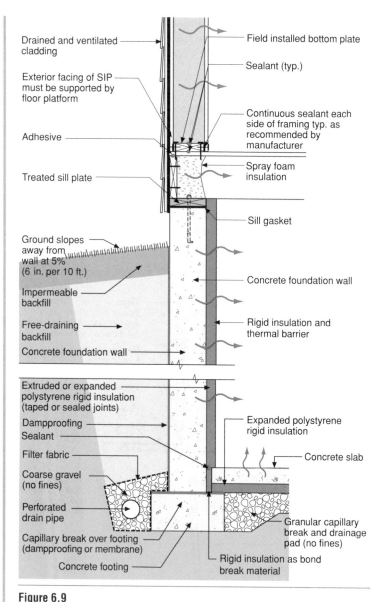

Drained and ventilated cladding

Exterior facing of SIP must be supported by floor platform

Adhesive

Treated sill plate

Ground slopes away from wall at 5% (6 in. per 10 ft.)

Impermeable backfill

Free-draining backfill

Concrete foundation wall

Extruded or expanded polystyrene rigid insulation (taped or sealed joints)

Dampproofing
Sealant

Filter fabric

Coarse gravel (no fines)

Perforated drain pipe

Capillary break over footing (dampproofing or membrane)

Concrete footing

Field installed bottom plate

Sealant (typ.)

Continuous sealant each side of framing typ. as recommended by manufacturer

Spray foam insulation

Sill gasket

Concrete foundation wall

Rigid insulation and thermal barrier

Expanded polystyrene rigid insulation

Concrete slab

Granular capillary break and drainage pad (no fines)

Rigid insulation as bond break material

Figure 6.9
Internally Insulated Concrete Basement with Wood Siding Above

- Concrete wall cold; can only dry to the interior if interior assemblies are vapor semi-permeable; low likelihood of mold
- Cold concrete wall must be protected from interior moisture-laden air in winter and in summer
- Basement floor slab is warm, can dry to the ground (since there is no under-slab vapor retarder) as well as to the interior; lowest likelihood of mold

Basements should be designed to dry to the interior (see Figure 6.9). These principles are often in conflict with some common misapplied energy conservation and moisture control practices – for example the use of sheet polyethylene as an interior vapor barrier.

Sheet polyethylene (or vapor barriers) should never be installed on the interior of interior basement insulation assemblies or on the interior of interior insulation in below grade wall assemblies in any climate as it prevents drying to the interior. The exception to this interior vapor barrier in basements rule is where drainage is provided between the interior vapor barrier and the assembly (i.e. exterior to the vapor barrier – see Figure 6.10 — Interior Drainage: Renovations and Figure 6.11 — Interior Drainage: New Construction).

Impermeable interior finishes should be avoided, such as vinyl wall coverings or oil (alkyd) based paints. In a similar vein, vinyl floor coverings should be avoided on basement floor slabs or on slab-on-grade construction unless a low water-to-cement ratio concrete is used (less than 0.45) installed directly over a polyethylene vapor barrier – and only where slab edges are protected from capillary water (see Figure 6.12 – Capillary Control For Monolithic Slab).

Slab Construction

Capillary control is necessary for slab-on-grade construction and crawlspaces (see Figure 6.12). Monolithic slabs need plastic ground covers that extend under the perimeter grade beam and upwards to grade. Additionally, the exposed portion of the slab edge that is exposed to the outside must be painted with latex paint to reduce water absorption and a capillary break must be installed under perimeter wall framing.

Interior perimeter drainage can also be used in new construction — particularly where impermeable rigid insulation is used on the interior of the foundation wall. This allows rigid insulation of greater than 1-inch to be used. And, if foil-faced rigid insulation is used — with the appropriate flame-spread and smoke-developed rating — it can be left exposed (i.e. interior gypsum board does not have to be installed as thermal barrier for fire protection. See Figure 6.11).

Also in renovations, the conditions under a slab may be difficult to determine, or once they are determined, it is found that a stone layer or polyethylene is not present. It may be necessary to provide "top side" control of water and vapor. This can be done several ways. If salts are not present in the ground, epoxy coatings or chemical sealers may be used. Salts lead to osmosis and osmotic pressures are typically greater than the bond strength of most coatings and sometimes exceed the cohesive strength of concrete (i.e. the coating is pushed off the slab or the

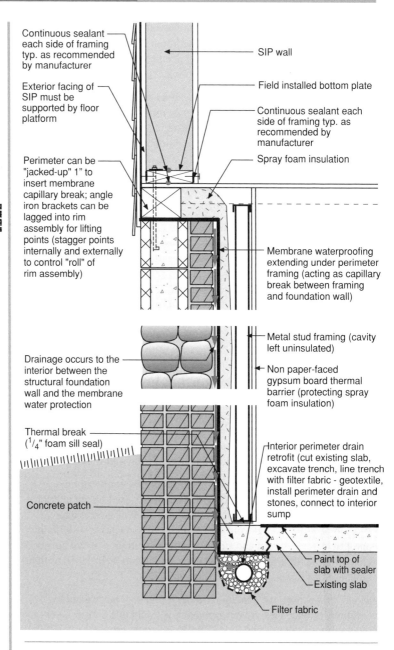

Continuous sealant each side of framing typ. as recommended by manufacturer

SIP wall

Exterior facing of SIP must be supported by floor platform

Field installed bottom plate

Continuous sealant each side of framing typ. as recommended by manufacturer

Perimeter can be "jacked-up" 1" to insert membrane capillary break; angle iron brackets can be lagged into rim assembly for lifting points (stagger points internally and externally to control "roll" of rim assembly)

Spray foam insulation

Membrane waterproofing extending under perimeter framing (acting as capillary break between framing and foundation wall)

Metal stud framing (cavity left uninsulated)

Drainage occurs to the interior between the structural foundation wall and the membrane water protection

Non paper-faced gypsum board thermal barrier (protecting spray foam insulation)

Thermal break ($\frac{1}{4}$" foam sill seal)

Interior perimeter drain retrofit (cut existing slab, excavate trench, line trench with filter fabric - geotextile, install perimeter drain and stones, connect to interior sump

Concrete patch

Paint top of slab with sealer

Existing slab

Filter fabric

Figure 6.10
Interior Drainage — Renovation

- Interior membrane waterproofing must be gas tight and vapor tight relative to the interior

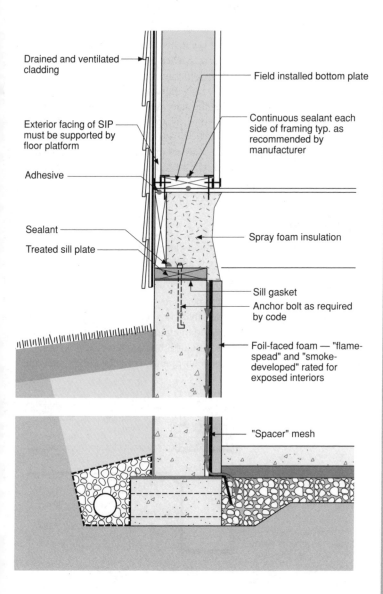

Drained and ventilated cladding

Field installed bottom plate

Exterior facing of SIP must be supported by floor platform

Continuous sealant each side of framing typ. as recommended by manufacturer

Adhesive

Sealant

Spray foam insulation

Treated sill plate

Sill gasket

Anchor bolt as required by code

Foil-faced foam — "flame-spread" and "smoke-developed" rated for exposed interiors

"Spacer" mesh

Figure 6.11
Interior Drainage — New Construction
- Interior rigid insulation must be gas tight and vapor tight relative to the interior
- This can also be a retrofit approach

concrete spalls/flakes apart). If salts are present, spacer systems that provide vapor control and drainage can be used over the top of existing slabs (see Figure 6.13).

A "floating floor" (see Figure 6.14) can also be used where moisture flow upwards is small – or where a finished wood floor (or carpet) is to be installed over a slab. Rigid insulation and plywood are installed on the top of the slab. In this assembly extruded polystyrene should be limited to $^3/_4$ - inch or less so that the slab can dry upwards (floors are different than walls with respect to permeability limits). Carpets should never be installed directly on below grade slabs unless slabs are insulated (below or on the top surface). Carpets on uninsulated slabs are cold resulting in sufficiently elevated relative humidities within the carpet to support dust mite and mold growth.

Exterior Drainage

It is always better to intercept groundwater before it gets to a foundation wall. Exterior perimeter drainage is always preferable to interior perimeter drainage.

However, in renovations, exterior perimeter drainage may not be present or may not be practical or possible. In such cases, interior perimeter drainage can be used and connected to an interior sump pump. Interior sump pits/crocks must be fitted with airtight gasketed covers to prevent soil gas entry. This interior perimeter drainage may be combined with

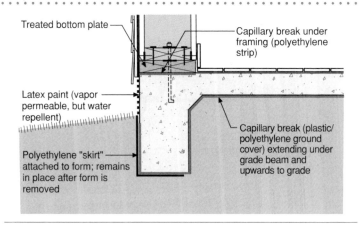

Treated bottom plate

Capillary break under framing (polyethylene strip)

Latex paint (vapor permeable, but water repellent)

Capillary break (plastic/ polyethylene ground cover) extending under grade beam and upwards to grade

Polyethylene "skirt" attached to form; remains in place after form is removed

Figure 6.12
Capillary Control for Monolithic Slab
- Never install a sand layer between a polyethylene ground cover and a slab; the sand layer becomes wet and holds water indefinitely; the sand can only dry upwards, not downwards, due to the polyethylene

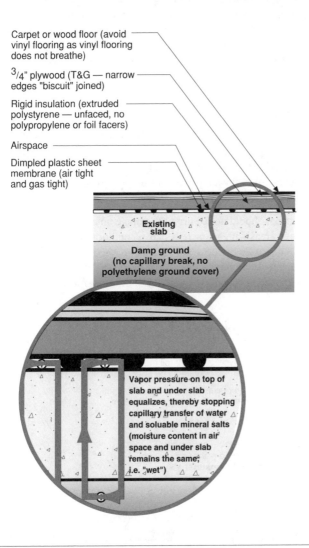

Carpet or wood floor (avoid vinyl flooring as vinyl flooring does not breathe)

$3/4$" plywood (T&G — narrow edges "biscuit" joined)

Rigid insulation (extruded polystyrene — unfaced, no polypropylene or foil facers)

Airspace

Dimpled plastic sheet membrane (air tight and gas tight)

Existing slab

Damp ground (no capillary break, no polyethylene ground cover)

Vapor pressure on top of slab and under slab equalizes, thereby stopping capillary transfer of water and soluable mineral salts (moisture content in air space and under slab remains the same; i.e. "wet")

Figure 6.13
Slab Top-Side Vapor Control — Airspace Approach
- Works in both new construction and rehabilitation
- Plywood glued (T&G edges) to itself not mechanically fastened (no screws or nails) through foam and dimpled plastic sheet membrane so that gas barrier/air barrier is not comprised
- Groundwater leakage can also be handled with this approach by draining the airspace to a sump or floor drain
- It is important to seal the sheet membrane around the foundation perimeter thereby isolating the airspace from the interior

an interior drainage layer. Where an interior drainage layer is used, it must be gas tight and vapor tight relative to the interior (see Figure 6.10). Another technique is to use an exterior impermeable material to minimize rain and groundwater entering below grade spaces (see Figure 6.15).

Crawlspaces

Crawlspaces should be designed and constructed to be dry and pest-free. A dry crawlspace is good for the inhabitants and good for building durability. A dry crawlspace is less likely to have pests and termites. Make sure you control rainwater, groundwater and provide drainage for potential plumbing leaks or flooding incidents.

Crawlspaces should not be used for storage unless they are designed as storage areas with a concrete slab, a conditioning system and ready access. Otherwise builders and contractors should use designs that discourage the use of crawlspaces for storage, and provide clear guidance to owners and occupants to avoid using this area for storage.

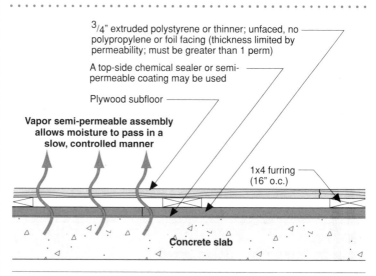

Figure 6.14
Slab Top-Side Vapor Control — Semi-Permeable Floating Floor
- Extruded polystyrene should be used due to its compressive strength (expanded polystyrene can be used if furring spacing is reduced to 12-inches o.c. or if plywood is supported directly on foam—i.e. no furring)
- Not applicable with visibly wet slabs and where efflorescence (salts) is visible
- Avoid vinyl flooring with this assembly as vinyl flooring does not breathe

Crawlspaces should ideally be designed and constructed as mini-basements, part of the house – within the building boundary. They should not be vented to the exterior. They should be insulated on their perimeters and should have a continuous sealed ground cover such as taped polyethylene. They should have perimeter drainage just like a basement (when the crawlspace ground level is below the ground level of the surrounding grade). Make sure there is good drainage away from crawlspaces.

While crawlspace venting has been viewed as good building practice and is still required by some codes, an unvented crawlspace with insulation on the perimeter performs better in terms of moisture, durability and pest control.

Perimeter insulation rather than floor insulation performs better in all climates. The crawlspace temperatures and relative humidity track that of the house. Crawlspaces insulated on the perimeter are warmer and drier than crawlspaces insulated between the crawlspace and the house. Cold surfaces that can condense water are minimized.

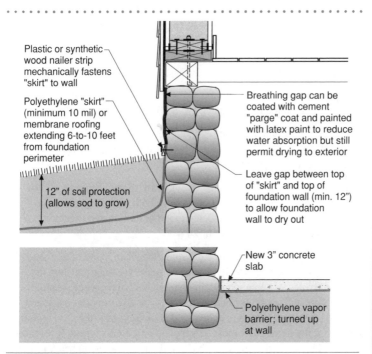

Plastic or synthetic wood nailer strip mechanically fastens "skirt" to wall

Polyethylene "skirt" (minimum 10 mil) or membrane roofing extending 6-to-10 feet from foundation perimeter

12" of soil protection (allows sod to grow)

Breathing gap can be coated with cement "parge" coat and painted with latex paint to reduce water absorption but still permit drying to exterior

Leave gap between top of "skirt" and top of foundation wall (min. 12") to allow foundation wall to dry out

New 3" concrete slab

Polyethylene vapor barrier; turned up at wall

Figure 6.15
Using an Impermeable Skirt Outside
• Prevents saturation of ground adjacent to existing foundation

A major source of summertime high humidity in crawlspaces is humid outside air entering through vents. When humid outside air comes into crawlspaces the relative humidity goes up. Since crawlspaces are cooler than the outside condensation may form on cold surfaces. Summertime ventilation in crawlspaces usually makes them wetter not drier. Wintertime ventilation makes crawlspaces colder and is not very effective at drying them. Additionally, wintertime ventilation increases the heat loss from the home – venting crawlspaces can waste energy, and can lead to freezing pipes and uncomfortable floors.

Note: The International Building Code (ICC) allows the construction of closed (unvented) — conditioned — crawlspaces. Contact code officials in the design phase to determine their requirements.

If it is not possible to treat the crawlspace as a part of the house such as in flood zones in coastal areas – or where it is not necessary such as in dry climates, it is important to construct the house such that the crawlspace is isolated from the house – outside of the building boundary. This can be accomplished by air sealing the boundary between the crawlspace and the house and by installing a vapor barrier on the underside of the floor assembly (see Figure 6.16). This vapor barrier needs to have sufficient thermal resistance to control condensation (in both summer and winter)— as such insulating sheathing is recommended in this location. A similar approach is recommended for homes on piers (see Figure 6.17).

No heating and cooling equipment or ductwork should be in the crawlspace if it is treated as an outside (vented) space.

In parts of the country where radon and pesticides in soil gases can be found, sub-slab passive ventilation is recommended (see Figure 6.5). This also helps keep a crawlspace drier.

If possible, seal the vents in an existing crawlspace. Build new crawlspaces without vents. Where homes have both a crawlspace and a basement they should be connected together and treated together as a conditioned space (see Figure 6.20).

It is always necessary to have a drying mechanism. One option is to passively connect the crawlspace to the house via floor registers or transfer grilles. The incidental air change that happens between the crawlspace and the house in this manner typically provides sufficient drying. A second option is to heat and cool them as if they are included as part of the home. Air must be supplied to the crawlspace from the home. This air can be returned back to the home or it can be exhausted (see Figure 6.23a through Figure 6.23f). A third option is a UL-approved dehumidifier plumbed to a sump pump or drain.

Some existing crawlspaces are sources of pollutants that cannot be satis-factorily removed or controlled. The most practical solution is to install a durable fan to exhaust air continuously from the crawlspace to the out-side. The fan should be rated for continuous duty and sized according to either ASHRAE Standard 62.2 (so that it also provides ventilation for the house if desired) or at a minimum rate of 20 cfm/1000 square feet otherwise. This reverses the flow air, pulling air from the house into the crawlspace and then out of the building (Figure 6.23d).

To keep them dry all crawlspaces should have:

- Continuous, durable ground cover or liner
- Rain water and groundwater control similar to a basement if the crawlspace is below the ground level of the surrounding grade
- Pest control measures as appropriate for the location
- Inside sloped to one or more low places for when a flooding in-cident occurs from a plumbing leak or rain entry – the low places should be either drained to daylight or a sump pump.

There are several ways to provide a durable ground cover or liner. The option used depends on the resources available, the frequency of people entering the crawlspace to either store possessions (not a good idea) or to maintain equipment and the severity of the pest problem.

Carpets

Installing carpets on cold, damp concrete floor slabs can lead to serious allergic reactions and other health-related consequences. It is not recom-mended that carpets be installed on basement concrete slabs unless the carpets can be kept dry and warm. In practice, this is not possible unless basement floor slab assemblies are insulated and basement areas are conditioned. Installing carpets on concrete slab foundations located at grade is risky unless the slab is insulated and the carpet and associated carpet pad are vapor permeable. Slabs on grade are typically warmer and much dryer than basement slabs.

Insects and Termites

There is no good way of dealing with termites. Borate-treated wood framing, cavity insulation (cellulose) and rigid foams are a promising approach, but long-term performance has yet to be demonstrated. Using a protective membrane or a stainless steel mesh with a polymer cement slurry as a termite barrier coupled with soil treatment seems to work on the few projects that have used the approach. However, there is no universal consensus on this matter as no long term performance infor-mation is available.

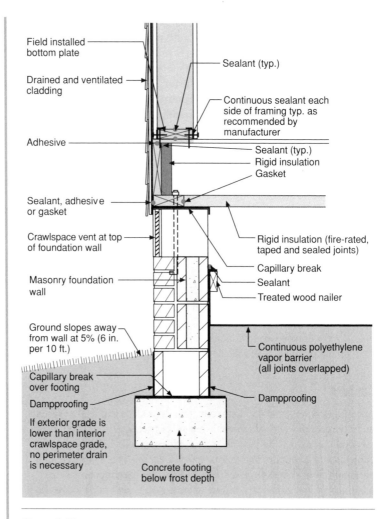

Figure 6.16
Vented Crawlspace

- Above grade wall construction recommended for severe cold climates, not for cold climates
- Rigid impermeable insulating sheathing protects underside of floor assembly from wetting during summer. Structural wood beams must also be similarly protected.
- Rigid insulation must be fire-rated if it is left exposed under the floor framing in the crawlspace
- Band joist assembly must be tight or entry of outside air will compromise the effectiveness of the floor cavity insulation
- Penetrations in bottom plates of interior and exterior partition walls should also be sealed to provide a degree of redundancy to the primary air flow retarder (the rigid insulation and band joist assembly)

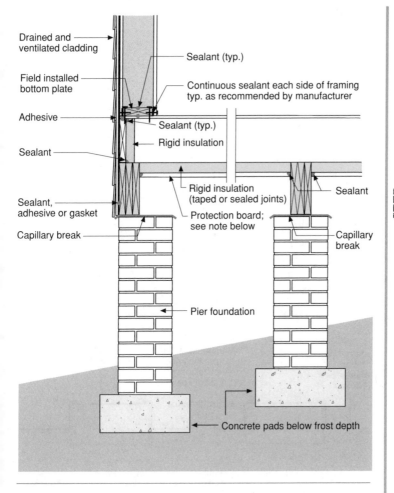

Figure 6.17
Pier Foundation
- Rigid impermeable insulating sheathing protects underside of floor assembly from wetting during summer
- Floor cavity insulation held down in contact with rigid insulation – air space above insulation provides warm floor during winter
- Band joist assembly must be tight or entry of outside air will compromise the effectiveness of the floor cavity insulation
- Penetrations in bottom plates of interior and exterior partition walls should also be sealed to provide a degree of redundancy to the primary air barrier (the rigid insulation and band joist assembly)
- Protection board is required for non-fire-rated insulations and in areas that may receive physical abuse. Acceptable materials are fire-rated gypsum board or finished fiber cement board

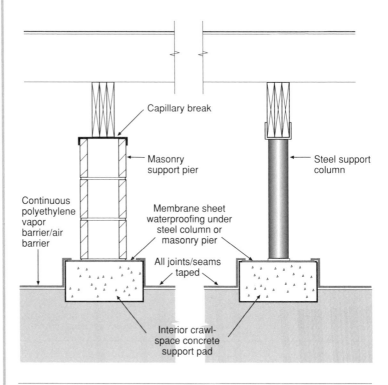

Capillary break

Masonry support pier

Steel support column

Continuous polyethylene vapor barrier/air barrier

Membrane sheet waterproofing under steel column or masonry pier

All joints/seams taped

Interior crawl-space concrete support pad

Figure 6.18
Air Barrier Continuity at Piers

- All joints and seams in polyethylene are taped
- Polyethylene ground cover taped to membrane sheet waterproofing at columns and piers

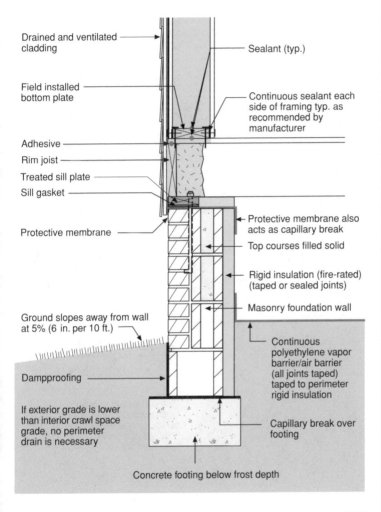

Drained and ventilated cladding

Sealant (typ.)

Field installed bottom plate

Continuous sealant each side of framing typ. as recommended by manufacturer

Adhesive

Rim joist

Treated sill plate

Sill gasket

Protective membrane

Protective membrane also acts as capillary break

Top courses filled solid

Rigid insulation (fire-rated) (taped or sealed joints)

Masonry foundation wall

Ground slopes away from wall at 5% (6 in. per 10 ft.)

Dampproofing

If exterior grade is lower than interior crawl space grade, no perimeter drain is necessary

Continuous polyethylene vapor barrier/air barrier (all joints taped) taped to perimeter rigid insulation

Capillary break over footing

Concrete footing below frost depth

Figure 6.19
Internally Insulated Concrete Crawlspace with Stucco Wall Above
- Masonry wall cold; can dry to exterior; low likelihood of mold
- Protective membrane acts as termite barrier
- Rigid insulation must be fire-rated if it is left exposed on the interior
- Building paper installed shingle fashion acts as drainage plane located behind rigid insulation

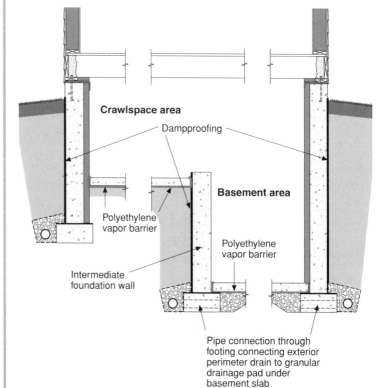

Crawlspace area

Dampproofing

Basement area

Polyethylene
vapor barrier

Polyethylene
vapor barrier

Intermediate
foundation wall

Pipe connection through
footing connecting exterior
perimeter drain to granular
drainage pad under
basement slab

Figure 6.20
Connecting Crawlspace and Basement

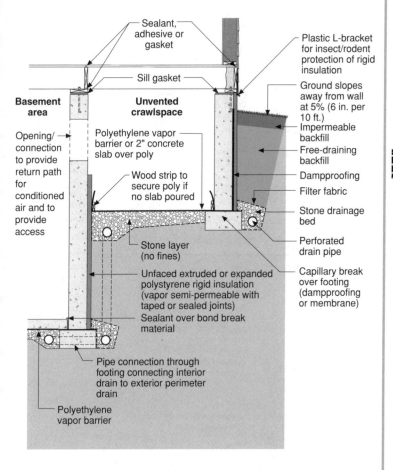

Figure 6.21
Connecting Crawlspace and Basement

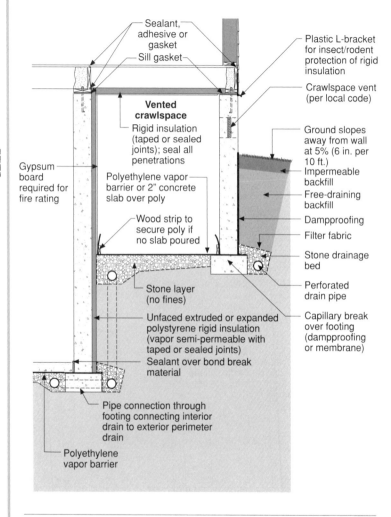

Sealant, adhesive or gasket

Sill gasket

Vented crawlspace

Rigid insulation (taped or sealed joints); seal all penetrations

Gypsum board required for fire rating

Polyethylene vapor barrier or 2" concrete slab over poly

Wood strip to secure poly if no slab poured

Stone layer (no fines)

Unfaced extruded or expanded polystyrene rigid insulation (vapor semi-permeable with taped or sealed joints)

Sealant over bond break material

Pipe connection through footing connecting interior drain to exterior perimeter drain

Polyethylene vapor barrier

Plastic L-bracket for insect/rodent protection of rigid insulation

Crawlspace vent (per local code)

Ground slopes away from wall at 5% (6 in. per 10 ft.)

Impermeable backfill

Free-draining backfill

Dampproofing

Filter fabric

Stone drainage bed

Perforated drain pipe

Capillary break over footing (dampproofing or membrane)

Figure 6.22
Vented Crawlspace Adjacent to Basement

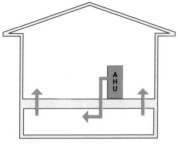

A: Supply air to crawlspace/passive return
- Minimum 2-4"x8" transfer grilles **to** house
- 50 cfm of flow per 1,000 ft² of crawlspace
- Air handler cycled at 5 minutes per hour

D: Exhaust fan in crawlspace
- Transfer air **from** house
- Fan sized at ASHRAE 62.2 whole house flow rates:
  7.5 cfm/person + 0.01 cfm/ft² of conditioned area
- For a 2,000 ft² 3 bedroom house w/ 4 occupants:
  4 x 7.5 cfm = 30 cfm
  2,000 ft² x 0.01 cfm = 20 cfm
  30 cfm + 20 cfm = 50 cfm (i.e. 50 cfm exhaust fan)
- Fan runs continuously

6

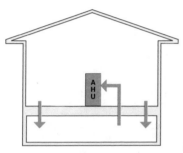

B: Return air from crawlspace
- Minimum 2-4"x8" transfer grilles **from** house
- 50 cfm of flow per 1,000 ft² of crawlspace
- Air handler cycled at 5 minutes per hour

E: Supply air to crawlspace/passive return
- Minimum 2-4"x8" transfer grilles **to** house
- 50 cfm of flow per 1,000 ft² of crawlspace

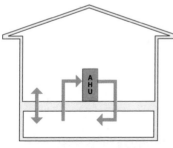

C: Supply and return to crawlspace
- Minimum 2-4"x8" transfer grilles **from** house through floor to equalize air pressure
- 50 cfm of flow per 1,000 ft² of crawlspace
- Air handler cycled at 5 minutes per hour

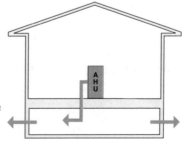

F: Supply air to crawlspace
- Floor air sealed
- 50 cfm of flow per 1,000 ft² of crawlspace
- Air handler cycled at 5 minutes per hour

Figure 6.23
Conditioning Crawlspaces

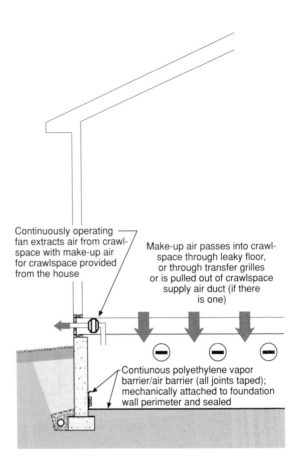

Continuously operating
fan extracts air from crawlspace with make-up air
for crawlspace provided
from the house

Make-up air passes into crawlspace through leaky floor,
or through transfer grilles
or is pulled out of crawlspace
supply air duct (if there
is one)

Contiunous polyethylene vapor
barrier/air barrier (all joints taped);
mechanically attached to foundation
wall perimeter and sealed

**Figure 6.24
Controlled Mechanical Ventilation, Soil Gas and Crawlspace Ventilation System**
- Crawlspace is conditioned (heated during the winter, cooled during the summer)
  either by make-up air pulled from the house or by a supply HVAC system duct
- Depressurization of crawlspace is facilitated by continuous exhaust from the
  crawlspace with make-up air for the crawlspace provided from the house common
  area
- Crawlspace ground cover is tighter than subfloor
- Crawlspace ventilation and house ventilation is provided by a single fan

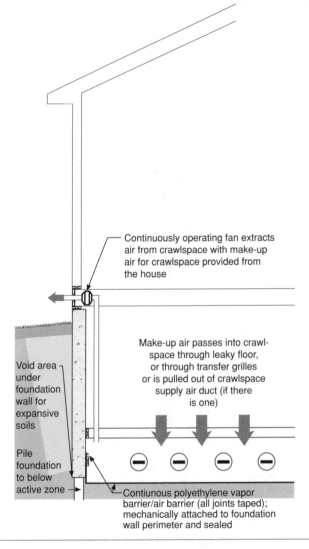

Continuously operating fan extracts air from crawlspace with make-up air for crawlspace provided from the house

Make-up air passes into crawl-space through leaky floor, or through transfer grilles or is pulled out of crawlspace supply air duct (if there is one)

Void area under foundation wall for expansive soils

Pile foundation to below active zone

Continuous polyethylene vapor barrier/air barrier (all joints taped); mechanically attached to foundation wall perimeter and sealed

Figure 6.25
Combined Controlled Ventilation, Soil Gas and Crawlspace Ventilation System
- Crawlspace is conditioned (heated during the winter, cooled during the summer) either by make-up air pulled from the house or by a supply HVAC system duct
- In regions with expansive soils and suspended wood basement floors over crawlspaces, depressurization of crawlspace can be facilitated by continuous exhaust from the crawlspace with make-up air for the crawlspace provided from the house common area
- Crawlspace ground cover is tighter than subfloor
- Crawlspace ventilation and house ventilation is provided by a single fan

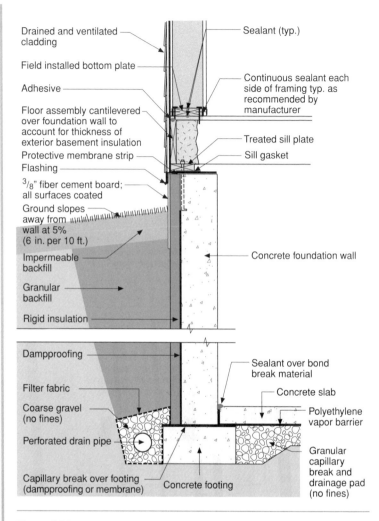

Drained and ventilated cladding

Field installed bottom plate

Adhesive

Floor assembly cantilevered over foundation wall to account for thickness of exterior basement insulation

Protective membrane strip

Flashing

$^3/_8$" fiber cement board; all surfaces coated

Ground slopes away from wall at 5% (6 in. per 10 ft.)

Impermeable backfill

Granular backfill

Rigid insulation

Dampproofing

Filter fabric

Coarse gravel (no fines)

Perforated drain pipe

Capillary break over footing (dampproofing or membrane)

Sealant (typ.)

Continuous sealant each side of framing typ. as recommended by manufacturer

Treated sill plate

Sill gasket

Concrete foundation wall

Sealant over bond break material

Concrete slab

Polyethylene vapor barrier

Granular capillary break and drainage pad (no fines)

Concrete footing

Figure 6.26
Externally Insulated Concrete Basement with Vinyl or Aluminum Siding Above
- Concrete wall warm, can dry to the interior; extremely low likelihood of mold
- Basement floor slab can dry to the interior
- Protective membrane acts as termite barrier
- Protective membrane can be adhesive-backed roll roofing or other UV resistant materials. Below grade sheet waterproofing or ice dam protection membranes can also be used if protected from UV exposure by using aluminum sheet stock or other alternative materials.
- Granular backfill helps drain water away from foundation wall

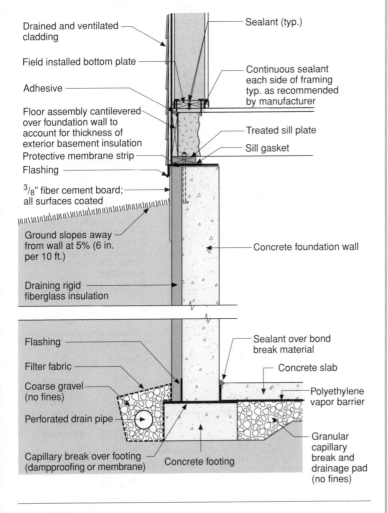

Drained and ventilated cladding

Sealant (typ.)

Field installed bottom plate

Continuous sealant each side of framing typ. as recommended by manufacturer

Adhesive

Floor assembly cantilevered over foundation wall to account for thickness of exterior basement insulation

Treated sill plate

Sill gasket

Protective membrane strip

Flashing

$^3/_8$" fiber cement board; all surfaces coated

Ground slopes away from wall at 5% (6 in. per 10 ft.)

Concrete foundation wall

Draining rigid fiberglass insulation

Flashing

Sealant over bond break material

Filter fabric

Concrete slab

Coarse gravel (no fines)

Polyethylene vapor barrier

Perforated drain pipe

Capillary break over footing (dampproofing or membrane)

Concrete footing

Granular capillary break and drainage pad (no fines)

Figure 6.27
Externally Insulated Concrete Basement with Wood Siding Above

- Draining rigid fiberglass insulation also acts as capillary break (no dampproofing required)
- Concrete wall warm, can dry to the interior and exterior (since no dampproofing); lowest likelihood of mold
- Basement floor slab can dry to the interior
- Protective membrane acts as termite barrier
- Protective membrane can be adhesive-backed roll roofing or other UV resistant materials. Below grade sheet waterproofing or ice dam protection membranes can also be used if protected from UV exposure by using aluminum sheet stock or other alternative materials.

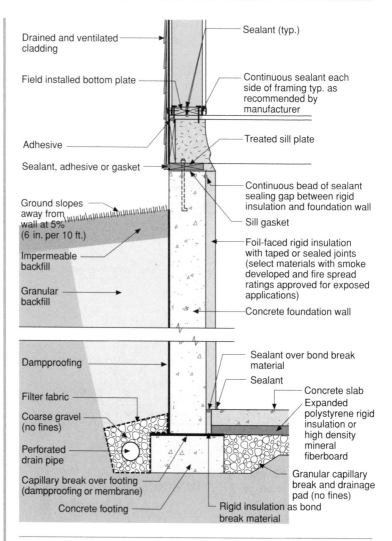

Drained and ventilated cladding

Sealant (typ.)

Field installed bottom plate

Continuous sealant each side of framing typ. as recommended by manufacturer

Adhesive

Treated sill plate

Sealant, adhesive or gasket

Continuous bead of sealant sealing gap between rigid insulation and foundation wall

Ground slopes away from wall at 5% (6 in. per 10 ft.)

Sill gasket

Impermeable backfill

Foil-faced rigid insulation with taped or sealed joints (select materials with smoke developed and fire spread ratings approved for exposed applications)

Granular backfill

Concrete foundation wall

Dampproofing

Sealant over bond break material

Filter fabric

Sealant

Coarse gravel (no fines)

Concrete slab

Expanded polystyrene rigid insulation or high density mineral fiberboard

Perforated drain pipe

Capillary break over footing (dampproofing or membrane)

Granular capillary break and drainage pad (no fines)

Concrete footing

Rigid insulation as bond break material

Figure 6.28
Internally Insulated Concrete Basement
- Cold concrete wall must be protected from interior moisture-laden air in winter and in summer
- Basement floor slab is warm, can dry to the ground (since no under slab vapor barrier) as well as to the interior; lowest likelihood of mold
- Concrete wall cold, cannot dry to interior; drying only possible to exterior at above grade portion of wall
- Due to low drying potential, interior impermeable rigid insulation should not be installed until moisture from concrete foundation wall has substantially dried/ equilibrated (typically 6 months or more) otherwise mold is possible

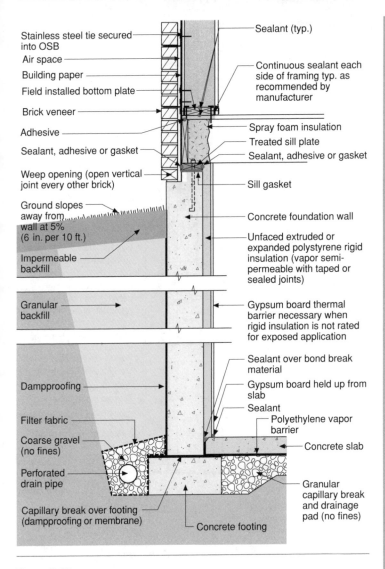

Stainless steel tie secured into OSB

Air space

Building paper

Field installed bottom plate

Brick veneer

Adhesive

Sealant, adhesive or gasket

Weep opening (open vertical joint every other brick)

Ground slopes away from wall at 5% (6 in. per 10 ft.)

Impermeable backfill

Granular backfill

Dampproofing

Filter fabric

Coarse gravel (no fines)

Perforated drain pipe

Capillary break over footing (dampproofing or membrane)

Sealant (typ.)

Continuous sealant each side of framing typ. as recommended by manufacturer

Spray foam insulation

Treated sill plate

Sealant, adhesive or gasket

Sill gasket

Concrete foundation wall

Unfaced extruded or expanded polystyrene rigid insulation (vapor semi-permeable with taped or sealed joints)

Gypsum board thermal barrier necessary when rigid insulation is not rated for exposed application

Sealant over bond break material

Gypsum board held up from slab

Sealant

Polyethylene vapor barrier

Concrete slab

Granular capillary break and drainage pad (no fines)

Concrete footing

Figure 6.29
Internally Insulated Concrete Basement with Brick Veneer Above

- Concrete wall is cold, can only dry to the interior if interior assemblies are vapor semi-permeable; mold possible if interior assemblies do not permit drying
- Cold concrete wall must be protected from interior moisture-laden air in winter and in summer
- Basement floor slab can dry to the interior
- Airspace behind brick veneer can be as small as $3/8$-inch; 1-inch is typical

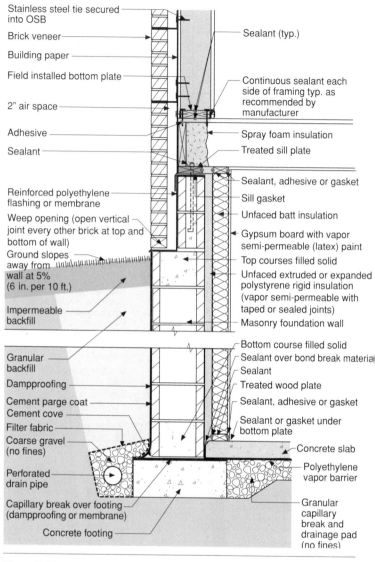

Stainless steel tie secured into OSB

Brick veneer

Building paper

Field installed bottom plate

2" air space

Adhesive

Sealant

Reinforced polyethylene flashing or membrane

Weep opening (open vertical joint every other brick at top and bottom of wall)

Ground slopes away from wall at 5% (6 in. per 10 ft.)

Impermeable backfill

Granular backfill

Dampproofing

Cement parge coat
Cement cove

Filter fabric

Coarse gravel (no fines)

Perforated drain pipe

Capillary break over footing (dampproofing or membrane)

Concrete footing

Sealant (typ.)

Continuous sealant each side of framing typ. as recommended by manufacturer

Spray foam insulation

Treated sill plate

Sealant, adhesive or gasket

Sill gasket

Unfaced batt insulation

Gypsum board with vapor semi-permeable (latex) paint

Top courses filled solid

Unfaced extruded or expanded polystyrene rigid insulation (vapor semi-permeable with taped or sealed joints)

Masonry foundation wall

Bottom course filled solid

Sealant over bond break material

Sealant

Treated wood plate

Sealant, adhesive or gasket

Sealant or gasket under bottom plate

Concrete slab

Polyethylene vapor barrier

Granular capillary break and drainage pad (no fines)

Figure 6.30
Internally Insulated Masonry Basement with Brick Veneer Above

- Masonry wall cold, can only dry to the interior if interior assemblies are vapor permeable; mold possible if interior assemblies do not permit drying
- Cold masonry wall must be protected from interior moisture-laden air in winter and in summer
- Basement floor slab can dry to the interior
- Airspace behind brick veneer must be ventilated top and bottom and a minimum 2-inch airspace is required

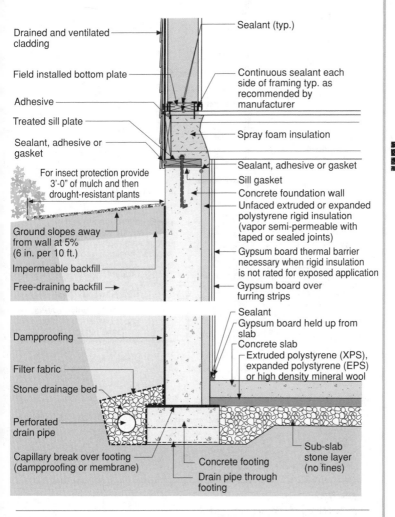

Sealant (typ.)

Drained and ventilated cladding

Field installed bottom plate

Continuous sealant each side of framing typ. as recommended by manufacturer

Adhesive

Treated sill plate

Sealant, adhesive or gasket

Spray foam insulation

For insect protection provide 3'-0" of mulch and then drought-resistant plants

Sealant, adhesive or gasket

Sill gasket

Concrete foundation wall

Unfaced extruded or expanded polystyrene rigid insulation (vapor semi-permeable with taped or sealed joints)

Ground slopes away from wall at 5% (6 in. per 10 ft.)

Impermeable backfill

Free-draining backfill →

Gypsum board thermal barrier necessary when rigid insulation is not rated for exposed application

Gypsum board over furring strips

Sealant

Gypsum board held up from slab

Concrete slab

Extruded polystyrene (XPS), expanded polystyrene (EPS) or high density mineral wool

Dampproofing

Filter fabric

Stone drainage bed

Perforated drain pipe

Capillary break over footing (dampproofing or membrane)

Concrete footing

Sub-slab stone layer (no fines)

Drain pipe through footing

Figure 6.31
Internally Insulated Concrete Basement

6

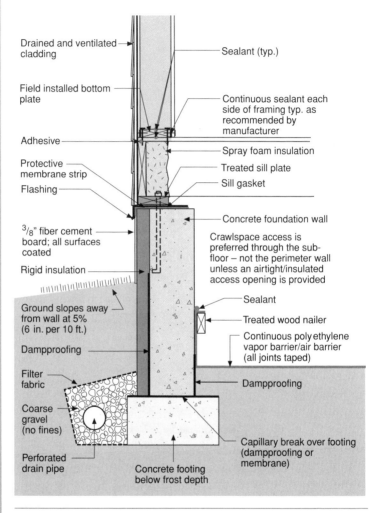

Drained and ventilated cladding

Field installed bottom plate

Adhesive

Protective membrane strip

Flashing

$^3/_8$" fiber cement board; all surfaces coated

Rigid insulation

Ground slopes away from wall at 5% (6 in. per 10 ft.)

Dampproofing

Filter fabric

Coarse gravel (no fines)

Perforated drain pipe

Sealant (typ.)

Continuous sealant each side of framing typ. as recommended by manufacturer

Spray foam insulation

Treated sill plate

Sill gasket

Concrete foundation wall

Crawlspace access is preferred through the sub-floor – not the perimeter wall unless an airtight/insulated access opening is provided

Sealant

Treated wood nailer

Continuous polyethylene vapor barrier/air barrier (all joints taped)

Dampproofing

Capillary break over footing (dampproofing or membrane)

Concrete footing below frost depth

Figure 6.32
Externally Insulated Concrete Crawlspace

- Concrete wall warm, can dry to the interior; extremely low likelihood of mold
- Protective membrane acts as termite barrier
- Perimeter drain is necessary since interior grade is lower than exterior grade
- Protective membrane can be adhesive-backed roll roofing or other UV resistant materials. Below grade sheet waterproofing or ice dam protection membranes can also be used if protected from UV exposure by using aluminum sheet stock or other alternative materials.

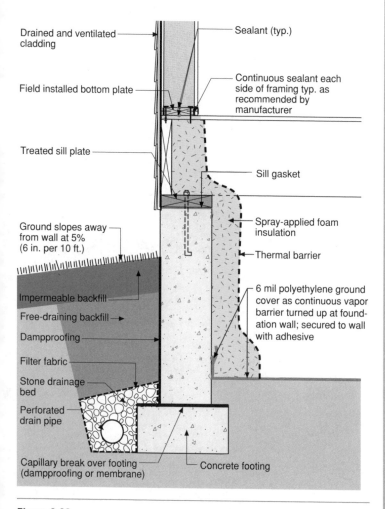

Drained and ventilated cladding

Sealant (typ.)

Field installed bottom plate

Continuous sealant each side of framing typ. as recommended by manufacturer

Treated sill plate

Sill gasket

Ground slopes away from wall at 5% (6 in. per 10 ft.)

Spray-applied foam insulation

Thermal barrier

Impermeable backfill

6 mil polyethylene ground cover as continuous vapor barrier turned up at foundation wall; secured to wall with adhesive

Free-draining backfill

Dampproofing

Filter fabric

Stone drainage bed

Perforated drain pipe

Capillary break over footing (dampproofing or membrane)

Concrete footing

Figure 6.33
Internally Insulated Concrete Crawlspace with Spray Foam
- A thermal barrier must be installed over spray foam insulations in crawlspaces

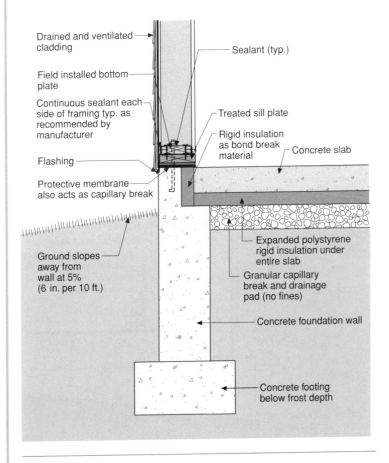

Drained and ventilated cladding

Sealant (typ.)

Field installed bottom plate

Continuous sealant each side of framing typ. as recommended by manufacturer

Treated sill plate

Rigid insulation as bond break material

Concrete slab

Flashing

Protective membrane also acts as capillary break

Ground slopes away from wall at 5% (6 in. per 10 ft.)

Expanded polystyrene rigid insulation under entire slab

Granular capillary break and drainage pad (no fines)

Concrete foundation wall

Concrete footing below frost depth

Figure 6.34
Slab with Concrete Perimeter and Vinyl or Aluminum Siding Above
- Protective membrane acts as termite barrier; sealed to slab
- Rigid insulation on frame wall extends downward below top of concrete foundation wall to shelter horizontal joint
- Floor slab is warm due to sub-slab rigid insulation under entire floor;
  Can dry to the ground (since there is no under slab vapor barrier, retarder insulation selected is semi-permeable) as well as to the interior, lowest likelihood of mold

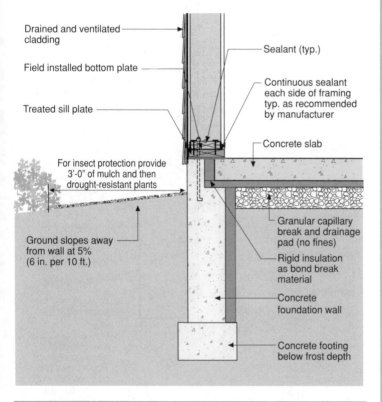

Drained and ventilated cladding

Field installed bottom plate

Treated sill plate

Sealant (typ.)

Continuous sealant each side of framing typ. as recommended by manufacturer

Concrete slab

For insect protection provide 3'-0" of mulch and then drought-resistant plants

Granular capillary break and drainage pad (no fines)

Ground slopes away from wall at 5% (6 in. per 10 ft.)

Rigid insulation as bond break material

Concrete foundation wall

Concrete footing below frost depth

Figure 6.35
Slab with Concrete Perimeter and Stucco Wall Above

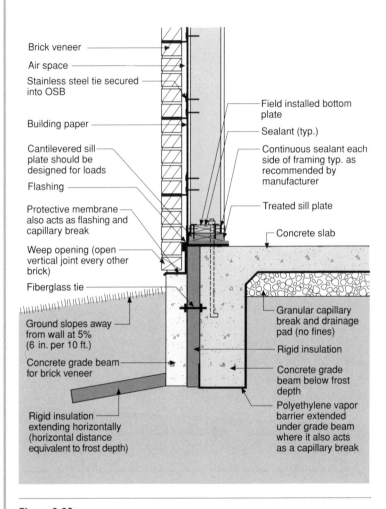

Brick veneer

Air space

Stainless steel tie secured into OSB

Building paper

Cantilevered sill plate should be designed for loads

Flashing

Protective membrane also acts as flashing and capillary break

Weep opening (open vertical joint every other brick)

Fiberglass tie

Ground slopes away from wall at 5% (6 in. per 10 ft.)

Concrete grade beam for brick veneer

Rigid insulation extending horizontally (horizontal distance equivalent to frost depth)

Field installed bottom plate

Sealant (typ.)

Continuous sealant each side of framing typ. as recommended by manufacturer

Treated sill plate

Concrete slab

Granular capillary break and drainage pad (no fines)

Rigid insulation

Concrete grade beam below frost depth

Polyethylene vapor barrier extended under grade beam where it also acts as a capillary break

Figure 6.36
Monolithic Slab with Brick Veneer Above
- Protective membrane acts as termite barrier and acts as flashing at base of brick veneer
- Grade beam for brick veneer cast simultaneously with monolithic slab
- Exterior horizontal rigid insulation provides frost protection
- Airspace behind brick veneer can be as small as $3/8$-inch; 1-inch is typical

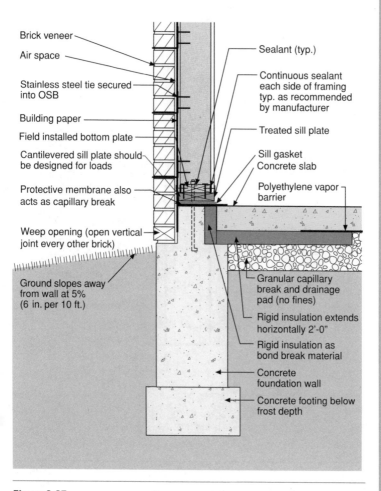

Brick veneer

Air space

Stainless steel tie secured into OSB

Building paper

Field installed bottom plate

Cantilevered sill plate should be designed for loads

Protective membrane also acts as capillary break

Weep opening (open vertical joint every other brick)

Ground slopes away from wall at 5% (6 in. per 10 ft.)

Sealant (typ.)

Continuous sealant each side of framing typ. as recommended by manufacturer

Treated sill plate

Sill gasket
Concrete slab

Polyethylene vapor barrier

Granular capillary break and drainage pad (no fines)

Rigid insulation extends horizontally 2'-0"

Rigid insulation as bond break material

Concrete foundation wall

Concrete footing below frost depth

Figure 6.37
Slab with Concrete Perimeter and Brick Veneer Above
- Protective membrane acts as termite barrier; sealed to slab
- Airspace behind brick veneer can be as small as $3/8$-inch; 1-inch is typical

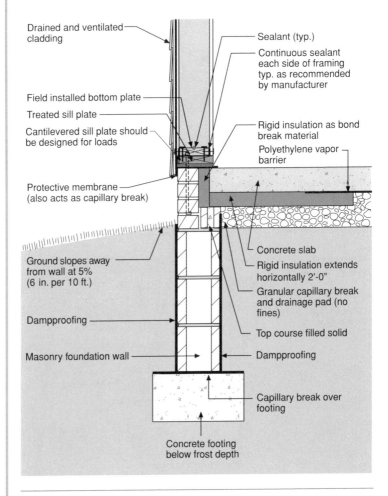

Figure 6.38
Slab with Masonry Perimeter and Wood Siding Above
- Protective membrane acts as termite barrier; sealed to slab

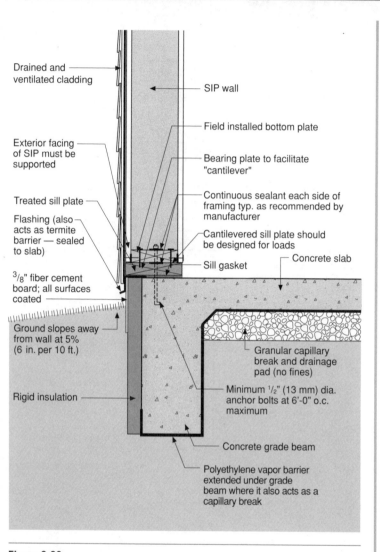

Drained and ventilated cladding

SIP wall

Field installed bottom plate

Exterior facing of SIP must be supported

Bearing plate to facilitate "cantilever"

Treated sill plate

Continuous sealant each side of framing typ. as recommended by manufacturer

Flashing (also acts as termite barrier — sealed to slab)

Cantilevered sill plate should be designed for loads

Sill gasket

Concrete slab

$3/8$" fiber cement board; all surfaces coated

Ground slopes away from wall at 5% (6 in. per 10 ft.)

Granular capillary break and drainage pad (no fines)

Rigid insulation

Minimum $1/2$" (13 mm) dia. anchor bolts at 6'-0" o.c. maximum

Concrete grade beam

Polyethylene vapor barrier extended under grade beam where it also acts as a capillary break

Figure 6.39
Monolithic Slab — SIP Above Grade Wall

- Vinyl and aluminum siding can be directly applied to housewraps as they are inherently "back-ventilated" due to their profile
- Drained and ventilated cladding such as vinyl siding installed directly over a water resistive barrier, wood siding or cement siding installed over a $1/4$-inch (6 mm) spacer strip over a water resistive barrier, cedar shingles installed over $3/8$-inch (9 mm) drainage mat over a water resistive barrier
- Spacer strip (i.e. "furring") can be as thin as $1/4$-inch (6 mm); cutting foam $1/4$-inch (6 mm) thick "fan-fold" siding backer into 2-inch (50 mm) wide strips is a fast, economical method of back-ventilating and draining siding

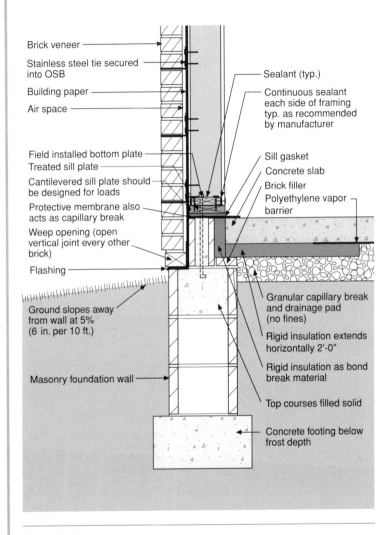

Brick veneer

Stainless steel tie secured into OSB

Building paper

Air space

Field installed bottom plate

Treated sill plate

Cantilevered sill plate should be designed for loads

Protective membrane also acts as capillary break

Weep opening (open vertical joint every other brick)

Flashing

Ground slopes away from wall at 5% (6 in. per 10 ft.)

Masonry foundation wall

Sealant (typ.)

Continuous sealant each side of framing typ. as recommended by manufacturer

Sill gasket

Concrete slab

Brick filler

Polyethylene vapor barrier

Granular capillary break and drainage pad (no fines)

Rigid insulation extends horizontally 2'-0"

Rigid insulation as bond break material

Top courses filled solid

Concrete footing below frost depth

Figure 6.40
Slab with Masonry Perimeter and Brick Veneer Above
- Protective membrane acts as termite barrier; sealed to slab
- Brick veneer corbelled outwards at base to provide drainage space
- Airspace behind brick veneer can be as small as $3/8$-inch; 1-inch is typical

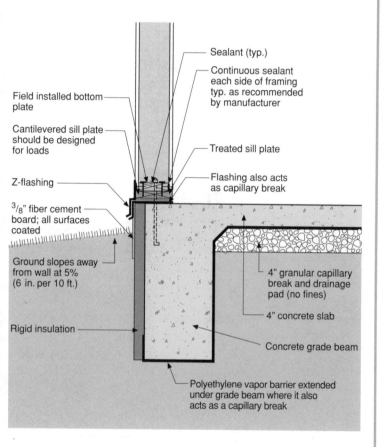

Sealant (typ.)

Continuous sealant each side of framing typ. as recommended by manufacturer

Field installed bottom plate

Cantilevered sill plate should be designed for loads

Treated sill plate

Z-flashing

Flashing also acts as capillary break

$^3/_8$" fiber cement board; all surfaces coated

Ground slopes away from wall at 5% (6 in. per 10 ft.)

4" granular capillary break and drainage pad (no fines)

4" concrete slab

Rigid insulation

Concrete grade beam

Polyethylene vapor barrier extended under grade beam where it also acts as a capillary break

Figure 6.41
Externally Insulated Monolithic Slab

6

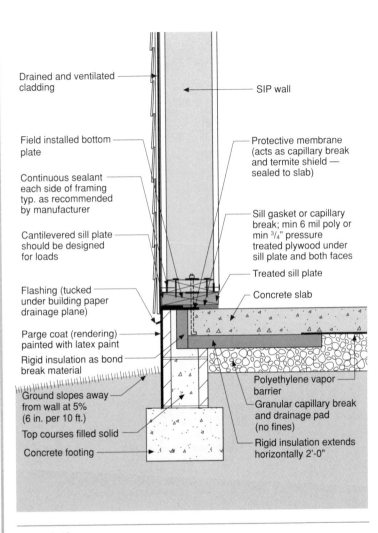

Drained and ventilated cladding

SIP wall

Field installed bottom plate

Protective membrane (acts as capillary break and termite shield — sealed to slab)

Continuous sealant each side of framing typ. as recommended by manufacturer

Sill gasket or capillary break; min 6 mil poly or min 3/4" pressure treated plywood under sill plate and both faces

Cantilevered sill plate should be designed for loads

Treated sill plate

Flashing (tucked under building paper drainage plane)

Concrete slab

Parge coat (rendering) painted with latex paint

Rigid insulation as bond break material

Polyethylene vapor barrier

Ground slopes away from wall at 5% (6 in. per 10 ft.)

Granular capillary break and drainage pad (no fines)

Top courses filled solid

Rigid insulation extends horizontally 2'-0"

Concrete footing

Figure 6.42
Slab with Masonry Perimeter — SIP Above Grade Wall
- Vinyl and aluminum siding can be directly applied to housewraps as they are inherently "back-ventilated" due to their profile
- Drained and ventilated cladding such as vinyl siding installed directly over a water resistive barrier, wood siding or cement siding installed over a 1/4-inch (6 mm) spacer strip over a water resistive barrier, cedar shingles installed over 3/8-inch (9 mm) drainage mat over a water resistive barrier
- Spacer strip (i.e. "furring") can be as thin as 1/4-inch (6 mm); cutting foam 1/4-inch (6 mm) thick "fan-fold" siding backer into 2-inch (50 mm) wide strips is a fast, economical method of back-ventilating and draining siding

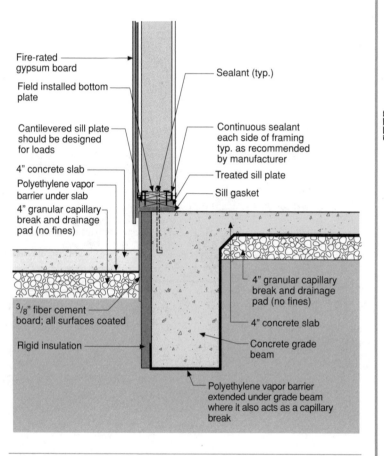

Fire-rated gypsum board

Field installed bottom plate

Cantilevered sill plate should be designed for loads

4" concrete slab

Polyethylene vapor barrier under slab

4" granular capillary break and drainage pad (no fines)

$^3/_8$" fiber cement board; all surfaces coated

Rigid insulation

Sealant (typ.)

Continuous sealant each side of framing typ. as recommended by manufacturer

Treated sill plate

Sill gasket

4" granular capillary break and drainage pad (no fines)

4" concrete slab

Concrete grade beam

Polyethylene vapor barrier extended under grade beam where it also acts as a capillary break

Figure 6.43
Garage Slab

6

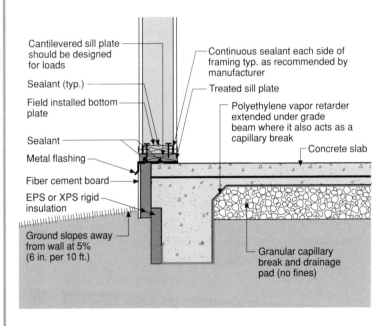

Cantilevered sill plate should be designed for loads

Sealant (typ.)

Field installed bottom plate

Sealant

Metal flashing

Fiber cement board

EPS or XPS rigid insulation

Ground slopes away from wall at 5% (6 in. per 10 ft.)

Continuous sealant each side of framing typ. as recommended by manufacturer

Treated sill plate

Polyethylene vapor retarder extended under grade beam where it also acts as a capillary break

Concrete slab

Granular capillary break and drainage pad (no fines)

Figure 6.44
Post-tensioned Slab

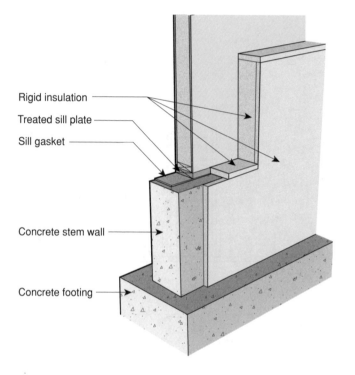

Rigid insulation

Treated sill plate

Sill gasket

Concrete stem wall

Concrete footing

Figure 6.45
Step Down Foundation Wall
• In basement assemblies and conditioned crawlspace assemblies that are internally insulated, it is important that rigid insulation "wraps" around exposed concrete/ block assemblies at "step downs" in order to control condensation, particularly during summer months

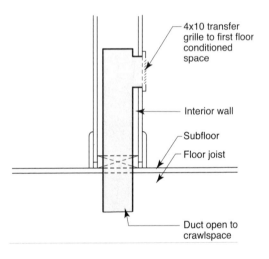

4x10 transfer grille to first floor conditioned space

Interior wall

Subfloor

Floor joist

Duct open to crawlspace

Figure 6.46
Transfer Grille to Crawlspace

Creature and Dust Control

Infestations of cockroaches, dust mites, mice and rats can all cause allergic reactions. Even after the pests are gone, their skin, hair and feces can remain and can trigger allergic reactions.

Making a home pest-resistant reduces exposure to allergens and asthma triggers released by the pests, and it can reduce the amount of pesticides used by the occupants.

Design and construct the building so it's easy for people to keep pests from colonizing. Take the following steps:

- Make it hard for them to get in by sealing the walls, ceilings, roofs and foundations

- If they do get in, make it hard for them to move around unseen by sealing passages through interior floors, walls and ceilings, kick spaces

- Make it hard for them to find water by: keeping liquid water out, making plumbing easy to inspect and repair, and insulating plumbing pipes to keep them warm (above dewpoint temperatures)

- Make it hard for them to find food using tight food storage, by keeping paper and wood products away from potential moisture sources, and by using pest-resistant materials

- Make directed use of low toxicity pesticides in locations that are heavily infested with problem creatures.

To Know the Critter is to Control The Critter

To actually do the things on the list, you must know the creature. The simplest, safest and most elegant controls are those that work with the creature's natural urges. Creatures that get eaten a lot don't like open spaces. Give them open spaces. No closed-in kick spaces, strips around

Design

buildings free of shrubs and organic mulch. Seal around pipes and wires to keep them out of walls.

Keeping Them Out

Keep them out by changing the surrounding landscape and by blocking pest entries and passages. Reduce food and water availability.

Keep bushes and trees at least 3 feet from homes. Bushes and trees near a home provide food, a living place and sheltered passage for pests such as rats, mice, bats, birds, roaches and ants.

Seal utility openings and joints between materials. Use corrosion-proof materials such as copper or stainless steel mesh. Rodents can chew through many materials and squeeze through tiny openings.

Reducing Food and Water

Provide places to store food that are dry and ventilated. Provide a place to store trash and to facilitate recycling.

Design and construct the home to be dry and to dry if and when it gets wet. Absolutely no installed carpet in areas prone to get wet: bathrooms, laundry rooms, kitchens, entryways and damp basements.

In cold climates, dust mites do not generally colonize buildings because buildings are too dry for much of the year. They colonize bedding, stuffed animals and favorite chairs because we humidify these things with our bodies. Control is by washing these items in hot water (greater than 130° Fahrenheit), which kills the mites and washes away allergens.

Pesticides

In the design and construction of new buildings, pesticides have a very limited and targeted role to play. In a neighborhood infested with a difficult species, like roaches or termites, use a limited amount of low toxicity pesticide in targeted locations. In high risk termite areas, exclusion and inspection detailing — plus a combination of treated wooden materials and soil treatment — is useful. For roaches, dusting with boric acid in areas that would be hard to treat later is an effective, low risk strategy. For example, dust with boric acid inside the kick space beneath sink, then seal the kick space as completely as possible.

To assess risk factors associated with a pesticide, look at:
- Registration, classification, use, mode of action
- Specificity, effectiveness, repellency
- Toxicity to humans

- Cautions on label
- Toxicity in the environment
- Resistant populations

Look especially for products like insect growth hormone regulators, which are species-specific, effective and have low toxicity for the applicators, occupants and the environment.

Don't spray pesticides; apply them directly to surfaces to be treated.

Dust

Stop the dust at the door. Vacuum and filter the rest away. And make it easy to clean.

Over two thirds of dust in houses originates outdoors, and is tracked in on feet. House dust is known to contain many hazardous materials. House dust is an asthma trigger.

Entry Control

Pave exterior walks. Use exterior grate track off, interior carpet mat and hard surface floors. Design entries so that there is room to remove and store coats, shoes and boots.

Use a three part track-off approach:

1. Permeable, rugged outdoor mat that collects gritty materials (or a grate over a collection hole is an alternative approach)

2. Rugged indoor mat that collects grit and water

3. A hard surface, easily mopped floor to collect very fine particles left by drying foot prints

Cleanable Surfaces

Whenever possible, replace carpets with smooth flooring which is easy to clean and less likely to retain dust. Use window treatments such as blinds or shades that can be easily wiped. Use hard surfaces rather than textiles. Use semi-gloss latex paints instead of flat or matte finishes. Such surfaces are easier to clean using mild soaps.

Filtration

Construct a tight building enclosure to keep out outside dust and provide filtration. Filters should be MERV 6 – 8 (35 percent or better ASHRAE dust spot efficiency).

Part II

General Contractor

All the general contractor has to do is build the building on time and on budget using imperfect materials and imperfect trades, under less than ideal conditions. The client even expects the building to work. There never seems to be enough time or money, but the job still has to get done. In this line of work, Murphy is an optimist.

In the old days, all you needed was good workmanship and good materials. Getting good workmanship today is hard enough given the state of the trades, but it is not enough. Good workmanship cannot compensate for bad design. A general contractor cannot just follow the plans. Plans rarely provide enough information to get the job done, and many times the plans are wrong, in which case, the general contractor has to catch the mistakes. When the plans don't provide enough information, the general contractor has to fill in the gaps. "Not my fault, I was just following the plans" or "Nobody told me I had to do it that way" doesn't work anymore. It's not fair, nor is it right, but it's often the way it is. In order to protect himself or herself, the general contractor has to know everything about everything. Easy, right?

Concerns

Everything is a concern to the general contractor, but of all the concerns, there is one that towers above the rest. Getting the right information to people when they need it in order to do their jobs is more important than anything else. Getting the materials and equipment to the people when they need it comes next. General contracting is all about the flow of information, materials and equipment to the right people at the right time.

Most mistakes happen because of a lack of information, followed by a lack of attention. Attention follows information. Understanding comes from having the right information. Once there is understanding, problems can be caught early and corrected by the people actually doing the work. It helps the general contractor to employ workers who understand how their jobs fit into the entire process.

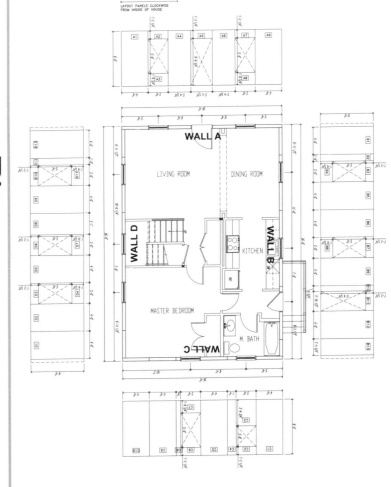

Figure 8.1
SIP Layout Diagram
- Panel, numbered by wall, shown with layout direction

Unfortunately, nowadays it is difficult to find fully trained and knowledgeable trades people. It seems that trades people don't take courses or classes anymore and that apprenticeship programs have fallen by the wayside. The depth of experience in the trades is often missing and the work force is very transient. Even when there has been training, it is often out of date or just plain wrong. In order to get the job done right, the general contractor has to train the trades himself, every day, day in and day out.

The most effective training approach is on-site training, beginning with the first day of work. This should occur during a one-hour period prior to commencing work. "This is what I want and why." "This is how I think you should do it, but I'm open to suggestions on how to do it simpler." "I'm available all day to answer questions."

Training is always easier if you have the right tools. Simple training tools, like visual aids posted on site for easy reference and use, work well. Posters illustrating key details can be developed for framers, electricians, insulators and drywallers.

Detailed panel layout drawings that illustrate the location of each panel and framing member are commonplace in SIP construction (Figure 8.1). Wherever possible, the same level of detail should be given to the balance of the construction drawing set. Well-coordinated foundation, panel, architectural, electrical and mechanical drawings can significantly reduce construction time as well as potential confusion. Supervisory time can also be reduced.

The better, the quicker and simpler the training, the better the subcontractors' prices the next time a job is bid.

The detailed panel drawings and posters developed for the installers, electricians, insulators and drywallers, coupled with checklists and addresses of suppliers, become key elements in developing "competitive pricing" during bid negotiations.

No one likes surprises. The better the information and the better the training, the fewer the surprises. When there are no surprises, you get good prices. Now we're talking.

Materials on the Building Site

Materials should be delivered to the site just before they are to be used. If they are not there, they don't get stolen, rained on, beat-up or destroyed. Of course if materials are not there when you need them, you also have big trouble. "Just-in-time delivery" is more than a slogan, it should be a way of life.

If you have to store materials at the job site, dumping them on the ground in a pond of water in everyone's way is not generally a good idea. Materials should be placed on skids raised off the ground and covered with material to shed water. Materials should be placed in a convenient location. Moving materials more than once is bad planning. A transport trailer makes a good storage shed if you can keep someone from hooking up their truck and pinching it.

For SIPs in particular, some general guidelines for handling material on site should be observed:

- Off-load panels in reverse order to installation sequence to minimize handling

- Do not place panel facings in direct contact with the ground

- Fully support panels when stacked

- Do not lift panels by upper facings

- Protect foam from direct exposure to sunlight

- Protect panels from rain and snow

- Protect panels with breathable covering when stored outside

- Cover panels with drainage plane and exterior cladding as soon as possible after installation

Don't get more than you need. If you get more than you need, it's never left over at the end of the job. It somehow disappears. On job sites the law of conservation of mass does not hold. Here's where detailed drawings and detailed take-offs pay for themselves.

Sites should be neat. Sites should be orderly. Sites should be clean. Clean, neat, orderly sites are safe, productive sites. He who makes a mess, cleans the mess. Those of us who were kids once, learned to clean up our toys when we were done. A job site should be run by the same rules.

"Drying in" the building as quickly as possible is a good idea. Roofing felt is relatively inexpensive and can be used to cover everything. Remember that wood loves water. Gypsum board loves water. Mold loves wood and gypsum board when it is wet. Mold is bad.

Materials that come to the job site "flat" and that need to be "flat" when installed should be stored "flat." Roofing shingles should be stored so that the bundles can lie flat without bending. Windows and sliding doors like to be "square." Store them "square." Remember that big piles of building materials can be very heavy. Heavy loads, concentrated on one spot for any appreciable time, can be a real problem. Distribute drywall and other heavy loads. Be smart. Think.

Concrete and Excavation

Concrete cracks. Concrete has always cracked. Concrete will always crack. Reinforcing concrete will not prevent it from cracking. It is not possible to build a crack-free concrete slab or foundation wall. However, it is possible to control the cracking process by deliberately cracking the concrete (Figures 9.1 and 9.2). These deliberate cracks are called control joints. Cracks do not naturally occur in straight lines, nor do they happen in predictable places; but control joints cause concrete to crack along straight lines and in predictable locations where builders can better deal with them. Home owners get annoyed at cracks in concrete, but home owners don't have a problem with control joints. Cracks are bad. Control joints are good.

Concrete also shrinks, creeps and moves. This is also true for masonry and brick, only more so. Masonry and brick swell when they get wet. Concrete can shrink while brick is swelling. Concrete moves. Masonry moves. Brick moves. Let them move.

When wood gets wet it expands; when it dries it shrinks. Wood is almost always in the process of either getting wet, absorbing moisture or drying. Therefore, wood is almost always moving. Wood has always moved and will always move. Nailing wood, screwing wood and gluing wood will not prevent it from moving. It is not possible to build a wood wall, floor, roof or foundation and not have it move. Let it move.

Mixing wood with concrete, masonry and brick makes building interesting but also makes buildings move. Buildings will always move. It is not possible to build buildings that do not move. Let them move.

Since buildings move, it is not possible to build one without holes. Builders can reduce the number of holes; builders can control the size of holes. Builders can control the types of holes. But make no mistake about it, there will be holes. The trick is to keep the water out, even though you have holes. Fortunately, water is lazy. Water will always

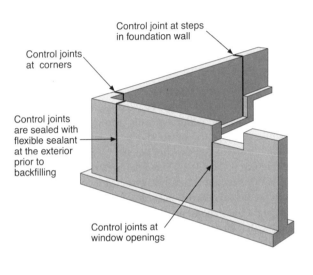

Control joint at steps
in foundation wall

Control joints
at corners

Control joints
are sealed with
flexible sealant
at the exterior
prior to
backfilling

Control joints at
window openings

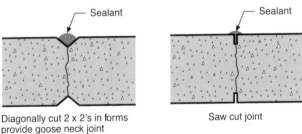

Sealant

Sealant

Diagonally cut 2 x 2's in forms
provide goose neck joint

Saw cut joint

Figure 9.1
Control Joints in Concrete Foundation Walls
- Control joints should be within 10 feet of corners
- Control joint spacing should be 20 feet maximum

Typical Driveway

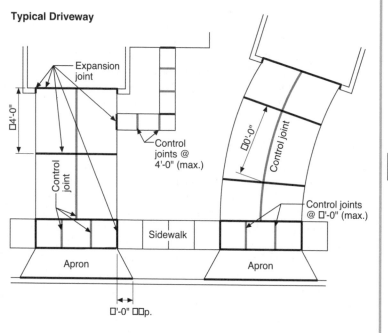

9

Control Joint

Expansion Joint

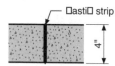

Figure 9.2
Control Joints and Expansion Joints in Exterior Concrete
- Control joints control shrinkage cracking
- Expansion joints control thermal movement

choose the easiest path to travel. If you provide an easy path for water to travel to a foundation drain, it will follow that path rather than a path through a foundation wall, even if the foundation wall has holes. And we know the foundation wall will have holes despite our best efforts.

Frost Movement

Frost exacerbates foundation movement. The key to frost management is also the key to water management. Keep water away from the foundation wall so that there is no water to freeze. Garages are most susceptible to frost damage due to lack of heat in a garage. Keep the water away from a garage foundation wall. If water freezes in the ground anyway, let the garage foundation move in a manner that won't destroy the house foundation (Figures 9.3 and 9.4).

Polyethylene Under Slabs

A sand layer is sometimes installed over a polyethylene vapor retarder located under a concrete slab. It is thought by some that the sand layer will protect the polyethylene from damage and act as a receptor for excess mix water in the concrete slab when the concrete is cast. This is an extremely bad idea because a reservoir of standing water can be created. If it rains during construction, if a wet cure is used, if excessive irrigation is used or if groundwater rises sufficiently to contact the underside of the polyethylene, water will enter the sand layer and be held in the sand layer by capillary forces, even after the groundwater level drops. Since the polyethylene is between the water-soaked sand and the ground, the only way for the water to get out is up into the building through the concrete slab by diffusion. The wetting of the sand by groundwater can take only minutes, but the drying out may take a decade.

The polyethylene under a concrete slab can function as an effective vapor barrier even if it has holes. It does not need to be protected. The best way to deal with excess mix water is to not have any. Use low water-to-cement ratio concrete with an accelerator or a super-plasticizer. It is faster and easier and, therefore, less expensive. The concrete costs a little more, but the labor is much less.

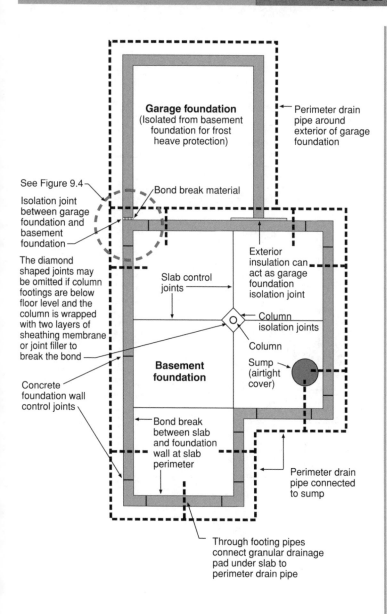

See Figure 9.4

Isolation joint between garage foundation and basement foundation

The diamond shaped joints may be omitted if column footings are below floor level and the column is wrapped with two layers of sheathing membrane or joint filler to break the bond

Concrete foundation wall control joints

Garage foundation
(Isolated from basement foundation for frost heave protection)

Bond break material

Perimeter drain pipe around exterior of garage foundation

Exterior insulation can act as garage foundation isolation joint

Slab control joints

Column isolation joints

Column

Basement foundation

Sump (airtight cover)

Bond break between slab and foundation wall at slab perimeter

Perimeter drain pipe connected to sump

Through footing pipes connect granular drainage pad under slab to perimeter drain pipe

Figure 9.3
Sub-Grade Drainage System
- Garage foundation isolated from basement foundation for frost protection
- Perimeter drain also protects garage foundation
- Joints should be sealed
- Floor slab joint spacing 20 feet maximum

9

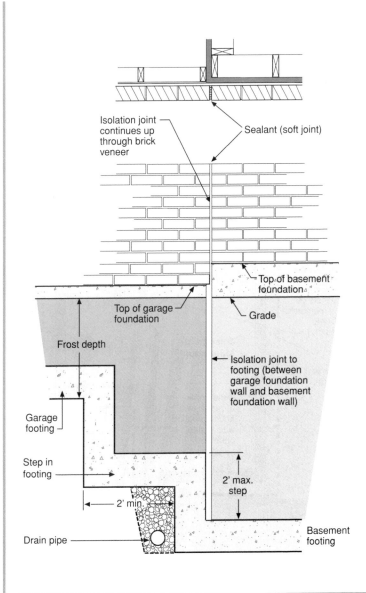

Isolation joint continues up through brick veneer

Sealant (soft joint)

Top of basement foundation

Top of garage foundation

Grade

Frost depth

Isolation joint to footing (between garage foundation wall and basement foundation wall)

Garage footing

Step in footing

2' max. step

2' min.

Drain pipe

Basement footing

Figure 9.4
Isolation Joint Between Garage and Basement Foundation
- If frost heave moves the garage the basement remains unaffected
- Step in footing should be less than 2 feet
- Distance between steps in footing should be more than 2 feet

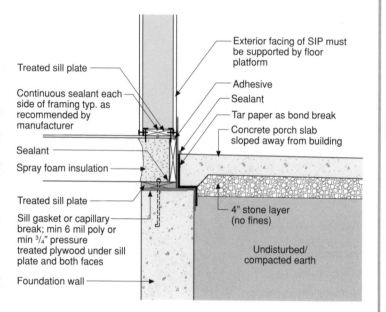

Exterior facing of SIP must be supported by floor platform

Treated sill plate

Continuous sealant each side of framing typ. as recommended by manufacturer

Adhesive

Sealant

Tar paper as bond break

Concrete porch slab sloped away from building

Sealant

Spray foam insulation

Treated sill plate

Sill gasket or capillary break; min 6 mil poly or min ³/₄" pressure treated plywood under sill plate and both faces

Foundation wall

4" stone layer (no fines)

Undisturbed/ compacted earth

Figure 9.5
Concrete Porch

- Detail above should be protected by an overhang where possible
- Where grade permits, step down concrete foundation to provide bearing for porch slab below level of moisture-sensitive materials

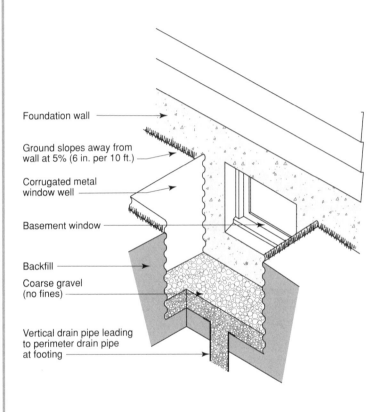

Foundation wall

Ground slopes away from wall at 5% (6 in. per 10 ft.)

Corrugated metal window well

Basement window

Backfill

Coarse gravel (no fines)

Vertical drain pipe leading to perimeter drain pipe at footing

Figure 9.6
Window Well at Basement Wall

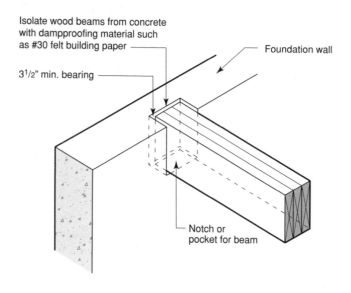

Isolate wood beams from concrete with dampproofing material such as #30 felt building paper

Foundation wall

3¹/₂" min. bearing

Notch or pocket for beam

9

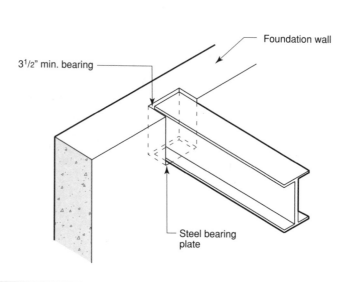

Foundation wall

3¹/₂" min. bearing

Steel bearing plate

Figure 9.7
Beam Pockets in Foundation Walls
- Isolate wood beams from concrete with dampproofing material such as #30 felt building paper

9

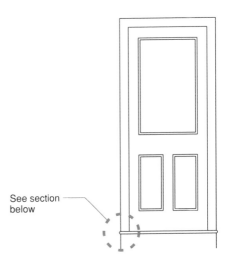

See section
below

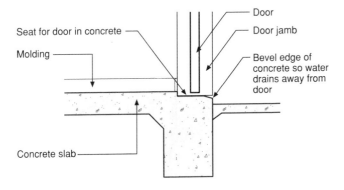

Seat for door in concrete

Molding

Concrete slab

Door

Door jamb

Bevel edge of
concrete so water
drains away from
door

Figure 9.8
Door Threshold Detail — Section
- Prevents damage to bottom of casings/leaks at front door

Assembly and Framing with SIPs

All residential building enclosures must:

- hold the building up
- keep the rain water out
- keep the wind out
- keep the water vapor out
- let the water and water vapor out if it gets inside
- keep the heat in during the winter
- keep the heat out during the summer

SIP construction has an advantage in that many of these enclosure functions are performed by a single component of the enclosure that can be quickly assembled on site.

However, SIPs can't perform all of these functions and, in a particular building, may not perform all of the functions that they could. SIP-hybrid assemblies are common, using combinations of wood, wood products, steel, masonry, concrete and Insulating Concrete Forms. All of the assembly elements used must work together to perform the functions listed above.

Concerns

As with wood frame construction, the single greatest concern with SIPs is their ability to control rain water entry. In this regard, SIPs should be treated similarly to wood frame construction where OSB or plywood is used as an exterior sheathing. Accordingly, an exterior drainage plane of a water resistive barrier (WRB) i.e. "housewrap" or "building wrap" or building paper installed shingle fashion and detailed at window openings in a similar manner to wood frame construction is recommended (see Chapter 2 — Rain, Drainage Planes and Flashings).

Since SIP components are rigid panels made from laminated or adhered elements they often move due to thermal induced moisture differentials between their wood-based hygroscopic facings. They bow and move differentially with the changing moisture contents of their exterior facings. This can result in the "telegraphing" of panel joints in roof assemblies under asphalt shingles.

And, as with any type of construction, in SIP buildings careful attention must be paid to joints and connections. Figure 10.1 identifies the primary areas of concern.

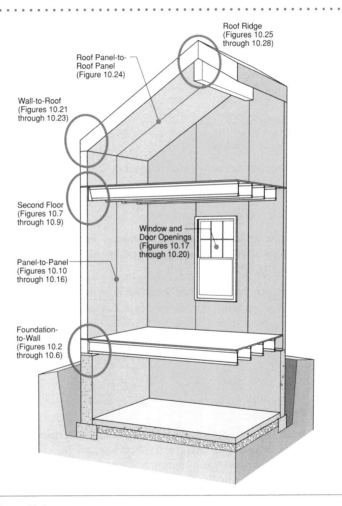

Figure 10.1
Key to SIPs Framing Drawings
  • The following pages show these details as numbered

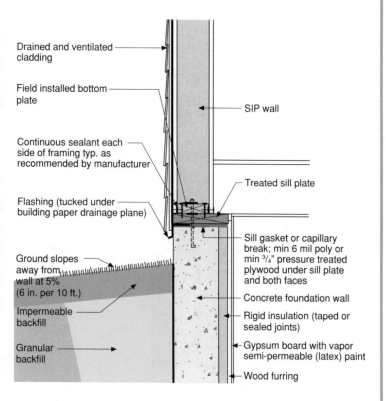

Drained and ventilated cladding

Field installed bottom plate

Continuous sealant each side of framing typ. as recommended by manufacturer

Flashing (tucked under building paper drainage plane)

Ground slopes away from wall at 5% (6 in. per 10 ft.)

Impermeable backfill

Granular backfill

SIP wall

Treated sill plate

Sill gasket or capillary break; min 6 mil poly or min $3/4$" pressure treated plywood under sill plate and both faces

Concrete foundation wall

Rigid insulation (taped or sealed joints)

Gypsum board with vapor semi-permeable (latex) paint

Wood furring

Figure 10.2
Internally Insulated Concrete Basement — SIP Above Grade Wall

- Vinyl and aluminum siding can be directly applied to housewraps as they are inherently "back-ventilated" due to their profile
- Drained and ventilated cladding such as vinyl siding installed directly over a water resistive barrier, wood siding or cement siding installed over a $1/4$-inch (6 mm) spacer strip over a water resistive barrier, cedar shingles installed over $3/8$-inch (9 mm) drainage mat over a water resistive barrier
- Spacer strip (i.e. "furring") can be as thin as $1/4$-inch (6 mm); cutting foam $1/4$-inch (6 mm) thick "fan-fold" siding backer into 2-inch (50 mm) wide strips is a fast, economical method of back-ventilating and draining siding

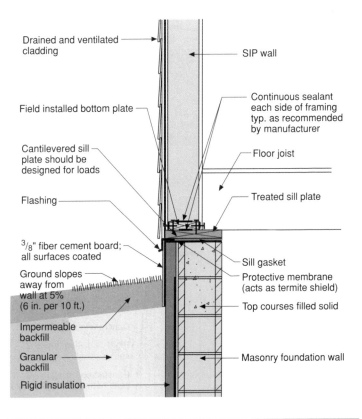

Drained and ventilated cladding

SIP wall

Continuous sealant each side of framing typ. as recommended by manufacturer

Field installed bottom plate

Floor joist

Cantilevered sill plate should be designed for loads

Treated sill plate

Flashing

$3/8$" fiber cement board; all surfaces coated

Sill gasket

Protective membrane (acts as termite shield)

Ground slopes away from wall at 5% (6 in. per 10 ft.)

Top courses filled solid

Impermeable backfill

Granular backfill

Masonry foundation wall

Rigid insulation

10

Foundation-to-Wall

Figure 10.3
Externally Insulated Masonry Basement — SIP Above Grade Wall

- Cantilever SIP over foundation wall
- Vinyl and aluminum siding can be directly applied to housewraps as they are inherently "back-ventilated" due to their profile
- Drained and ventilated cladding such as vinyl siding installed directly over a water resistive barrier, wood siding or cement siding installed over a $1/4$-inch (6 mm) spacer strip over a water resistive barrier, cedar shingles installed over $3/8$-inch (9 mm) drainage mat over a water resistive barrier
- Spacer strip (i.e. "furring") can be as thin as $1/4$-inch (6 mm); cutting foam $1/4$-inch (6 mm) thick "fan-fold" siding backer into 2-inch (50 mm) wide strips is a fast, economical method of back-ventilating and draining siding

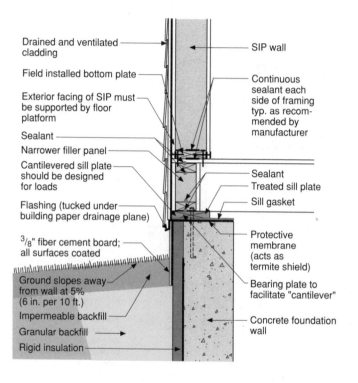

Drained and ventilated cladding

Field installed bottom plate

Exterior facing of SIP must be supported by floor platform

Sealant

Narrower filler panel

Cantilevered sill plate should be designed for loads

Flashing (tucked under building paper drainage plane)

$3/8$" fiber cement board; all surfaces coated

Ground slopes away from wall at 5% (6 in. per 10 ft.)

Impermeable backfill

Granular backfill

Rigid insulation

SIP wall

Continuous sealant each side of framing typ. as recommended by manufacturer

Sealant

Treated sill plate

Sill gasket

Protective membrane (acts as termite shield)

Bearing plate to facilitate "cantilever"

Concrete foundation wall

10

Foundation-to-Wall

Figure 10.4
Externally Insulated Concrete Basement — SIP Above Grade Wall
- Cantilever SIP over foundation wall
- Vinyl and aluminum siding can be directly applied to housewraps as they are inherently "back-ventilated" due to their profile
- Drained and ventilated cladding such as vinyl siding installed directly over a water resistive barrier, wood siding or cement siding installed over a $1/4$-inch (6 mm) spacer strip over a water resistive barrier, cedar shingles installed over $3/8$-inch (9 mm) drainage mat over a water resistive barrier
- Spacer strip (i.e. "furring") can be as thin as $1/4$-inch (6 mm); cutting foam $1/4$-inch (6 mm) thick "fan-fold" siding backer into 2-inch (50 mm) wide strips is a fast, economical method of back-ventilating and draining siding.

10
Foundation-to-Wall

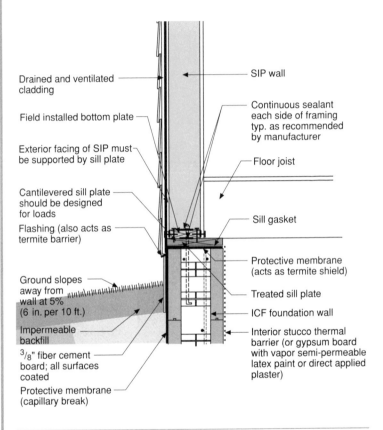

Drained and ventilated cladding

Field installed bottom plate

Exterior facing of SIP must be supported by sill plate

Cantilevered sill plate should be designed for loads

Flashing (also acts as termite barrier)

Ground slopes away from wall at 5% (6 in. per 10 ft.)

Impermeable backfill

$^3/_8$" fiber cement board; all surfaces coated

Protective membrane (capillary break)

SIP wall

Continuous sealant each side of framing typ. as recommended by manufacturer

Floor joist

Sill gasket

Protective membrane (acts as termite shield)

Treated sill plate

ICF foundation wall

Interior stucco thermal barrier (or gypsum board with vapor semi-permeable latex paint or direct applied plaster)

Figure 10.5
SIP Wall on ICF Foundation
- Cantilever SIP over foundation wall
- Vinyl and aluminum siding can be directly applied to housewraps as they are inherently "back-ventilated" due to their profile
- Drained and ventilated cladding such as vinyl siding installed directly over a water resistive barrier, wood siding or cement siding installed over a $^1/_4$-inch (6 mm) spacer strip over a water resistive barrier, cedar shingles installed over $^3/_8$-inch (9 mm) drainage mat over a water resistive barrier
- Spacer strip (i.e. "furring") can be as thin as $^1/_4$-inch (6 mm); cutting foam $^1/_4$-inch (6 mm) thick "fan-fold" siding backer into 2-inch (50 mm) wide strips is a fast, economical method of back-ventilating and draining siding

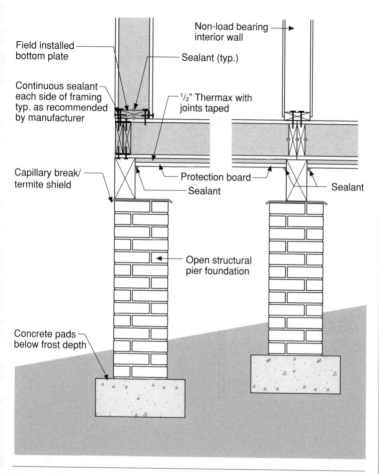

Non-load bearing interior wall

Field installed bottom plate

Sealant (typ.)

Continuous sealant each side of framing typ. as recommended by manufacturer

¹/₂" Thermax with joints taped

Capillary break/ termite shield

Protection board

Sealant

Sealant

Open structural pier foundation

Concrete pads below frost depth

10
Foundation-to-Wall

Figure 10.6
SIP Floor Over an Open Crawlspace

- "Thermax" is a foil-faced rigid insulation that has excellent "flame spread" and "smoke developed" characteristics
- The foil facing on the rigid insulation provides an exterior vapor barrier that protects the SIP floor system from evaporated groundwater and humid exterior "ventilation" air
- "Protection board" is typically a fiber cement board or tile backer that provides physical protection to the foil-faced rigid insulation from vermin and other small animals

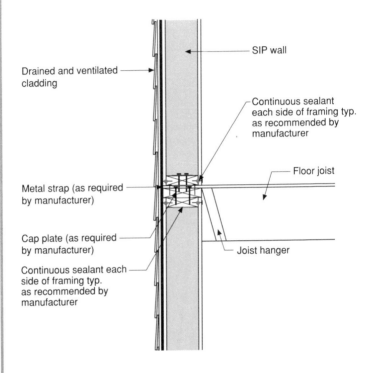

Drained and ventilated cladding

SIP wall

Continuous sealant each side of framing typ. as recommended by manufacturer

Floor joist

Metal strap (as required by manufacturer)

Cap plate (as required by manufacturer)

Joist hanger

Continuous sealant each side of framing typ. as recommended by manufacturer

10

Second Floor

Figure 10.7
Hanging Floor

- Vinyl and aluminum siding can be directly applied to housewraps as they are inherently "back-ventilated" due to their profile
- Drained and ventilated cladding such as vinyl siding installed directly over a water resistive barrier, wood siding or cement siding installed over a $1/4$-inch (6 mm) spacer strip over a water resistive barrier, cedar shingles installed over $3/8$-inch (9 mm) drainage mat over a water resistive barrier
- Spacer strip (i.e. "furring") can be as thin as $1/4$-inch (6 mm); cutting foam $1/4$-inch (6 mm) thick "fan-fold" siding backer into 2-inch (50 mm) wide strips is a fast, economical method of back-ventilating and draining siding

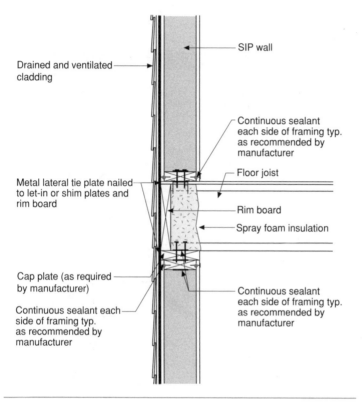

Drained and ventilated cladding

SIP wall

Continuous sealant each side of framing typ. as recommended by manufacturer

Floor joist

Metal lateral tie plate nailed to let-in or shim plates and rim board

Rim board

Spray foam insulation

Cap plate (as required by manufacturer)

Continuous sealant each side of framing typ. as recommended by manufacturer

Continuous sealant each side of framing typ. as recommended by manufacturer

Second Floor

Figure 10.8
Rim Board

- Vinyl and aluminum siding can be directly applied to housewraps as they are inherently "back-ventilated" due to their profile
- Drained and ventilated cladding such as vinyl siding installed directly over a water resistive barrier, wood siding or cement siding installed over a $\frac{1}{4}$-inch (6 mm) spacer strip over a water resistive barrier, cedar shingles installed over $\frac{3}{8}$-inch (9 mm) drainage mat over a water resistive barrier
- Spacer strip (i.e. "furring") can be as thin as $\frac{1}{4}$-inch (6 mm); cutting foam $\frac{1}{4}$-inch (6 mm) thick "fan-fold" siding backer into 2-inch (50 mm) wide strips is a fast, economical method of back-ventilating and draining siding

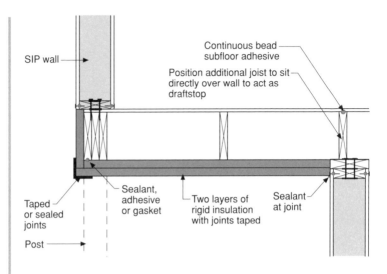

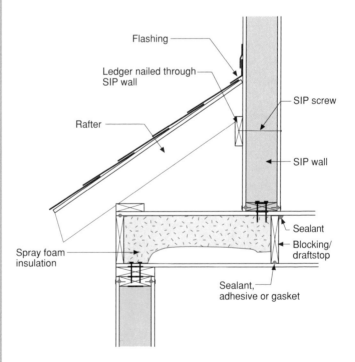

Figure 10.9
Cantilever/Overhanging Floors

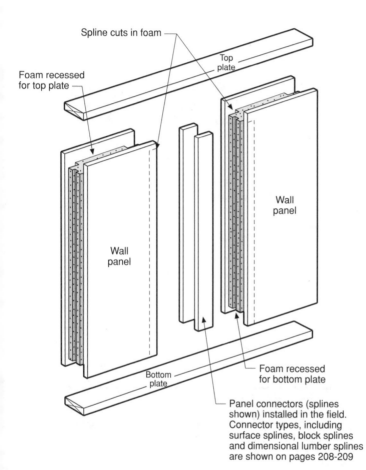

Spline cuts in foam

Top plate

Foam recessed for top plate

Wall panel

Wall panel

Foam recessed for bottom plate

Bottom plate

Panel connectors (splines shown) installed in the field. Connector types, including surface splines, block splines and dimensional lumber splines are shown on pages 208-209

10
Panel-to-Panel

Figure 10.10
SIP Wall Assembly Overview

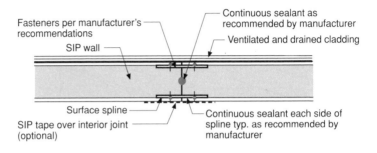

Fasteners per manufacturer's recommendations

SIP wall

Continuous sealant as recommended by manufacturer

Ventilated and drained cladding

Surface spline

SIP tape over interior joint (optional)

Continuous sealant each side of spline typ. as recommended by manufacturer

Figure 10.11
Surface Spline

10
Panel-to-Panel

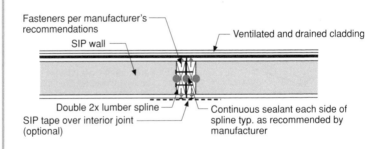

Fasteners per manufacturer's recommendations

SIP wall

Ventilated and drained cladding

Double 2x lumber spline

SIP tape over interior joint (optional)

Continuous sealant each side of spline typ. as recommended by manufacturer

Figure 10.12
Dimensional Lumber Spline

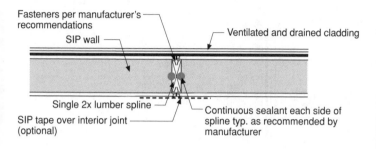

Fasteners per manufacturer's recommendations

Ventilated and drained cladding

SIP wall

Single 2x lumber spline

SIP tape over interior joint (optional)

Continuous sealant each side of spline typ. as recommended by manufacturer

Figure 10.13
Single Dimensional Lumber Spline

10

Panel-to-Panel

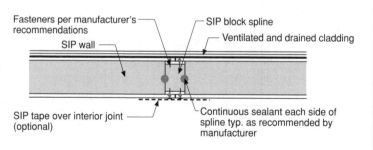

Fasteners per manufacturer's recommendations

SIP block spline

SIP wall

Ventilated and drained cladding

SIP tape over interior joint (optional)

Continuous sealant each side of spline typ. as recommended by manufacturer

Figure 10.14
Block Spline

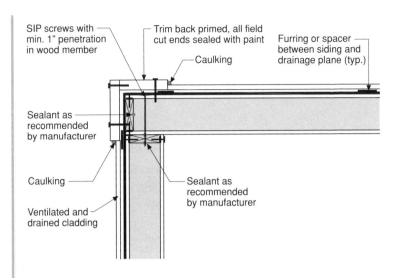

SIP screws with min. 1" penetration in wood member

Trim back primed, all field cut ends sealed with paint

Caulking

Furring or spacer between siding and drainage plane (typ.)

Sealant as recommended by manufacturer

Caulking

Ventilated and drained cladding

Sealant as recommended by manufacturer

10

Panel-to-Panel

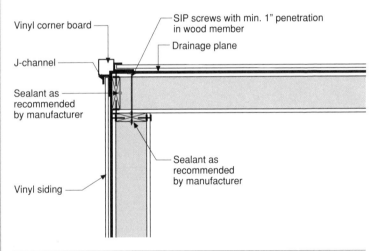

Vinyl corner board

SIP screws with min. 1" penetration in wood member

J-channel

Drainage plane

Sealant as recommended by manufacturer

Vinyl siding

Sealant as recommended by manufacturer

**Figure 10.15
Exterior Corner and Trim Detail—Ventilated Cladding**

- Vinyl and aluminum siding can be directly applied to housewraps as they are inherently "back-ventilated" due to their profile
- Drained and ventilated cladding such as vinyl siding installed directly over a water resistive barrier, wood siding or cement siding installed over a $1/4$-inch (6 mm) spacer strip over a water resistive barrier, cedar shingles installed over $3/8$-inch (9 mm) drainage mat over a water resistive barrier
- Spacer strip (i.e. "furring") can be as thin as $1/4$-inch (6 mm); cutting foam $1/4$-inch (6 mm) thick "fan-fold" siding backer into 2-inch (50 mm) wide strips is a fast, economical method of back-ventilating and draining siding

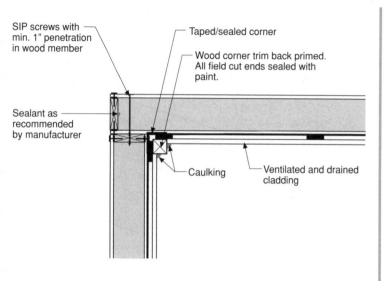

SIP screws with min. 1" penetration in wood member

Taped/sealed corner

Wood corner trim back primed. All field cut ends sealed with paint.

Sealant as recommended by manufacturer

Caulking

Ventilated and drained cladding

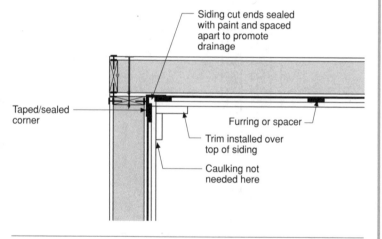

Siding cut ends sealed with paint and spaced apart to promote drainage

Taped/sealed corner

Furring or spacer

Trim installed over top of siding

Caulking not needed here

10

Panel-to-Panel

Figure 10.16
Interior Corner and Trim Detail—Ventilated Cladding

- Vinyl and aluminum siding can be directly applied to housewraps as they are inherently "back-ventilated" due to their profile
- Drained and ventilated cladding such as vinyl siding installed directly over a water resistive barrier, wood siding or cement siding installed over a $1/4$-inch (6 mm) spacer strip over a water resistive barrier, cedar shingles installed over $3/8$-inch (9 mm) drainage mat over a water resistive barrier
- Spacer strip (i.e. "furring") can be as thin as $1/4$-inch (6 mm); cutting foam $1/4$-inch (6 mm) thick "fan-fold" siding backer into 2-inch (50 mm) wide strips is a fast, economical method of back-ventilating and draining siding

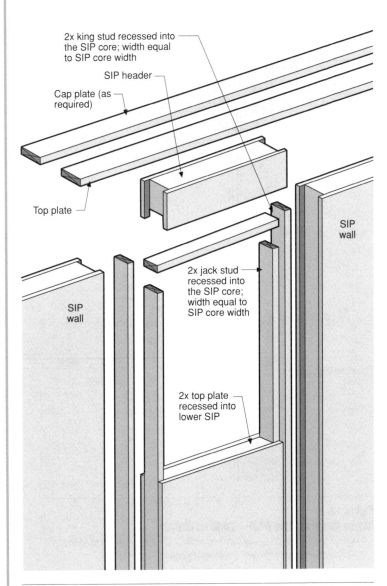

2x king stud recessed into
the SIP core; width equal
to SIP core width

SIP header

Cap plate (as
required)

Top plate

10

Windows & Doors

SIP
wall

2x jack stud
recessed into
the SIP core;
width equal to
SIP core width

SIP
wall

2x top plate
recessed into
lower SIP

SIP
wall

Figure 10.17
SIP Load Bearing Window/Sliding Door Opening

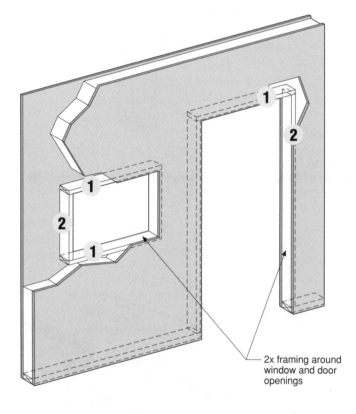

Windows & Doors

2x framing around
window and door
openings

Figure 10.18
SIP Window and Door Openings
• Head and sill framing (**1** above) must be installed before jamb framing (**2** above)

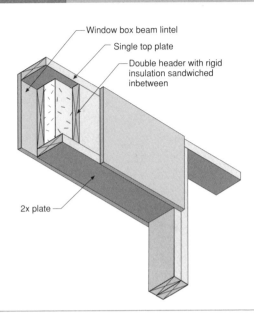

10

Windows & Doors

Figure 10.19
Headers in SIP Construction—Load-Bearing Built-Up Header with Rigid Insulation

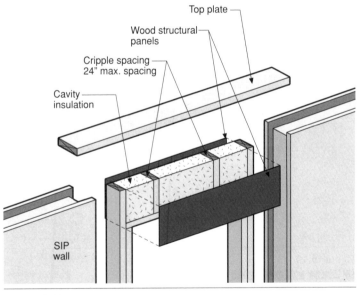

Figure 10.20
Headers in SIP Construction—Load-Bearing Build-Up Header with Cavity Insulation

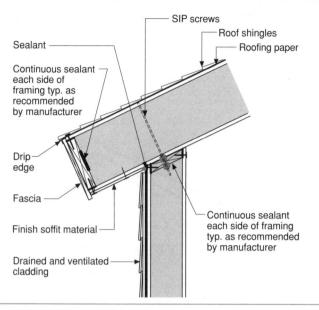

Sealant —

Continuous sealant each side of framing typ. as recommended by manufacturer

SIP screws

Roof shingles

Roofing paper

Drip edge

Fascia —

Finish soffit material —

Continuous sealant each side of framing typ. as recommended by manufacturer

Drained and ventilated cladding

Figure 10.21
Beveled SIP Wall

10

Wall-to-Roof

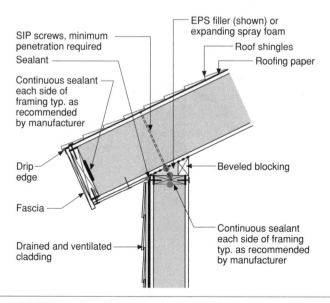

SIP screws, minimum penetration required

Sealant —

Continuous sealant each side of framing typ. as recommended by manufacturer

EPS filler (shown) or expanding spray foam

Roof shingles

Roofing paper

Drip edge

Fascia —

Beveled blocking

Continuous sealant each side of framing typ. as recommended by manufacturer

Drained and ventilated cladding

Figure 10.22
Beveled Blocking

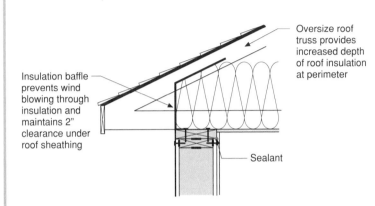

Oversize roof truss provides increased depth of roof insulation at perimeter

Insulation baffle prevents wind blowing through insulation and maintains 2" clearance under roof sheathing

Sealant

10

Wall-to-Roof

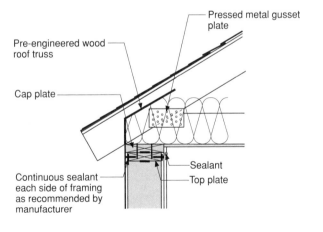

Pressed metal gusset plate

Pre-engineered wood roof truss

Cap plate

Continuous sealant each side of framing as recommended by manufacturer

Sealant

Top plate

Figure 10.23
SIPs Wall to Truss Roof

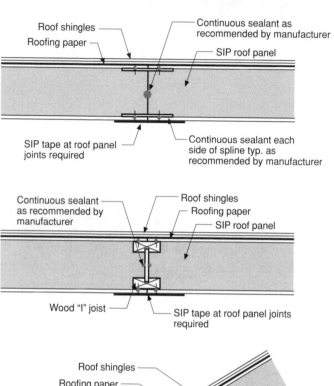

Roof shingles

Roofing paper

Continuous sealant as recommended by manufacturer

SIP roof panel

SIP tape at roof panel joints required

Continuous sealant each side of spline typ. as recommended by manufacturer

Continuous sealant as recommended by manufacturer

Roof shingles

Roofing paper

SIP roof panel

Wood "I" joist

SIP tape at roof panel joints required

10

Panel-to-Panel

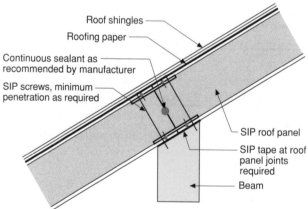

Roof shingles

Roofing paper

Continuous sealant as recommended by manufacturer

SIP screws, minimum penetration as required

SIP roof panel

SIP tape at roof panel joints required

Beam

Figure 10.24a
SIPs Roof Panel Joints

10

Roof Ridge

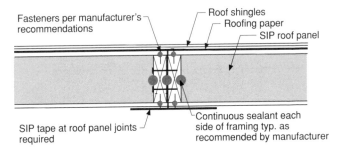

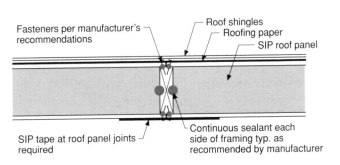

Figure 10.24b
SIPs Roof Ridge—Dimensional Lumber Splines

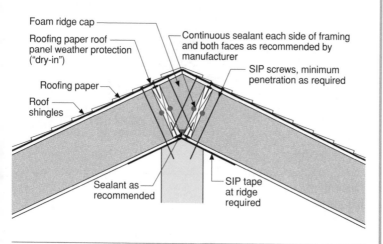

Figure 10.25
SIPs Roof Ridge—Foam Cap Detail

Roof Ridge

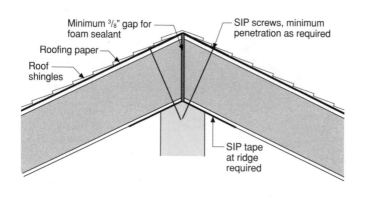

Figure 10.26
Beveled SIP Ridge Detail

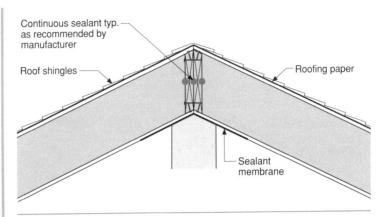

Continuous sealant typ.
as recommended by
manufacturer

Roof shingles

Roofing paper

Sealant
membrane

**Figure 10.27
SIPs Roof Ridge**
- Shows dimensional lumber spline between SIP panels with offset structural
  members below

10

Roof Ridge

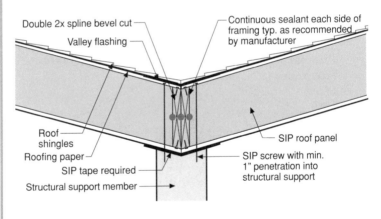

Double 2x spline bevel cut

Valley flashing

Continuous sealant each side of
framing typ. as recommended
by manufacturer

Roof
shingles

Roofing paper

SIP tape required

Structural support member

SIP roof panel

SIP screw with min.
1" penetration into
structural support

**Figure 10.28
SIPs Roof Valley Detail**
- Shows dimensional lumber spline at valley intersection between SIP roof panels
  with structural member below

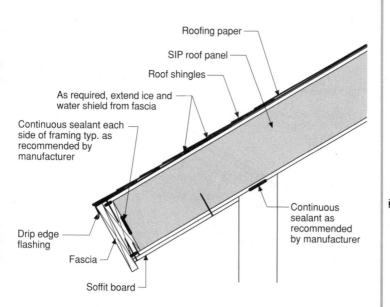

Roofing paper

SIP roof panel

Roof shingles

As required, extend ice and water shield from fascia

Continuous sealant each side of framing typ. as recommended by manufacturer

Drip edge flashing

Fascia

Soffit board

Continuous sealant as recommended by manufacturer

10

Figure 10.29
Eaves Detailing A
- Shows dimensional lumber inset into SIP roof panel at roof edge with soffit boards flush to panel (sloped soffit) and fascia board flush to end of panel

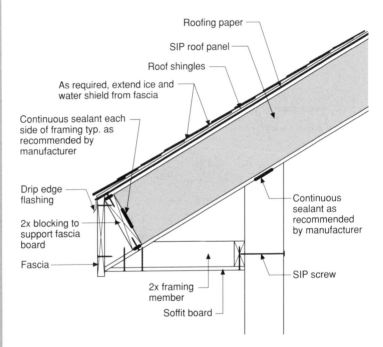

Roofing paper

SIP roof panel

Roof shingles

As required, extend ice and water shield from fascia

Continuous sealant each side of framing typ. as recommended by manufacturer

Drip edge flashing

2x blocking to support fascia board

Fascia

Continuous sealant as recommended by manufacturer

SIP screw

2x framing member

Soffit board

Figure 10.30
Eaves Detailing B
- Shows dimensional lumber framing for horizontal soffit and vertical fascia

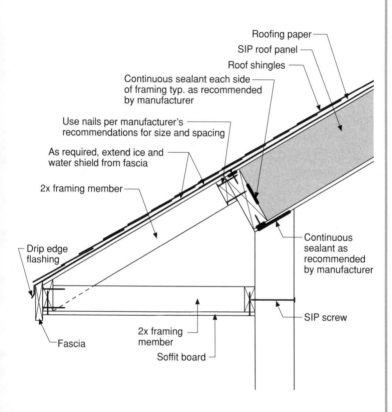

Roofing paper

SIP roof panel

Roof shingles

Continuous sealant each side of framing typ. as recommended by manufacturer

Use nails per manufacturer's recommendations for size and spacing

As required, extend ice and water shield from fascia

2x framing member

Drip edge flashing

Continuous sealant as recommended by manufacturer

SIP screw

Fascia

2x framing member

Soffit board

10

Figure 10.31
Eaves Detailing C
• Shows dimensional lumber framing for roof overhang

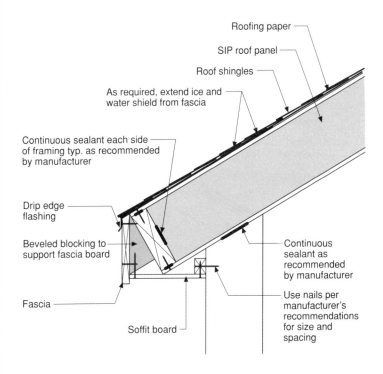

Roofing paper

SIP roof panel

Roof shingles

As required, extend ice and water shield from fascia

Continuous sealant each side of framing typ. as recommended by manufacturer

Drip edge flashing

Beveled blocking to support fascia board

Fascia

Soffit board

Continuous sealant as recommended by manufacturer

Use nails per manufacturer's recommendations for size and spacing

Figure 10.32
Eaves Detailing D

- Shows minimal dimensional lumber framing for narrow overhang with horizontal soffit and vertical fascia

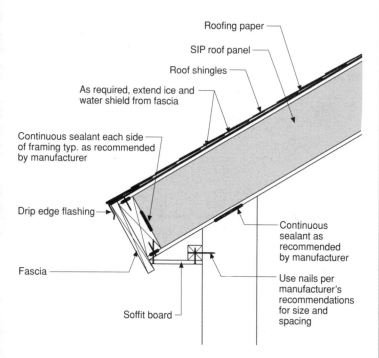

Roofing paper

SIP roof panel

Roof shingles

As required, extend ice and water shield from fascia

Continuous sealant each side of framing typ. as recommended by manufacturer

Drip edge flashing

Fascia

Soffit board

Continuous sealant as recommended by manufacturer

Use nails per manufacturer's recommendations for size and spacing

Figure 10.33
Eaves Detailing E
- Shows minimal dimensional lumber framing for narrow overhang with horizontal soffit and angled fascia flush with end of SIP roof panel

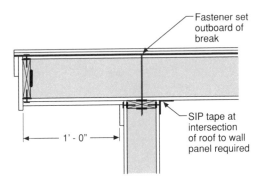

Fastener set outboard of break

1' - 0"

SIP tape at intersection of roof to wall panel required

Figure 10.34
Rake Detail

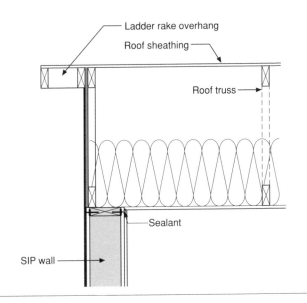

Ladder rake overhang

Roof sheathing

Roof truss

Sealant

SIP wall

Figure 10.35
Rake Detail

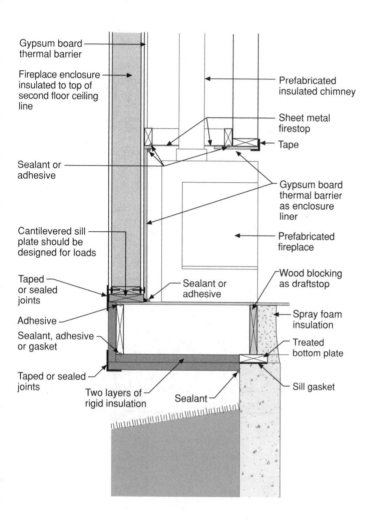

Gypsum board thermal barrier

Fireplace enclosure insulated to top of second floor ceiling line

Prefabricated insulated chimney

Sheet metal firestop

Tape

Sealant or adhesive

Gypsum board thermal barrier as enclosure liner

Prefabricated fireplace

Cantilevered sill plate should be designed for loads

Taped or sealed joints

Sealant or adhesive

Wood blocking as draftstop

Adhesive

Spray foam insulation

Sealant, adhesive or gasket

Treated bottom plate

Taped or sealed joints

Two layers of rigid insulation

Sealant

Sill gasket

Figure 10.36
Fireplace Section

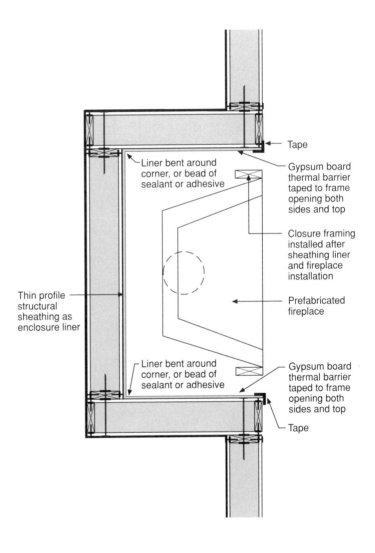

Tape

Gypsum board thermal barrier taped to frame opening both sides and top

Liner bent around corner, or bead of sealant or adhesive

Closure framing installed after sheathing liner and fireplace installation

Thin profile structural sheathing as enclosure liner

Prefabricated fireplace

Liner bent around corner, or bead of sealant or adhesive

Gypsum board thermal barrier taped to frame opening both sides and top

Tape

Figure 10.37
Fireplace Plan

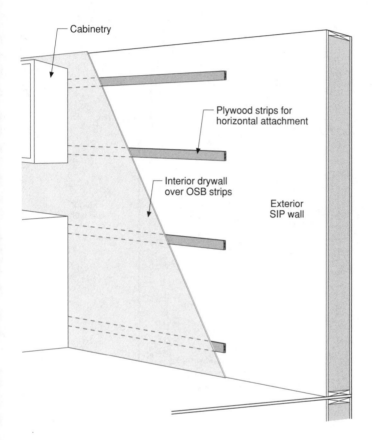

Cabinetry

Plywood strips for
horizontal attachment

Interior drywall
over OSB strips

Exterior
SIP wall

10

Figure 10.38
Framing Behind Cabinets
- Plywood provides good structural support for cabinet installation
- Plywood is "vapor open"—it allows drying towards the interior

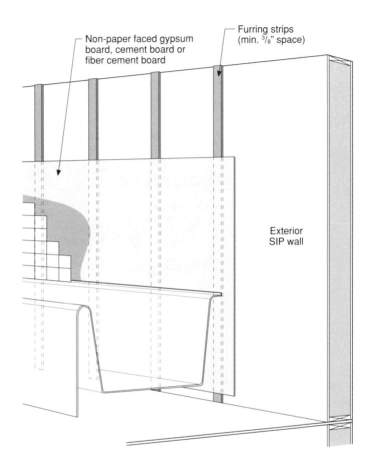

Non-paper faced gypsum board, cement board or fiber cement board

Furring strips (min. $^3/_8$" space)

Exterior SIP wall

**Figure 10.39
Framing Behind Tub—Water Management and Vapor-Open Detail**

HVAC

Two heating and cooling approaches are common in residential construction: those with forced air and those without. Three controlled ventilation approaches are common in residential construction: exhaust systems, supply systems and balanced systems (Figures 11.1, 11.2, 11.3). When mixed and matched all these systems have to:

- heat when it's cold
- cool when it's hot
- humidify when it's dry
- dehumidify when it's wet
- bring in outside air
- distribute outside air
- exhaust strong pollutant point sources
- filter the air
- do all this when needed without noise, vibration, drafts and odors

Concerns

The first choice a builder makes is which type of energy source to use: combustion, electricity or the sun (if we split hairs, the sun is the source of all energy, except nuclear generated electricity - where we split atoms). Choosing between combustion, electricity or the sun requires the wisdom of Solomon, the intelligence of Newton and the wit of Wilde (the reason we have trouble with this choice is that none of these people are alive to actually ask). Wars have been fought over less. Sometimes no choice is possible. We will assume that some type of rational choice will be made.

If a combustion energy source is selected, combustion appliances should not be subject to backdrafting or spillage of combustion products. If electricity is selected, resistance heating should be avoided except in cases where building enclosures are so ultra-efficient that conventional thinking does not apply. In all cases, utilizing the sun for at least a partial contribution should be considered.

The second choice a builder makes is to use forced air or not. If air conditioning is desired (and by air conditioning we mean cooling), forced air systems usually become a necessity. If air conditioning is not a requirement, either forced air or radiant heating systems are options. Arguing the merits of forced air versus radiant systems can be compared to arguing about politics, religion or philosophy (we need to ask those dead guys again). Again, we will assume that some type of rational choice will be made.

Forced air heating and cooling systems involve an air handler with a cooling coil (such as a furnace with an A/C coil or a fan-coil unit with an A/C coil and a heating coil coupled to a hot water heater). The air handler is typically connected to a supply and return ductwork system.

Radiant heating systems are those whose principal mode of heat transfer is radiation (sometimes coupled with convective heat transfer). Included are hot water or steam radiators, hot water baseboard heaters, electric baseboard convectors, radiant hot water floor piping, electric radiant panels and wood stoves. There are some radiant cooling systems available, but they are rare.

The third choice a builder makes is how to ventilate. Why do we need to ventilate? We need to ventilate to protect building occupants and the building. Ventilation controls odors and airborne contaminants. Ventilation also can control interior moisture levels.

Ventilation Requirements

Building tight is right. Buildings can never be built too tight. However, they can be under ventilated.

All buildings require controlled ventilation systems. SIP buildings are inherently "tight" and therefore, for all intents and purposes, have almost no "natural" ventilation. "Natural" in this case means "leaky," "unreliable," "random," "intermittent," and otherwise not good. SIP buildings absolutely, positively require controlled ventilation systems.

There are two kinds of ventilation: spot ventilation ("point source exhaust") and dilution ventilation. Both are necessary. Spot ventilation deals with point sources of pollution such as bathrooms and kitchens. Dilution ventilation deals with low-level pollutants throughout the home.

This ventilation is in addition to the use of operable windows.

Every home needs to have exhaust from kitchens and from bathrooms.

In kitchens, recirculating fans should be avoided because they become breeding grounds for biologicals, a major source of odors, and in all cases allow grease vapors to coat surfaces throughout the home. Kitchen range hoods must be exhausted to the outside to remove moisture, odors and other pollutants.

Bathroom fans must exhaust to the exterior — even bathrooms with operable windows. No exceptions. Low sone fans (less than 3 sones) are recommended because they are quiet (so they are more likely to be used) and more durable (in order to make them quiet they must be made durable).

Dilution ventilation can be provided three ways: exhaust (Figure 11.1), supply (Figure 11.2) or balanced (Figure 11.3). In all cases, it should be continuous and fan powered.

The key to dilution ventilation is good distribution. Outside air should be provided throughout the house. Forced air duct systems can be excellent distribution systems (either by directly providing outside air or by providing mixing of interior air). Where duct distribution systems do not exist, multiport exhaust strategies can be used.

Adding controlled ventilation in hot-humid climates can seem at first to be a contradiction. Supplying outside air increases interior moisture levels and the latent load. Isn't this bad? Yes, but people also need outside air and outside air is required to dilute interior contaminants emitted from furnishings, the building structure and occupant activities. The key is to only supply the amount of outside air that is needed — and not more. And then address the resulting latent (interior humidity) load.

The contradiction gets worse when you consider the effect of duct leakage. Most ductwork and air handlers leak and are located outside of the conditioned space in vented attics, vented crawlspaces or garages. This results in excessive air change. That's right, most houses in humid climates are over-ventilated when the air handler operates. So you'd have to be crazy to add controlled ventilation? Well, no. The key is to get rid of the duct leakage induced air change which is uncontrolled and then add controlled ventilation. This approach typically results in a lower latent load. It is not unusual to have more than 150 to 200 cfm of duct leakage induced air change. This is replaced by 50 to 60 cfm of controlled ventilation after the duct leakage is eliminated.

Relying on duct leakage-induced air change to provide ventilation causes other problems. The outside air that is induced to enter often enters from the attic, crawlspace or garage — locations that are not conducive to the highest quality of outside air by virtue of temperature, humidity or contaminants.

The ideal approach to ventilation in hot-humid climates is to properly size equipment and minimize the need for outside air. The air should be obtained in a controlled manner (mechanically with a fan). The air

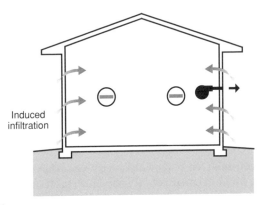

Figure 11.1
Exhaust Ventilation System

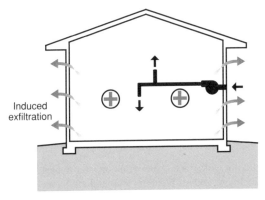

Figure 11.2
Supply Ventilation System

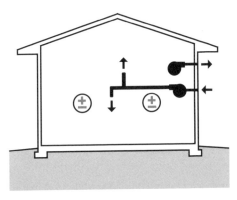

Figure 11.3
Balanced Ventilation System

should be conditioned where it comes into the building. It should be dehumidified by cooling it below its dewpoint (typically below 55° F) and used to maintain the building enclosure at a slight positive pressure relative to the exterior. By doing so, it can be used to control the infiltration of exterior hot, humid air. Furthermore, the building enclosure should be built in a manner that aids in the pressurization of the building. Tight construction with ductwork and air handling located within conditioned spaces is recommended.

Dehumidification

It is common to attempt to use dilution (controlled air change by an exhaust, supply or balanced ventilation system) during heating periods (cold, dry winter months) to limit/control interior moisture levels. During cooling periods (hot, sometimes humid, summer months) the dehumidification characteristics of air conditioning (mechanical cooling) systems are used to reduce interior moisture levels.

However, dilution ventilation during the winter and air conditioning during the summer will not likely be able to control interior moisture levels in hot-humid climates without supplemental dehumidification. Furthermore spring or fall conditions, when neither heating nor cooling occurs and exterior humidity is high will lead to even more difficult interior moisture control problems. In hot-humid climates, the winters are particularly mild and the exterior air during the winter period is humid. Dilution (or air change) will not remove much moisture under these conditions since the incoming air is humid. Air change is still required to remove/dilute interior pollutants. However, air change will not remove moisture. Under such conditions a dehumidification system is needed. A stand alone dehumidifier or a ventilating dehumidifier is recommended.

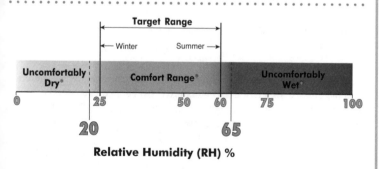

Figure 11.4
Relative Humidity and Comfort
  * For 80% or more of the occupants in a space

Similarly, under part load conditions in the summer or especially during the spring or fall (when the outside air is humid, but at the same temperature or slightly higher than the interior) when the air conditioner does not operate much, dehumidification may also be needed. Air conditioning will only remove moisture from the interior air when the air conditioning system is cooling the interior air. If there is not much need (demand) for cooling, dehumidification by the air conditioning system will not occur. Again, under such conditions a dehumidification system is needed and can be supplied by a stand alone dehumidifier or a ventilating dehumidifier.

Dehumidifiers or ventilating dehumidifiers should be selected with a minimum capacity of 40 to 60 pints per day. Interior relative humidities should always be maintained below 60%. In homes with carpets over slab-on-grade, interior RH should be kept below 50% to control dust mites. Dehumidifier capacity should be rated at 75°F and 50% RH.

It is recommended that dehumidifiers with enhanced recuperative dehumidification cycles be used. These types of dehumidifiers add a recuperative heat exchanger to the conventional dehumidification cycle. They typically require only $1/3$ of the electrical power and operating cost as conventional dehumidifiers.

Heat Recovery (HRV) or Energy Recovery (ERV) Systems

Although almost any controlled ventilation approach works with SIP buildings, most systems installed in SIP buildings are heat recovery (HRV) or energy recovery (ERV) systems. These types of systems are arguably the best type of ventilation technology available and tend to resonate with purchasers of premium high performance building enclosures such as SIPs.

HRV's and ERV's are balanced whole-house ventilation systems that exhaust and supply air in roughly equal amounts. Inside air is exhausted to the outdoors and outside air is supplied indoors. Balanced ventilation, by definition, does not affect the pressure of an interior space relative to outdoors.

Balanced ventilation systems with heat recovery (i.e. "HRV's") use a heat exchanger that transfers some heat between the exhaust air stream and the outside air stream. No moisture is exchanged between the air streams. This means that in cold months, the heating load due to ventilation will be less, and in hot months only the sensible cooling load due to ventilation will be less – the latent load will actually increase. Hence, HRV's are principally a "cold climate" system or a "dry climate" system.

Balanced ventilation systems with energy recovery (i.e. "ERV's") also use a heat exchanger, but both heat and moisture are exchanged between the air streams. This means that in cold, dry months, the heating load due to ventilation will be less, and the house interior moisture level will be higher than it otherwise would have been without energy recovery. In hot, humid months, the total cooling load (both sensible and latent) due to ventilation will be less. Hence, ERV's are principally a "hot humid" or "mixed humid" system.

It is important to note that while with ERV's less heat and moisture will come in from outdoors, an ERV can neither cool nor dehumidify the interior space. ERV's do not "make cold" and do not "make dry" – they only "maintain cold and dry." ERV's do not replace air conditioners and they do not replace dehumidifiers. Small energy-efficient building enclosures in hot humid climates typically need air conditioners, dehumidifiers and ERV's.

Ventilation Rates

How much air do you need? ASHRAE Standard 62.2 provides guidance. Somewhere between 10 cfm and 20 cfm per person when the building is occupied. If a building doesn't have strong interior pollutant sources, as low as 10 cfm per person will work. If a building has strong interior pollutant sources, not even 20 cfm per person will be enough. What are strong interior pollutant sources? Smokers. Damp basements. Pets that are not house trained. Unvented gas fireplaces or space heaters. Unusual hobby activities. Gas ovens and gas cooktops. Generally, if you keep the water out of a building, vent combustion appliances to the exterior, don't smoke, and don't have unusual habits or an uncommon lifestyle, 10 cfm per person will be just fine.

How do you decide how many people live in a house? A good rule of thumb is to take the number of bedrooms and add 1. This assumes two people in the master bedroom and one person in each additional bedroom. The following ventilation requirements result when you follow ASHRAE Standard 62.2.

- 7.5 cfm/person plus 0.01 cfm/ft^2 of conditioned floor area

- For a 2,000 ft^2 three bedroom house with 4 occupants:

  4 x 7.5 cfm = 30 cfm (people load)

  2,000 ft^2 x 0.01 cfm/ft^2 = 20 cfm (house/furnishing load)

  30 cfm (people load) + 20 cfm (house/furnishings load) = 50 cfm

Ventilation air should be provided when the building is occupied. Why ventilate when no one is in the building? Ventilation air should also be distributed (circulated) when the building is occupied.

Indoor Humidity and Airborne Pollutants

Indoor humidity and airborne pollutants are both controlled by ventilation.

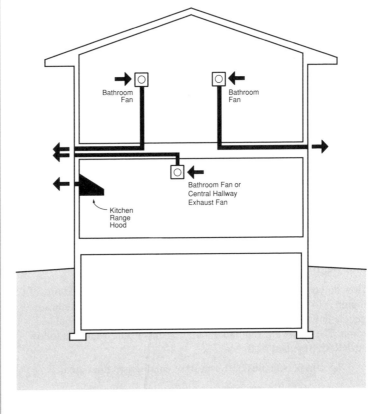

Figure 11.5
Exhaust Ventilation System with Point Source Exhaust

- Individual exhaust fans pull interior air out of bathrooms. One of these fans is selected to also serve as the exhaust ventilation fan for the entire building with a run time based on time of occupancy. Alternatively, an additional centrally located (hallway) exhaust fan can be installed.
- Replacement air is drawn into bathrooms from hallways and bedrooms providing circulation and inducing controlled infiltration of outside air.
- Kitchen range hood provides point source exhaust as needed.
- Always use sealed combustion appliances.

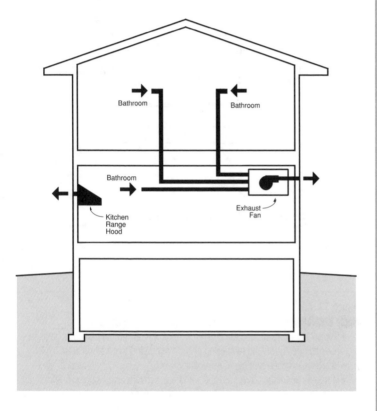

11

Figure 11.6
Central Exhaust Ventilation System

- A single exhaust fan is ducted to individual bathrooms pulls interior air out of bathrooms
- Replacement air is drawn into bathrooms from hallways and bedrooms providing circulation and inducing controlled infiltration of outside air.
- Run time is based on time of occupancy.
- Individual bathroom fans are eliminated.
- Kitchen range hood provides point source exhaust as needed.
- Always use sealed combustion appliances.

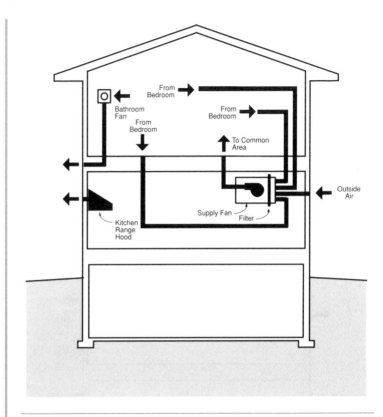

Figure 11.7
Supply Ventilation System with Circulation and Point Source Exhaust
- Supply fan brings in outside air and mixes it with air pulled from bedrooms to provide circulation and tempering prior to supplying to common area.
- Run time is based on time of occupancy.
- In supply ventilation systems, and with heat recovery ventilation, pre-filtration is recommended as debris can affect duct and fan performance reducing air supply.
- Kitchen range hood provides point source exhaust as needed.
- Always use sealed combustion appliances.

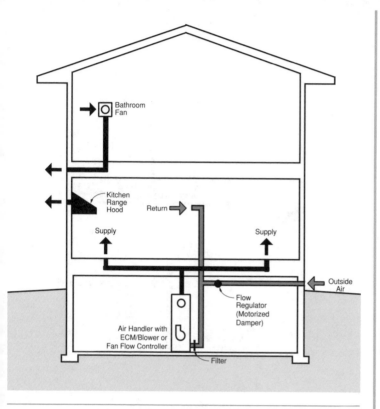

Figure 11.8
Supply Ventilation System Integrated with Heating and A/C

- Air handler with ECM/blower runs continuously (or operated based on time of occupancy) pulling outside air into the return system.
- A flow regulator (motorized damper) provides fixed outside air supply quantities independent of air handler blower speed.
- House forced air duct system provides circulation and tempering.
- Point source exhaust is provided by individual bathroom fans and a kitchen range hood.
- In supply ventilation systems, and with heat recovery ventilation, pre-filtration is recommended as debris can affect duct and fan performance reducing air supply.
- Kitchen range hood provides point source exhaust as needed.
- Outside air duct should be insulated and positioned so that there is a fall/slope toward the outside to control any potential interior condensation. Avoid using long lengths of flex duct that may have a dip that could create a reservoir for condensation.
- Mixed return air temperatures (return air plus outside air) should not be allowed to drop below 50° Fahrenheit at the design temperature in order to control condensation of combustion gases on heat exchanger surfaces
- Always use sealed combustion appliances.

Construction

Balanced Ventilation System Using a Supply Ventilation System Integrated with Heating and A/C with a Stand Alone Central Exhaust

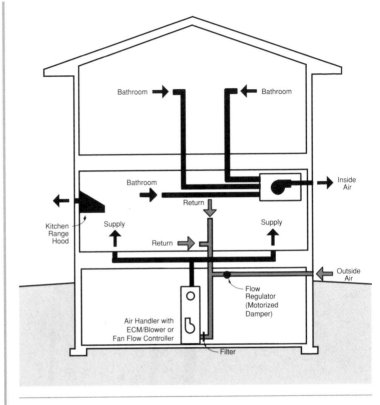

Figure 11.9
Balanced Ventilation System Using a Supply Ventilation System Integrated with Heating and A/C with a Stand Alone Central Exhaust

- The supply system integrated with heating and A/C as in Figure 11.8.
- A central exhaust system is added as in Figure 11.6. Both systems are operated simultaneously.
- Run time is based on time of occupancy.
- Air handler with ECM/blower runs continuously (or operated based on time of occupancy) pulling outside air into the return system.
- In supply ventilation systems, and with heat recovery ventilation, pre-filtration is recommended as debris can affect duct and fan performance reducing air supply.
- Kitchen range hood provides point source exhaust as needed.
- Outside air duct should be insulated and positioned so that there is a fall/slope toward the outside to control any potential interior condensation. Avoid using long lengths of flex duct that may have a dip that could create a reservoir for condensation.
- Mixed return air temperatures (return air plus outside air) should not be allowed to drop below 50° Fahrenheit at the design temperature in order to control condensation of combustion gases on heat exchanger surfaces
- Always use sealed combustion appliances.

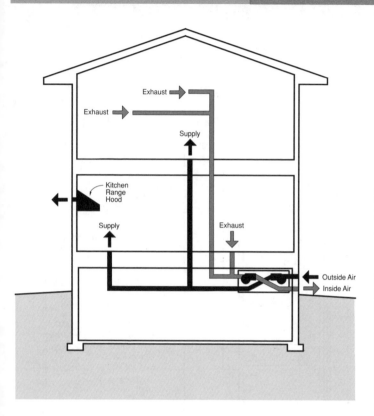

Figure 11.10
Balanced Ventilation System with Heat Recovery with a Heat Recovery Ventilator (HRV) or with an Energy Recovery Ventilator (ERV)

- The ventilation system has a separate duct system and is not integrated with the heating and A/C system.
- Run time is based on time of occupancy.
- Exhausts are typically from bathrooms and supplies are typically to bedrooms.
- In supply ventilation systems, and with heat recovery ventilation, pre-filtration is recommended as debris can affect duct and fan performance reducing air supply.
- Always use sealed combustion appliances.

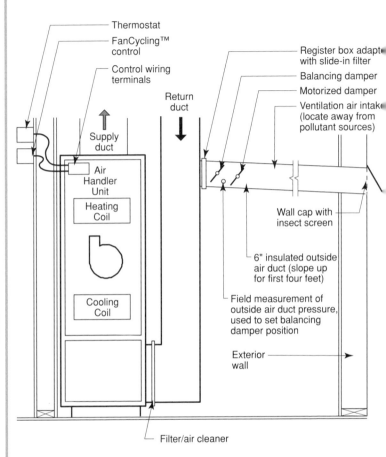

Figure 11.11
Supply Ventilation Integration

- Outside air duct should be insulated and positioned so that there is a fall/slope toward the outside to control any potential interior condensation. Avoid using long lengths of flex duct that may have a dip and could create a reservoir for condensation
- Motorized damper allows control of ventilation air duty cycle separate from air handler duty cycle
- Controller can be mounted on the air handler, or in the main space near the thermostat
- Balancing damper adjusted to provide required flow
- Mixed return air temperatures (return air plus outside air) should not be allowed to drop below 50° Fahrenheit at the design temperature in order to control condensation of combustion gases on heat exchanger surfaces

Most individuals are comfortable where relative humidity is in the 20 percent to 65 percent range (see Figure 11.4)

During the coldest part of the winter, indoor relative humidity should be kept low — but in the comfort range (see Figure 11.4). During summer months, indoor relative humidity (in air conditioned buildings) should not exceed 70 percent for extended periods of time (more than several days). In hot and humid climates this may only be possible with supplemental dehumidification (a stand alone dehumidifier plumbed to a condensate drain) — especially in small units with very little solar heat gain.

Recommended Not-to-Exceed Interior Relative Humidities*

Zone 5   35% relative humidity

Zone 6   30% relative humidity

Zone 7   25% relative humidity
(and higher)

> * During winter (December, January, February)

Formaldehyde and other emissions from particleboard can be harmful. To reduce emissions from particleboard surfaces, reduce the amount of particleboard. Use wire shelving in closets. Wire shelving is easy to clean and permits air circulation. With kitchen and bathroom cabinets constructed from particleboard, the exposed particleboard sources can be sealed with 100 percent acrylic paint or clear sealant.

Since most ventilation system airflow across the building enclosure is in the 50 cfm or less range, the effect on building pressures is typically small. However, in general, exhaust ventilation systems have a slight depressurization effect on building enclosures; supply ventilation systems have a slight pressurization effect on building enclosures, and balanced ventilation systems have no effect on building air pressures. See Figures 11.5 through 11.11 for more detail on different types of ventilation systems. Note that the figures show side wall locations for the exit or entrance point of ventilation ducts because venting through the ceiling plane is not desirable due to the difficulties in air sealing fan housings and the effect of thermosiphoning on airflows.

Furnace fans or air handler fans should not run continuously unless at reduced speed using electrically commutated motors (ECM). These types of motors are typically found only on premium units.

Even with efficient electric motors and blowers HVAC units should not run continuously if outside air ducted into the air handling system will only occur when the coils are energized. If blowers are run continuously, re-evaporation of condensate off the cooling coil will occur and condensation of humidity contained in ducted outside air can occur on cold ductwork (i.e. ductwork cooled by cold air coming off energized coils). This can be avoided by cycling the air handler such that once

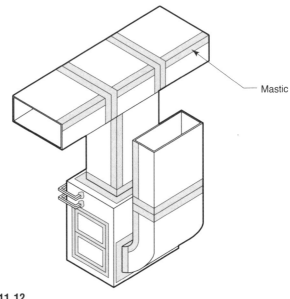

Mastic

Figure 11.12
Air Handler Air Sealing

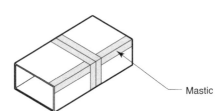

Mastic

Figure 11.13
Rigid Duct Air Sealing

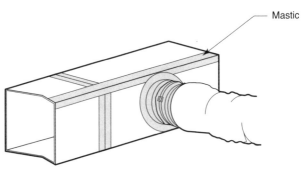

Mastic

Figure 11.14
Flex Take-off from Rigid Air Sealing

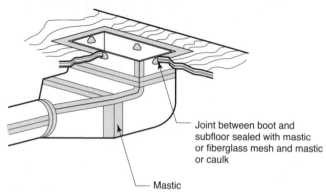

Joint between boot and subfloor sealed with mastic or fiberglass mesh and mastic or caulk

Mastic

Figure 11.15
Floor Boot Air Sealing

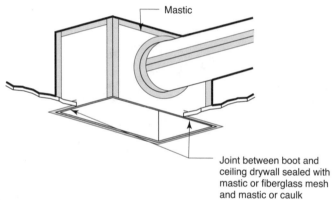

Mastic

Joint between boot and ceiling drywall sealed with mastic or fiberglass mesh and mastic or caulk

Figure 11.16
Ceiling Boot Air Sealing

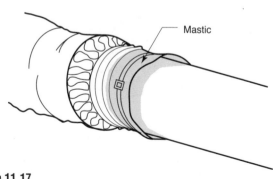

Mastic

Figure 11.17
Rigid to Flex Air Sealing

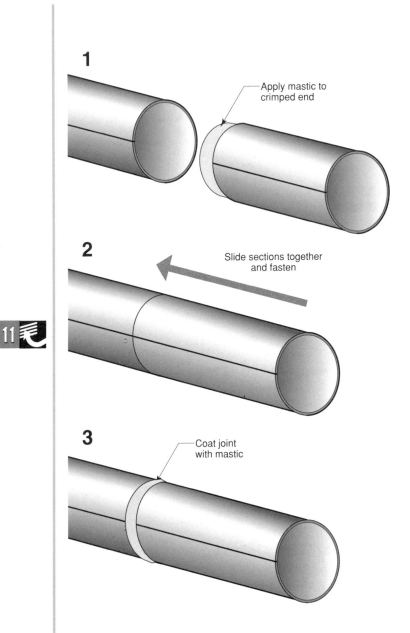

1

Apply mastic to crimped end

2

Slide sections together and fasten

3

Coat joint with mastic

Figure 11.18
Sheet Metal Duct Sealing

coils are de-energized, blowers are also shutdown for 15 minutes to allow ductwork to warm-up and condensate to drain from wet coil and drain pans.

A flow controller with a motorized damper can be used in a system where outside air is ducted to the return side of the air handler. When the air handler is operating and the motorized damper is open, outside air is brought into the building and distributed. The controller will only operate the blower with the damper open if the coils are energized or with a time-delay where the blower is shutdown for a given period after coils are de-energized to allow for system condensate drainage and duct system warming. This approach will also allow the blower to cycle several minutes each hour even if heating or cooling is not required. This will bring in outside air throughout the year in cases where the outside air supply is provided by the blower independent of thermostat control. The motorized damper prevents overventilation during long blower duty cycles.

Exhaust fans extracting less than 50 cfm will typically not increase radon ingress, soil gas ingress or backdrafting problems with fireplaces or wood stoves due to their negligible effect on building air pressures. Similarly, supply fans supplying less than 50 cfm will typically not increase wall and roof cavity interstitial moisture problems. Larger exhaust air flows may lead to unacceptably high negative air pressures (above 5 Pascals negative is considered unacceptable by some codes, 3 Pascals or less positive or negative is a recommended maximum allowable design metric for pressure differentials). Larger supply air flows may lead to moisture concerns in building enclosure wall and roof assemblies that are not designed to dry towards the exterior or that do not have a provision to control condensing surface temperatures.

Combustion Appliances

Spillage or backdrafting of combustion appliances is unacceptable. Only sealed combustion, direct vented, power vented or induced draft combustion appliances should be installed inside conditioned spaces for space conditioning or for domestic hot water. Traditional gas water heaters with draft hoods are prone to spillage and backdrafting. They should be avoided. Gas ovens, gas stoves or gas cooktops should only be installed with an exhaust range hood directly vented to the exterior. Wood-burning fireplaces or gas-burning fireplaces should be supplied with glass doors and exterior combustion air ducted to the firebox. Wood stoves should have a direct ducted supply of combustion air. Unvented (ventless) gas fireplaces or gas space heaters should never be installed. Sealed combustion direct vent gas fireplaces are an acceptable alternative. Portable kerosene heaters should never be used indoors. Figures 11.21 through 11.24 describe several different systems for safely installing gas fired furnaces and hot water tanks.

Garages

Ideally, garages should not be connected to a home. Discrete, separate garages constructed away from homes are preferred. If garages are connected to a home, they should be ventilated to the exterior with a passive vent stack (a "chimney" to the outside — 6-inch duct). Air handling devices such as furnaces or air conditioners should never be located in garages. Nor should forced air ductwork. Weatherstrip the door between the garage and the home and air seal the common wall.

When ductwork passes through a chase or a floor above a garage or adjacent to an exterior wall bordering a garage, it is important that the ductwork be sealed airtight against the migration of pollutants from the garage to inside the home.

Smoke

Smoking should not occur in homes. If you must smoke, smoke outside. Candles and incense produce soot as do fireplaces and wood stoves. Soot can be unhealthy.

Recirculating Fans

Recirculating range hoods and recirculating bathroom fans should be avoided due to health concerns. If recirculating range hood filters are not regularly replaced and units not regularly cleaned, they become a breeding ground for biologicals and a major source of odors.

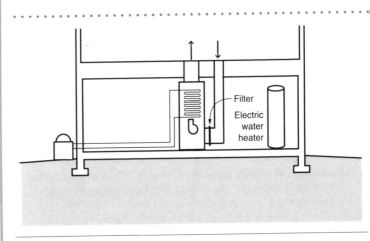

Figure 11.19
Air-to-Air Heat Pump
- Heating and cooling provided by an electrically driven heat pump with exterior air used as a heat source/sink

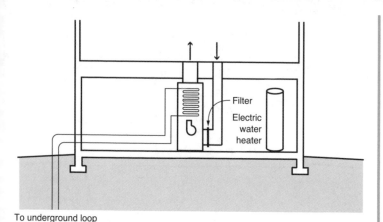

To underground loop

Figure 11.20
Ground Source Heat Pump
- Heating and cooling provided by an electrically driven heat pump with ground used as a heat source/sink

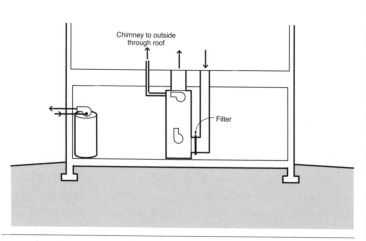

Figure 11.21
Sealed Combustion Power Vented Gas Water Heater, Induced Draft Gas Furnace
- Water heater combustion air supplied directly to water heater from exterior via duct; products of combustion exhausted directly to exterior also via duct.
- Furnace flue gases exhausted to the exterior using a fan to induce draft; combustion air taken from the interior

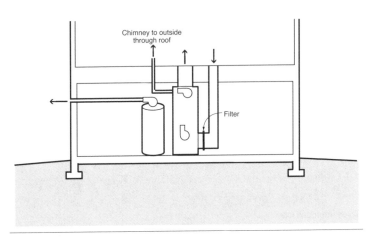

Figure 11.22
Power Vented Gas Water Heater, Induced Draft Gas Furnace
- Water heater flue gases exhausted to the exterior using a fan to maintain draft; combustion air taken from the interior
- Furnace gases exhausted to the exterior using a fan to induce draft; combustion air taken from the interior

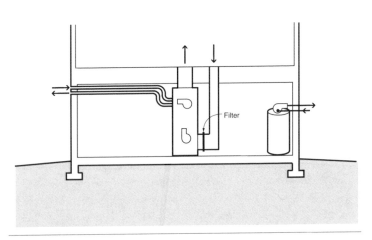

Figure 11.23
Sealed Combustion Power Vented Gas Water Heater, Sealed Combustion Power Vented Furnace
- Water heater combustion air supplied directly to water heater from exterior via duct; products of combustion exhausted directly to exterior also via duct.
- Furnace flue gases exhausted to the exterior using a fan; combustion air supplied directly to furnace from exterior via duct.

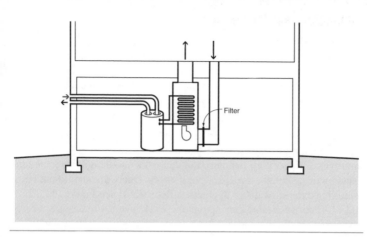

Figure 11.24
Sealed Combustion Power Vented Gas Water Heater
- Water heater flue gases exhausted to exterior using a fan; combustion air supplied directly to water heater from exterior via duct
- No furnace; heat provided by hot water pumped through a water-to-air heat exchanger (fan-coil)

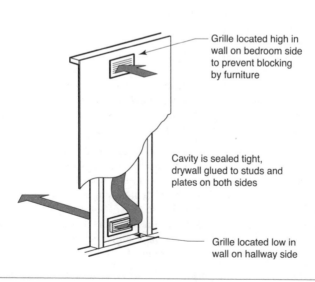

Grille located high in wall on bedroom side to prevent blocking by furniture

Cavity is sealed tight, drywall glued to studs and plates on both sides

Grille located low in wall on hallway side

Figure 11.25
Transfer Grille

Air Handlers and Ductwork

Equipment should be sized correctly and return air flow paths should be planned. If a similar floor plan is constructed several times in a subdivision and sited with different orientations, heat gain and heat loss calculations should be done for each orientation. Equipment should be specifically selected for each orientation.

Furnaces, air handlers and ductwork should always be located within conditioned spaces and allow for easy access to facilitate servicing, filter replacement, drain pan cleaning, and future replacement as technology improves. Furnaces, air handlers and ductwork should not be located in vented attics, vented crawlspaces or garages. Ductwork should not be located in exterior walls or in concrete floor slabs. See Figures 11.30 and 11.31 for suggested conceptual ductwork layouts. In designs where ducts are unavoidably located in an unconditioned space, they should be sealed airtight and insulated (Figure 11.29).

Ductwork, furnaces and air handlers should be sealed against air leakage. The only place air should be able to leave the supply duct system and the furnace or air handling unit is at the supply registers. The only place air should be able to enter the return duct system and the furnace or air handling unit is at the return grilles. A forced air system should be able to be pressure tested the way a plumber pressure tests a plumbing system for leaks. Builders don't accept leaky plumbing systems, they should not accept leaky duct systems.

Supply systems should be sealed with mastic in order to be airtight. All openings (except supply registers), penetrations, holes and cracks should be sealed with mastic or fiberglass mesh and mastic. Tape, especially duct tape, does not work and should not be used. Sealing of the supply system includes sealing the supply plenum, its attachment to the air handler or furnace, and the air handler or furnace itself. Joints, seams and openings on the air handler, furnace or ductwork near the air handler or furnace should be sealed with both fiberglass mesh and mastic due to greater local vibration and flexure. See Figures 11.12 through 11.18 for suggested ways to air seal your ductwork.

Return systems should be "hard" ducted and sealed with mastic in order to be airtight. Building cavities should never be used as return ducts. Stud bays or cavities should not be used for returns. Panned floor joists should not be used. Panning floor joists and using stud cavities as returns leads to leaky returns and the creation of negative pressure fields within interstitial spaces. Carpet dust marking at baseboards, odor problems, mold problems and pollutant transport problems typically occur when building cavities are used as return ducts.

The return side of the air handler or furnace also must be sealed, especially the filter access. The filter access should be easy to get at and have a gasketed airtight fitting door. Gaskets also need to be used around the filters in order to avoid bypass of air around the filters.

All supply registers should have clear access to a return grille in order to prevent the pressurization of bedrooms and the depressurization of common areas. Bedrooms should either have a direct-ducted return or a transfer grille. Undercutting of bedroom doors rarely works and should not be relied upon to relieve bedroom pressurization. A central "hard" ducted return that is airtight and coupled with transfer grilles to relieve bedroom pressurization significantly outperforms a return system with leaky ducted returns in every room, stud bays used as return ducts and panned floor joists. See Figures 11.25 through 11.27 for effective transfer grille details.

The design of HVAC ductwork is important as to whether extensive mold growth will occur or not. If debris can readily collect on the internal surface of ductwork, mold growth is more likely. On the other hand, if the internal surface is smooth like bare galvanized metal, debris is much less likely to collect and mold to grow. For most residential homes, the use of internal duct liners in the HVAC system is not necessary or desired. Porous liners (fibrous glass) should never be used for sound attenuation. Normally liners are only necessary near fan discharge and inlet plenums. If liner is used, only "tough" liner (smooth coated fibrous glass) should be specified and then only for short distances from the fan (normally less than ten feet). Internal liners should never be used in fresh air intakes or return air ductwork. Internal porous liners should never be used near moisture sources, only smooth surface closed cell foam liners should be used. Air handling units, if insulation is necessary, should be insulated on the exterior or double walled (metal insulation metal). If perforated metal is used adjacent to the airstream, the fibrous glass inside the liner needs to be protected by plastic film.

Cooling Coils and Drain Pans

The most common mold amplification sites identified are the cooling coils and adjacent areas of the HVAC system. The cooling coils discussed here are not the condenser coils located outside your house, these are located inside ductwork inside the house near the furnace heating coils. There are three potential growth sites in the cooling coil area:

- The cooling coils — Debris can build up on the cooling coils (especially on the upstream side of the coils) and act as a food source for the mold. This area is a high humidity area during the cooling season.

- The cooling coil drainage area — Debris can build up in the drainage pans and act as a food source for the mold to grow in this area. In addition, the debris can block the drainage from the cooling coils and cause water to be sprayed or leaked onto the ductwork down-

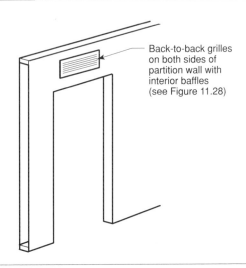

Figure 11.26
Transfer Grille — Over Door Opening
- Relieves pressure differences between spaces
- Interior baffles control sound and light transfer
- Door undercut of 1-inch minimum still required

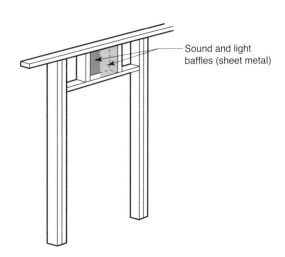

Figure 11.27
Transfer Grille — Construction

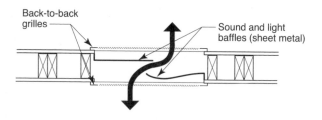

Figure 11.28
Transfer Grille — Section
• Typically 6x20

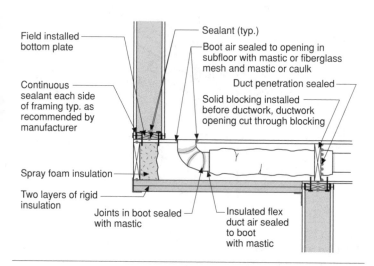

Figure 11.29
Ducts in Cantilevered Spaces or Serving Bedrooms Over Garages
- Avoid whenever possible
- Use insulated ducts
- Air seal all joints with mastic including boot penetrations through subfloors and duct penetrations through draftstops
- Consider spraying boot exterior with foam insulation

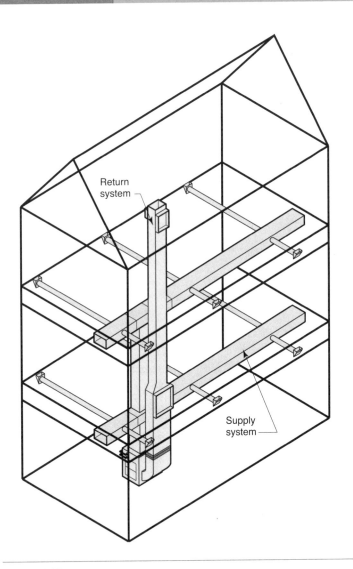

Figure 11.30
Air Handler and Duct Layout
- Air handler centrally located to minimize duct runs
- No ductwork in exterior walls or attic
- No returns in basement
- Return high in hallway of upper floor
- Return low in hallway of main level
- Only fully "hard"-ducted returns when connected directly to air handler; no panned floor joist returns; no stud cavity returns
- Either return ducts in bedrooms or transfer grilles

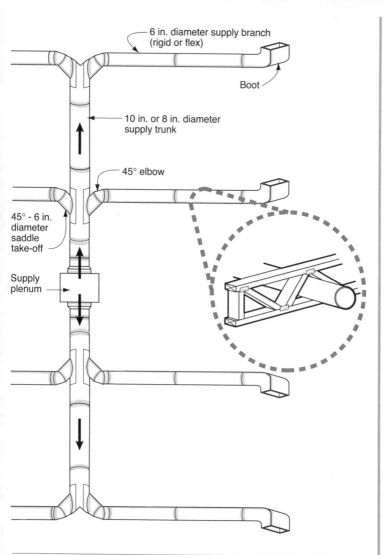

6 in. diameter supply branch
(rigid or flex)

Boot

10 in. or 8 in. diameter
supply trunk

45° elbow

45° - 6 in.
diameter
saddle
take-off

Supply
plenum

Figure 11.31
Supply Duct System
- Must be sized/designed on a case-by-case basis
- Supply duct system sized to fit within 14-inch deep or 12-inch deep open webbed floor trusses.
- Trunk ducts can be 10-inch diameter for 14-inch deep floor trusses or 8-inch diameter for 12-inch deep floor trusses depending on air flows and heat losses
- Branch supply ducts can be insulated flex
- Rounded ducts, 45° take-offs and 45° elbows reduce air flow resistance so ducts can be made smaller to fit in floor system

stream from the cooling coils. Drainage systems which are not properly engineered will not drain and will allow standing water to accumulate in the drainage pans and/or adjacent ductwork. Double-sloped smooth surface drainage pans are recommended. Drainage pans must slope to the middle of the pan and the middle should slope to one end and a trap installed. Pitch of $^1/_4$-inch per foot is acceptable but this slope needs to be in both directions. The depth of the trap should be 1 x the static pressure present in the cooling coil drainage pan location. Normally a 3-inch trap is needed for most residential homes. The drainage pan must drain to leave puddles no larger than 2-inches in diameter and no more than $^1/_8$-inch deep.

- Ductwork downstream and adjacent to cooling coils — Internal ductwork surfaces within 10 feet up and downstream of the cooling coils are the most critical. Internal ductwork surfaces need to have a smooth washable surface to avoid the collection of debris. Internal ductwork surfaces which have a rough surface will collect debris from the air being circulated. Mold grows on the debris which has collected on the internal surfaces. Rough, porous internal liners (fibrous glass) should not be used in high humidity areas of the HVAC system because these materials readily collect debris and are impossible to clean. The goal in the operation of the HVAC system is to control the population of mold. All cooling coil areas need to have easy accessible "gasketed clean-out doors" upstream and downstream of cooling coils. A single large access door, which allows access to both the up and downstream areas of the cooling coils is adequate in many cases. The cooling coil area needs to be cleaned with a cleaning solution in the early spring or late fall of each year. This cleaning needs to include ductwork three feet upstream and downstream of the cooling coils.

System Sizing

Equipment should be sized correctly and return air flow paths should be planned. If a similar floor plan is constructed several times in a subdivision and sited with different orientations, heat gain and heat loss calculations should be done for each orientation. Equipment should be specifically selected for each orientation.

Incorrectly sized equipment can lead to operational and cost problems. Oversizing or undersizing heat pump systems with resistance strip backup (supplemental) heat can alter the thermal balance point and increase resistance strip heat use and, therefore, operating costs.

Oversizing air conditioning and heat pump systems can increase cycling losses, induce high wear and lead to loss of comfort control. During cooling periods, the dehumidification capabilities of the air conditioning system are used to control interior humidity. Oversizing of air conditioning equipment can lead to high interior humidity problems in humid climates since oversized equipment will not run for extended periods of time, and, therefore, will dehumidify less than properly sized equipment.

Incorrectly sized ductwork that is improperly laid out can also lead to operational and cost problems. Heat pumps and air conditioning systems lose significant operating system efficiencies if air flow volumes across the coils are reduced as a result of improperly sized ducts, duct leakage or blockages due to layout, improper installation or a lack of servicing. If equipment is not located so it is accessible, dirty coils and dirty filters will occur from a lack of servicing and result in a reduction of air flow. Too little air across the indoor coil can potentially lower the coil temperature to the point of ice formation and create serious damage.

Correct heat gain and heat loss determination is necessary in order to size and select equipment and systems. The Air Conditioning Contractors Association (ACCA) provides a recognized standard procedure in the publication, *Manual J*. Size of ductwork and distribution system calculation procedures are outlined in a second publication, *Manual D*. However, users of these procedures are cautioned against using default values or rules of thumb for air leakage inputs.

Exterior coils of air conditioning and heat pump systems located under decks or adjacent to vegetation will experience recirculation of air, resulting in greater operating losses.

Incorrectly selected controls, or controls adjusted incorrectly, can result in significant operational losses. Strip heat should be kept off with an outdoor thermostat that only allows operation when outdoor temperature is below the calculated balance point (e.g. 20°F). Heat strips should be installed in banks of 5 kW or less and each bank should have its own outdoor thermostat.

Thermostats for forced air systems are low voltage and typically have a built-in anticipation circuit, and a manual changeover switch or a heating/cooling lockout to prevent cross-cycling ("dueling") between heating and cooling modes. If thermostats have setback settings, they should have a ramped recovery or intelligent recovery feature that limits use of heat strips (supplementary heat) during the recovery period.

Improperly charged systems can significantly affect efficiency. Overcharging or undercharging refrigerants by 10 or 15 percent reduces equipment efficiency by 10 or 15 percent.

Incorrectly selected blower speeds can also result in significant operational losses. Blower speeds are usually different for cooling modes and heating modes. Approximately 425 to 450 cfm of air flow per ton of cooling is typically required over dry coils (400 cfm per ton for wet coils). Significantly less air flow is usually required through the same system during heating periods, and may vary further under different heating modes. Three to five blower speed settings are common and are usually set manually. Some units use two speeds, one for cooling, and a lower speed for heating. Blowers that automatically adjust for changes in duct resistance are also available.

Air Filtration

One of the best methods of controlling dirt and debris in the air conveyance system is using good quality filters to remove particulates from the airstream. In the past, it has been common to use one-thick low efficiency "boulder catcher" filters. These are no longer considered adequate. Air filters are primarily tested using the American Society of Heating, Refrigeration and Air Conditioning Engineers Society (ASHRAE) Standard 52.2. Filters are rated from a MERV 1 (typical furnace filter) to MERV 16 (typical HEPA filter). A practical filter which does an excellent job is a MERV 8 filter. A big problem with better filters is the pressure drop across the filter (how hard it is to move air through the filter). The higher the pressure drop, the harder it is to move air through the filter.

Why don't we just use HEPA filters in the furnace? The problem is pressure drop across the filter. At the present time, most furnace blowers are not designed to pull air through a HEPA filter. Some specially designed blowers for furnaces can handle HEPA filters but the typical furnace blower is not able to.

Large Exhaust Fans

Large exhaust fans and appliances such as whole house fans, attic ventilation fans, indoor grills, clothes dryers, fireplaces and kitchen exhaust range hoods can significantly depressurize buildings.

Whole house fans should only be used with windows open in order to relieve building pressures.

Attic ventilation fans should never be installed. A correctly constructed attic makes attic ventilation fans unnecessary. An incorrectly constructed attic should be repaired, not saddled with an energy wasting and problem-creating attic ventilation fan.

Kitchen exhaust range hoods should not be oversized. Anything larger than 100 cfm exhaust capacity for a kitchen exhaust range hood should be carefully integrated into the entire design of the building. This is best done by providing an interlocked make-up fan. Similarly, indoor barbecue grills should only be installed with a provision for an interlocked make-up air system.

Clothes Dryers

Nothing practical can be done with the large unbalanced air flows created by standard clothes dryers except to reduce the impact of the negative effects by installing only sealed combustion, direct vent, induced draft or power vented combustion furnaces and water heaters. By the way, never duct a standard clothes dryer into the house. The resulting moisture load is more difficult to deal with than an intermittent pressure imbalance. Additionally, lint and other particulates are known to aggravate allergies and contribute to dustmarking on interior finishes.

It is important that dryers be located so that exhaust ducting can be installed within the manufacturers' limitations on length and number of elbows. If long lengths and excessive elbows are unavoidable a booster fan designed for dryer use should be provided.

Alternatively, condensing clothes dryers should be considered. These are electric clothes dryers that do not vent to the outside. Moisture is condensed and drained into a plumbing drain. These devices are particularly attractive in hot-humid climates as they do not increase the latent load.

Central Vacuum Systems

These units should discharge to the outside of the house due to indoor air quality concerns. Their impact on house pressure is minimal because of run time.

Plumbing

Plumbing systems have to:

- supply cold water
- supply hot water
- remove gray water and solid wastes
- not leak water, odors or air

Concerns

Plumbing system penetrations can be a major source of air leakage. Don't put plumbing in outside walls. Let us repeat that for those that may not get it. Don't put plumbing in outside walls. Holes in outside walls cause drafts; outside walls get cold. Pipes freeze. Owners get annoyed. Get it?

Plumbing penetrations through rim joists should be sealed with expanding foam or caulk. Vent stacks penetrating into attics should be sealed with flexible seals to handle expansion of pipes. See Figures 12.1 through 12.3 for details.

Openings in concrete slabs for tubs and showers must be sealed with concrete; avoid "earth" or "dirt" surfaces.

Tubs and Shower Stalls

Tubs, shower stalls, and one-piece tub-shower enclosures installed on exterior walls can be one of the single largest sources of air leakage across a building enclosure. It is essential that rigid draftstopping material is installed prior to tub and shower stall installation. With one-piece tub-shower enclosures, the entire height of the interior surface of the exterior wall should be insulated and sheathed prior to tub-shower enclosure installation.

Water Consumption

Low-flow toilets and shower heads should be installed to minimize water consumption. Pressure balanced shower controls should be used to reduce the dangers of scalding.

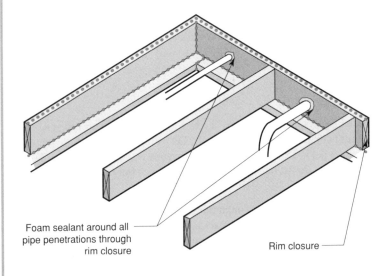

Foam sealant around all pipe penetrations through rim closure

Rim closure

Figure 12.1
Rim Penetrations

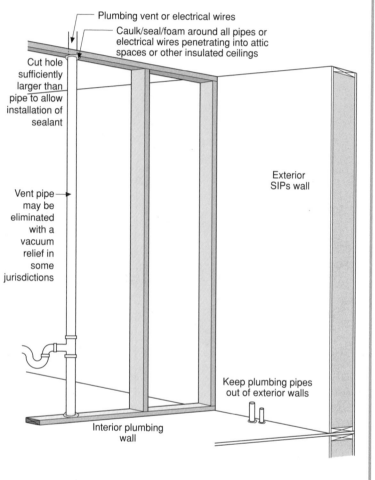

Plumbing vent or electrical wires

Caulk/seal/foam around all pipes or electrical wires penetrating into attic spaces or other insulated ceilings

Cut hole sufficiently larger than pipe to allow installation of sealant

Exterior SIPs wall

Vent pipe may be eliminated with a vacuum relief in some jurisdictions

Keep plumbing pipes out of exterior walls

Interior plumbing wall

Figure 12.2
Locating Plumbing Pipes

- Where connections are made to toilets and pedestal sinks and exposed piping, chrome plated or other surface finished materials should be considered for aesthetic reasons

- Sealants should be flexible, non-hardening

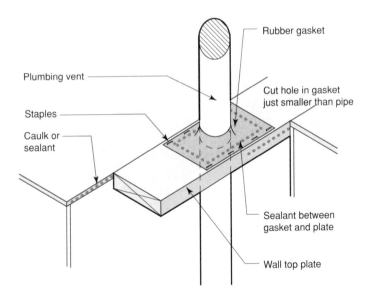

Rubber gasket

Plumbing vent

Cut hole in gasket just smaller than pipe

Staples

Caulk or sealant

Sealant between gasket and plate

Wall top plate

Figure 12.3
Vent Stack Penetration to Attic
• Prefabricated roof vent pipe flashings can be adapted to use as air sealing gaskets

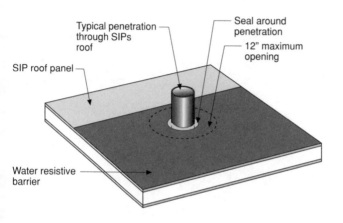

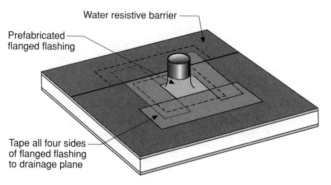

**Figure 12.4
Vent Stack Penetration Through Roof**

12

Electrical

Electrical systems have to:

- supply electricity
- supply communication and control signals
- not leak air

Concerns

Electrical system penetrations through the building enclosure can be a major source of air leakage.

SIP construction reduces air leakage pathways in exterior walls but builders should be aware that service chases cut in panels and pathways through internal walls and roof structures can lead to air leakage problems.

SIP manufacturers recommend installing electrical systems in interior walls wherever possible. There are two approaches to installation of wires and boxes in exterior walls: in service chases through panel cores or in perimeter baseboard chases. Perimeter baseboard chases are preferred. Service chases within panel cores should be sealed with expanding foam or caulk (Figure 13.2). Airtight outlet boxes should be installed where electrical services are specified in insulated ceilings. Specialized boxes are available. Alternatively, sealants can be used to seal penetrations in standard outlet boxes. See Figure 13.3 for details.

Electrical penetrations through rim joists should be sealed with expanding foam or caulk. Wires penetrating into attics, and through top and bottom plates in exterior walls should be sealed with expanding foam or caulk. Air can also leak through service penetrations in studs where interior walls intersect exterior walls. These penetrations should also be sealed (Figure 13.1).

13

Recessed light fixtures in insulated ceilings should be insulation cover (IC) rated fixtures which are airtight and can be covered with insulation. Recessed light fixtures installed in dropped ceilings or soffits need to be draftstopped (Figure 13.4b).

Where electrical panels are installed on exterior walls, air sealing of all penetrations is necessary.

Lighting fixtures, locations and approaches should be selected in conjunction with daylighting design. Energy-efficient lighting fixtures, bulbs and controls should be specified.

13

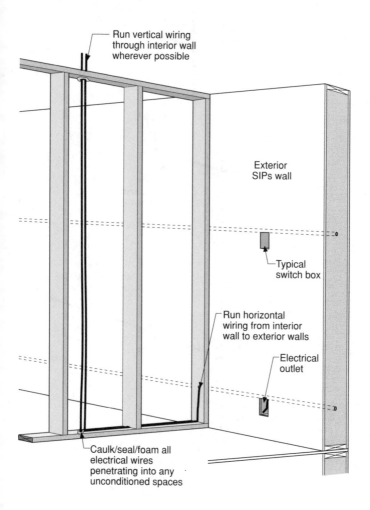

Run vertical wiring through interior wall wherever possible

Exterior SIPs wall

Typical switch box

Run horizontal wiring from interior wall to exterior walls

Electrical outlet

Caulk/seal/foam all electrical wires penetrating into any unconditioned spaces

13

Figure 13.1
Sealing Electrical Wires

- Run low voltage wires in plastic conduit to allow for future upgrade or service
- Some codes require wires to be held up from bottom plates 6-inches to 8-inches to protect wires from future drilling of holes through plates

13

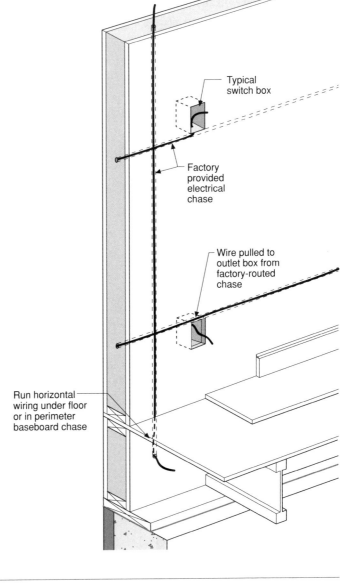

Typical switch box

Factory provided electrical chase

Wire pulled to outlet box from factory-routed chase

Run horizontal wiring under floor or in perimeter baseboard chase

Figure 13.2
Sealing Vertical Service Chase

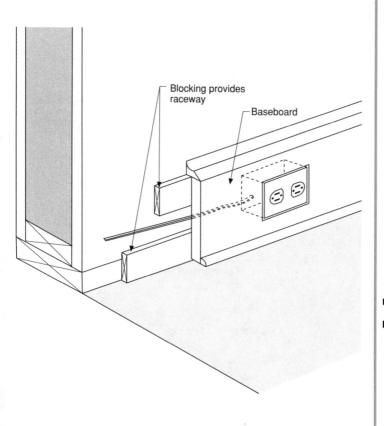

Blocking provides raceway

Baseboard

Figure 13.3
Perimeter Baseboard Service Chase

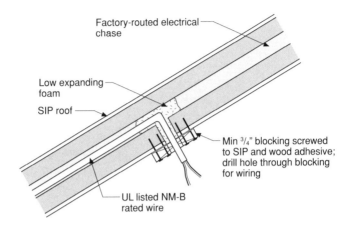

Factory-routed electrical chase

Low expanding foam

SIP roof

Min ³/₄" blocking screwed to SIP and wood adhesive; drill hole through blocking for wiring

UL listed NM-B rated wire

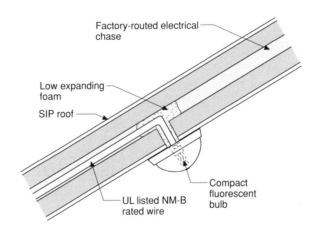

Factory-routed electrical chase

Low expanding foam

SIP roof

Compact fluorescent bulb

UL listed NM-B rated wire

13

Figure 13.4a
Ceiling Fixture Attachment

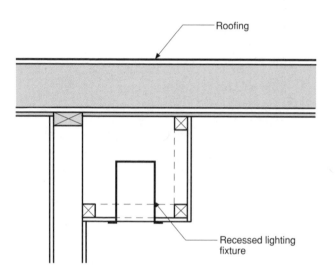

Roofing

Recessed lighting fixture

13

Figure 13.4b
Blocking and Sealing Around Recessed Lights in Interior Soffits or Dropped Ceiling
• Alternatively, interior soffit can be constructed after gypsum board installation

13 ∞

Appendix I
Design Data

	Heating Degree Days, Base 65°F	Cooling Degree Days, Base 65°F	Temperature, °F				Annual Precip. (in)	Winter Design Temp (°F)	Summ Design Ter Dry Bulb
			Dec	Jan	Feb	Average			
Abilene, TX	2624	N/A	42	44	47	44.3	19.2	20	99
Albuquerque, NM	4350	N/A	36	35	38	36.3	7.3	16	94
Amarillo, TX	4258	1354	38	35	40	37.7	20	11	95
Asheville, NC	4308	787	40	37	40	39.0	47.6	14	85
Aspen, CO	8850	N/A	21	22	24	22.5	21.0	-6	81
Atlanta, GA	2991	1667	45	45	46	45.3	51	22	92
Austin, TX	1688	3016	52	50	54	52.0	31.9	28	98
Bakersfield, CA	2122	N/A	47	46	51	48.0	3.9	32	101
Baltimore, MD	4654	1137	37	33	35	35.0	40.8	13	91
Biloxi, MS	1171	3201	54	52	55	53.7	62	31	92
Bismarck, ND	8802	471	16	9	16	13.7	16.8	-16	90
Boise, ID	5727	807	31	30	36	32.3	12.2	9	94
Boston, MA	5630	777	34	29	31	31.3	42.5	12	87
Brownsville, TX	635	3888	62	60	63	61.7	26.2	39	93
Buffalo, NY	6692	548	30	25	26	27.0	40.5	5	84
Burlington, VT	7665	489	24	18	19	20.3	36.1	-6	84
Calgary, AB	9195	73	19	16	21	19	16.2	-15	59
Charleston, SC	2013	2266	50	48	48	48.7	51.5	27	91
Charleston, WV	4476	1031	37	33	36	35.3	42.5	11	90
Charlotte, NC	3341	1582	43	41	44	42.7	43.1	22	93
Chattanooga, TN	3587	1544	42	39	43	41.3	53.5	18	93
Cheyenne, WY	7388	273	28	27	29	28.0	15.5	0	85
Chicago, IL	6498	830	28	22	27	25.7	36.3	-1	88
Cleveland, OH	6121	702	31	27	29	29.0	38.7	6	86
Corpus Christi, TX	1016	3439	59	56	60	58.3	30.1	35	94
Columbia, SC	2649	1966	47	45	48	46.7	50	24	95
Dallas, TX	2407	2603	47	44	49	46.7	33.7	22	100
Denver, CO	6128	696	31	31	33	31.7	15.8	3	90
Des Moines, IA	6436	1052	26	20	26	24.0	34.7	-4	90
Detroit, MI	6422	736	29	24	26	26.3	32.9	5	87
Duluth, MN	9724	189	14	8	13	11.7	31.0	-16	81
Edmonton, AB	10275	51	12	8	13	11	19	-21	62

I

Figure A.1
Climate Data (Imperial Units)

	Heating Degree Days, Base 65°F	Cooling Degree Days, Base 65°F	Temperature, °F				Annual Precip. (in)	Winter Design Temp (°F)	Summer Design Temp (°F)	
			Dec	Jan	Feb	Average			Dry Bulb	Wet Bulb
TX	2700	N/A	44	44	49	45.7	6.3	24	98	64
OR	4546	300	41	40	43	41.3	49.4	22	89	66
ers, FL	225	3702	68	66	66	66.7	53	41	93	80
CA	2612	N/A	43	43	50	45.3	8.0	30	100	69
ay, WI	7963	463	21	15	19	18.3	29.2	-8	85	72
NS	7861	187	27	21	22	23	57.2	2	66	78
, CT	6104	759	30	26	29	28.3	46.2	6	88	72
MT	7975	277	22	19	26	22.3	11.3	-10	87	59
, TX	1599	2700	54	51	51	52.0	46.1	32	94	77
olis, IN	5521	1042	32	27	31	30.0	41.0	3	88	74
nal Falls, MN	10269	233	9	2	9	6.7	24.0	-23	83	67
, MS	2467	2215	49	45	49	47.6	55.4	25	95	76
ville, FL	1434	2551	56	54	57	55.7	51.3	32	94	77
t, FL	100	4798	71	70	71	70.7	40	57	90	78
e, TN	3937	1266	41	38	42	40.3	47.1	19	92	73
arles, LA	1209	2922	54	51	54	53.0	55	27	95	80
as, NV	2709	N/A	45	46	50	47.0	2.0	28	106	65
n, KY	4683	1140	36	32	36	34.7	45	8	91	73
ck, AR	3155	2005	43	40	45	42.7	51	20	96	77
eles, CA	1348	N/A	56	56	56	56.0	7.7	40	89	70
e, KY	4514	1288	37	33	37	35.7	44	10	93	74
, TX	3431	1689	41	39	43	41.0	19	15	96	69
GA	2334	2125	49	46	49	48.0	44.6	25	93	76
, OR	4611	725	38	38	43	39.7	19	23	94	67
s, TN	3082	2118	43	40	44	42.3	52	18	95	76
FL	200	4198	69	68	69	68.7	55.9	47	90	77
ee, WI	7087	616	26	21	25	24.0	34.8	-2	86	72
s-St.Paul, MN	7876	699	19	13	19	17.0	29.4	-11	88	71
AL	1702	2627	53	51	54	52.7	64	29	93	77
mery, AL	2224	2212	49	47	51	49.0	53.4	25	93	76
, QC	8134	435	21	14	17	17	38.5	-7	70	83
e, TN	3729	1616	41	37	41	39.7	47	14	94	74
eans, LA	1513	2655	55	53	55	54.3	61.9	33	92	78
a City, OK	3659	1859	40	36	41	39.0	33	13	97	74
pley AP, NE	6311	1095	27	21	27	25.0	30.2	-2	92	75

I

	Heating Degree Days, Base 65°F	Cooling Degree Days, Base 65°F	Temperature, °F				Annual Precip. (in)	Winter Design Temp (°F)	Summ Design Tem Dry Bulb
			Dec	Jan	Feb	Average			
Orlando, FL	686	3381	62	60	62	61.3	48.1	38	93
Ottawa, ON	8284	440	19	13	16	16	37.1	-7	69
Phoenix, AZ	1766	N/A	52	52	54	52.7	5.2	34	107
Pittsburgh, PA	5829	726	32	28	31	30.3	37.9	7	86
Portland, ME	7318	347	27	22	24	24.3	45.8	2	83
Portland, OR	4522	371	41	39	43	41.0	36	23	85
Providence, RI	5754	714	33	29	30	30.7	46.5	10	86
Raleigh/Durham, NC	3659	1859	42	40	43	41.7	41	20	92
Rapid City, SD	7211	598	26	22	27	25.0	16.6	-5	91
Reno, NV	5600	493	33	33	38	34.7	7.5	13	92
Richmond, VA	3963	1348	40	38	40	39.3	43	17	92
Roswell, NM	3793	N/A	38	40	44	40.7	8.7	18	98
Sacramento, CA	2502	N/A	46	45	49	46.7	13.6	32	98
Salt Lake City, UT	5631	1066	30	29	34	31.0	16.5	11	94
San Antonio, TX	1644	2996	53	50	55	52.7	31	30	97
San Diego, CA	1458	N/A	57	56	57	56.7	6.6	44	80
San Francisco, CA	3015	N/A	49	48	52	49.7	15.6	38	77
Saskatoon, SK	10534	210	6	1	9	5	14	-26	63
Savannah, GA	1847	2365	51	49	52	50.7	49.2	27	93
Seattle/Tacoma, WA	4424	190	41	40	43	41.3	40	26	80
Shreveport, LA	2264	2368	49	46	50	48.3	46	25	96
Spokane, WA	6820	394	28	27	32	29.0	16.7	7	89
St. Louis, MO	4758	1534	35	30	35	33.3	38	6	94
Tallahassee, FL	1705	2518	53	52	55	53.3	65.7	30	92
Tampa, FL	725	3427	62	60	62	61.3	43.9	40	91
Toronto, ON	7318	454	47	21	22	23	31.2	2	70
Tucson, AZ	1800	N/A	52	51	52	51.7	9.7	32	102
Tulsa, OK	3691	2017	40	36	41	39.0	41	13	98
Tupelo, MS	3079	1908	44	40	44	42.7	56	19	94
Vancouver, BC	5268	80	38	38	41	39	47.2	24	64
Washington, DC	4224	973	36	31	34	33.7	40	17	91
Wilmington, NC	2470	1926	48	46	48	47.3	54.3	26	91
Winnipeg, MB	10400	334	6	0	8	5	20.2	-22	68

I

	Heating Degree Days, Base 18°C	Cooling Degree Days, Base 18°C	Temperature, °C				Annual Precip. (mm)	Winter Design Temp (°C)	Summer Design Temp (°C)	
			Dec	Jan	Feb	Average			Dry Bulb	Wet Bulb
e, TX	1459	N/A	5.6	6.7	8.3	6.9	488	-6.7	37	22
erque, NM	2419	N/A	2.2	1.7	3.3	2.4	185	-8.9	1.1	16
o, TX	2367	753	2.4	1.7	4.4	3.2	508	-12	35	19
lle, NC	2395	438	4.4	2.8	4.4	3.9	1209	-10	29	22
CO	4921	N/A	-6.1	-5.6	-4.4	-5.2	533	-14	27	15
, GA	1663	927	7.2	7.2	7.8	7.4	1295	-5.6	33	23
TX	939	1677	11	10	12	11	810	-2.2	37	23
field, CA	1180	N/A	8.3	7.8	11	8.9	99	0	38	21
ore, MD	2588	632	3	0.6	2	2	1036	-11	33	24
MS	651	1780	12	11	13	12	1575	-0.6	33	27
ck, ND	4894	262	-9	-13	-9	-10	427	-27	32	19
ID	3184	449	-0.6	-1	2	0.2	310	-13	34	17
, MA	3130	432	1	-2	-0.6	-0.4	1080	-11	31	22
sville, TX	353	2162	17	16	17	17	665	4	34	25
, NY	3721	305	-1	-4	-3	-3	1029	-15	29	21
ton, VT	4262	272	-4	-8	-7	-7	917	-21	29	21
y, AB	5108	40	-7	-9	-6	-8	413	-26	15	26
ston, SC	1119	1260	10	9	9	9.3	1308	-3	33	26
ston, WV	2484	573	3	1	2	2	1080	-12	32	23
tte, NC	1858	880	6	5	7	6	1095	-6	34	23
nooga, TN	1994	858	6	4	6	5	1359	-8	34	23
nne, WY	4108	152	-2	-3	-2	-2	394	-18	29	14
o, IL	3613	461	-2	-6	-3	-4	922	-18	32	23
and, OH	3403	390	-1	-3	-2	-2	983	-14	30	22
s Christi, TX	565	1912	15	13	16	15	25	2	34	26
bia, SC	1473	1093	8	7	9	8	1270	-4	35	24
TX	1338	1447	8	7	9	8	856	-6	38	24
, CO	3407	387	-1	-1	1	-1	401	-16	32	15
oines, IA	3578	585	-3	-7	-3	-4	881	-20	32	23
, MI	3571	409	-2	-4	-3	-3	836	-15	30	22
, MN	5407	105	-10	-13	-11	-11	787	-27	27	19
ton, AB	5708	28	-7	-9	-6	-8	413	-26	15	26

I

Figure A.2
Climate Data (Metric Units)

	Heating Degree Days, Base 18°C	Cooling Degree Days, Base 18°C	Temperature, °C Dec	Jan	Feb	Average	Annual Precip. (mm)	Winter Design Temp (°C)	Summer Design Temp Dry Bulb
El Paso, TX	1501	N/A	7	7	9	8	160	-4	37
Eugene, OR	2528	167	5	5	6	5	1255	-6	32
Fort Myers, FL	125	2058	20	19	19	19	1346	5	34
Fresno, CA	1452	N/A	6	6	10	7	203	-1	38
Green Bay, WI	4427	257	-6	-9	-7	-8	742	-22	29
Halifax, NS	4367	104	-3	-6	-6	-5	1452	-17	19
Hartford, CT	3394	422	-1	-3	-2	-2	1173	-14	31
Helena, MT	4434	154	-6	-7	-3	-5	287	-23	31
Houston, TX	889	1501	12	11	11	11	1171	0	34
Indianapolis, IN	3070	579	0	-3	-1	-1	1041	-16	31
International Falls, MN	5710	130	-13	-17	-13	-14	610	-31	28
Jackson, MS	1372	1232	9	7	9	9	1407	-4	35
Jacksonville, FL	797	1418	13	12	14	13	1303	0	34
Key West, FL	55.6	2668	22	21	22	22	1016	14	32
Knoxville, TN	2189	704	5	3	6	5	1196	-7	33
Lake Charles, LA	672	1625	12	11	12	12	1397	-3	35
Las Vegas, NV	1506	N/A	7	8	10	8	51	-2	41
Lexington, KY	2604	634	2	0	2	1	1143	-13	33
Little Rock, AR	1754	1115	6	4	7	6	1295	-7	36
Los Angeles, CA	749	N/A	13	13	13	13	196	4	32
Louisville, KY	2510	716	3	1	3	2	1118	-12	34
Lubbock, TX	1908	939	5	4	6	5	483	-9	36
Macon, GA	1298	1182	9	8	9	9	1133	-4	34
Medford, OR	2564	403	3	3	6	4	483	-5	34
Memphis, TN	1714	1178	6	4	7	6	1321	-8	35
Miami, FL	111	2334	21	20	21	20	1420	8	32
Milwaukee, WI	3940	342	-3	-6	-4	-4	884	-19	30
Minneapolis-St.Paul, MN	4379	389	-13	-11	-13	-8	747	-24	31
Mobile, AL	946	1461	12	11	12	12	1626	-2	34
Montgomery, AL	1237	1230	9	8	11	9	1356	-4	35
Montreal, QC	4519	242	-6	-10	-8	-8	979	-22	21
Nashville, TN	2073	898	5	3	5	4	1194	14	34
New Orleans, LA	841	1476	13	12	13	12	1572	1	33
Oklahoma City, OK	2034	1033	4	2	5	4	838	-11	36
Omaha Eppley AP, NE	3509	609	-3	-6	-3	-4	767	-19	33

I

	Heating Degree Days, Base 18°C	Cooling Degree Days, Base 18°C	Temperature, °C				Annual Precip. (mm)	Winter Design Temp (°C)	Summer Design Temp (°C)	
			Dec	Jan	Feb	Average			Dry Bulb	Wet Bulb
o, FL	381	1880	17	16	17	16	1222	3	34	24
, ON	4602	245	-7	-11	-9	-9	944	-22	21	29
ix, AZ	982	N/A	29	29	12	12	132	1	42	22
rgh, PA	3241	404	0	-2	-1	-1	963	-14	30	21
d, ME	4069	193	-3	-6	-4	-4	1163	-17	28	21
d, OR	2514	206	5	4	6	5	914	-5	29	19
ence, RI	3199	397	1	-2	-1	-1	1181	-12	30	22
/Durham, NC	2034	1034	6	4	6	5	1041	-7	33	24
City, SD	4009	332	-3	=6	-3	-4	422	-21	33	18
NV	3114	274	1	1	3	2	191	-11	33	16
ond, VA	2203	749	4	3	4	4	1092	-8	33	24
ll, NM	2109	N/A	3	4	7	5	221	-8	37	19
nento, CA	1391	N/A	8	7	9	8	345	0	37	21
ke City, UT	3131	593	-1	-2	1	-1	419	-12	34	17
tonio, TX	914	1666	12	10	13	12	787	-1	36	23
ego, CA	811	N/A	14	13	14	14	168	7	27	21
ancisco, CA	1676	N/A	9	9	11	10	396	3	25	17
oon, SK	5852	117	-14	-17	-13	-15	350	-32	17	29
ah, GA	1027	1315	11	9	11	10	1250	-3	34	25
Tacoma, WA	2460	106	5	4	6	5	1016	-3	27	18
port, LA	1259	1317	9	8	10	9	1168	-4	36	24
ne, WA	3792	219	-2	-3	0	-2	424	-14	32	16
is, MO	2645	853	2	-1	2	1	965	-14	34	24
ssee, FL	948	1400	12	11	13	12	1669	-1	33	24
, FL	403	1905	17	16	17	16	1115	4	33	25
o, ON	4066	252	-3	-6	-5	-5	793	-17	21	29
n, AZ	1000	N/A	11	11	11	11	246	0	39	19
OK	2052	1121	4	2	5	4	1041	-11	37	24
, MS	1712	11	24	22	7	6	1422	-7	34	25
uver, BC	2927	44	4	3	5	4	1199	-5	18	23
ngton, DC	2349	541	2	-1	1	1	1016	-8	33	23
gton, NC	1373	1071	9	8	9	9	1379	-3	33	26
eg, MB	5778	186	-14	-18	-14	-15	514	-30	20	29

I

I

Appendix II
Air Leakage Testing, Pressure Balancing, and Combustion Safety

Air leakage testing is a method for determining the total leakage area of a building enclosure or the leakage of air distribution systems (ductwork leakage in ducted forced air space conditioning systems). Air leakage testing is not a method for determining the actual air leakage or air change which occurs through the building enclosure under the influence of air pressure differences created by wind, stack action (the buoyancy of heated air) and mechanical systems (duct leakage and unbalanced forced air systems).

Air leakage testing for both building enclosures and ductwork is based on the fundamental properties of air flow through openings. The amount of air flow through an opening is determined by two principle factors:

- the area/size/geometry of the opening
- the air pressure difference across the opening

The three parameters — air flow, area and air pressure difference — can be related to each other by applying a simple mathematical relationship. Measuring two of the three parameters and applying the mathematical relationship can determine the third parameter. For example, if the air flow through an opening is measured, as well as the air pressure difference across the opening when air flow is occurring, the area of the opening can be calculated by applying the mathematical relationship. Applying this relationship to a flow rate of 1,000 cfm through an opening with an air pressure differential of 50 Pascals across the opening obtains a mathematically calculated area of approximately 1 square foot. In other words 1,000 cfm air flow occurs through a 1 square foot opening as a result of an air pressure difference of 50 Pascals.

II

Air Leakage Testing of Building Enclosures

Air leakage testing of building enclosures involves placing a large calibrated fan in an exterior door and creating an air flow through the fan. The calibrated fan is often referred to as a "blower door." Exhausting air depressurizes the building. Supplying air pressurizes the building. When air is exhausted from a building through a blower door, air leaks into the building through openings to replace the air exhausted. If sufficient air is exhausted to overcome any naturally occurring pressures, the quantity of air exhausted will equal the quantity of air supplied. The quantity of air exhausted through the blower door can be readily measured. This exhaust quantity can be equated to the air leaking into the building enclosure through all of the openings in the building enclosure. If the air pressure difference between the interior of the building enclosure and the exterior is also measured, this can be used to approximate the air pressure difference across all of the openings in the building enclosure.

By determining the quantity of air exhausted and the air pressure difference across the building enclosure, the combined air flow through all of the openings in the building enclosure as well as the air pressure difference across all of the openings is known. Applying a mathematical relationship converts the combined air flow and air pressure difference to the combined leakage area of all of the openings in the building enclosure. In this manner a blower door can determine the combined area of all of the openings in a building enclosure, including random cracks, flaws, openings built into the building as a result of the building process, without actually determining where the leaks and openings are.

The procedure can also be applied to building enclosures pressurized by calibrated fans. Either depressurization or pressurization can be employed. Depressurization is more common in building enclosure leakage testing as a result of tradition rather than accuracy (the procedures were initially popularized in cold climates where pressurization during the heating season typically created comfort problems during testing).

Air leakage test results are expressed several ways. Test results can be presented as a flow rate at 50 Pascals air pressure difference (CFM50). In other words, the volume flow rate of air extracted out of the building enclosure necessary to depressurize the building enclosure 50 Pascals relative to the exterior is measured and reported. The combined or equivalent leakage area of the building (EqLA) in square inches can be determined from the CFM50 measurement by the application of the mathematical relationship.

The combined leakage area of a building enclosure can also be compared to the total surface area of the building enclosure using a parameter called a leakage ratio. Leakage ratios are typically expressed as square inches of leakage for every 100 square feet of building enclosure

II

area (or cm²/100m² SI). In this manner the measured EqLA is related to the measured surface area of the building enclosure.

Test results can also be expressed in the form of air changes per hour at a pressure difference of 50 Pascals (ach @ 50 Pa). In this approach, the volume flow rate extracted out of the building is related to the volume of the building enclosure. For example, consider a blower door extracting air out of a building enclosure at a rate of 1,000 cubic feet (304.8 m³) per minute establishing an air pressure difference of 50 Pa. This is equivalent to an air extraction rate of 60,000 cubic feet (18,288 m³) per hour. If the volume of the conditioned space is 10,000 cubic feet (3,048 m³), this would result in 6 air changes per hour at a 50 Pascal air pressure difference (60,000/10,000 = 6). A flow rate of 1,000 cfm through an opening with a 50 Pascals air pressure difference was previously determined to require a 1 foot square opening. In other words, for this particular volume of building, 6 ach @ 50 Pa is equivalent to 1 foot square of leakage or an EqLA of 1 foot square (0.30 m²) or 144 square inches (365.8 cm²). If the surface area of the building enclosure was approximately 3,000 square feet (914.4 m²), the leakage ratio would be approximately 4.8 square inches (12.2 cm²) of leakage for every 100 square feet (30.5 m²) of building enclosure surface area (3,000/100 = 30 and 144/30 = 4.8).

The following information all describes the same building. It came from the blower door test conducted on the building described in the previous example.

$$CFM50 = 1,000$$

$$EqLA = 144 \text{ in}^2 (365.8 \text{ cm}^2)$$

6 ach @ 50 Pa (where building volume is 10,000 ft³/3,048 m³)

Leakage Ratio = 4.8 in²/100 ft² (12.2 cm²/30.5 m²)
where building enclosure surface area is 3,000 ft²/914.4 m²)

Not all of these values are always determined or recorded. All can be related to each other and the building enclosure tested. The leakage ratio value is the most descriptive as it can be used to compare buildings of differing volumes and surface areas to each other. Since the other values are related to specific buildings with given building volumes and building surface areas, comparisons between buildings of diverse construction are less meaningful. However, where buildings are of approximately the same floor area and volume, all of the values provide reasonably comparative information.

Air leakage testing of building enclosures is typically conducted as a method of quality control to ensure that control of air flow occurs in

II

constructed buildings. It is also used to identify leakage areas which may have been missed during construction thereby facilitating repairs and remediation.

Air Leakage Testing of Air Distribution Systems

Air leakage testing of air distribution systems is similar to air leakage testing of building enclosures in that both procedures involve using a calibrated fan to create an air pressure difference. In addition, both procedures require that air flows through the calibrated fans and pressure differentials be determined.

Air leakage testing of air distribution systems involves sealing the supply and return registers and depressurizing the system using a calibrated fan. In this approach, the ductwork and the air handler is considered a closed system. The calibrated fan, sometimes referred to as a "duct blaster" is typically attached to the air handler. The quantity of air moved by the duct blaster to pressurize or depressurize the system is directly related to the leakage area of the system. By determining the quantity of air supplied by the calibrated fan and the air pressure difference between the ductwork and the conditioned space, the combined air flow through all of the leakage openings in the air distribution system is determined.

Air leakage test results for air distribution systems are often presented as the flow rate through the calibrated fan required to pressurize or depressurize the duct system to a specific pressure differential. For example CFM25 values are typical. A reading of CFM25 = 60 cfm translates to: an air flow rate of 60 cfm through the calibrated fan (duct blaster) depressurized the air distribution system (ductwork and air handler) to a negative of 25 Pascals (0.1" w.c.) relative to the conditioned space.

Air leakage testing of air distribution systems is typically conducted as a method of quality control to ensure control of air flow occurs in air distribution systems. It is also used to identify leakage areas thereby facilitating repairs and remediation.

Pressure Balancing

II

Air pressure differentials between conditioned spaces and the surroundings, as well as between rooms and between building assemblies and rooms, affect the health, safety and durability of the building enclosure.

Infiltration of humid air during cooling periods is a concern as is the exfiltration of interior heated, moist air during heating periods. Infiltration of soil gas (moisture, radon, pesticides, other) below grade or from crawlspaces and slabs is a concern throughout the year. High interior negative air pressures can lead to the spillage and backdrafting of combustion appliances such as fireplaces, wood stoves, combustion water heaters and furnaces. Finally, significant depressurization can lead to flame roll out and fire in some combustion appliances such as furnaces and water heaters.

With respect to combustion appliances, installation of appliances which are not sensitive to negative air pressures as well as limiting the negative air pressures which can occur within building enclosures is an appropriate strategy for control.

With respect to the infiltration of exterior pollutants such as soil gas, pesticides, radon and below grade moisture, limiting the negative air pressure which can occur, providing positive air pressurization of building enclosures (or portions of building enclosures) as well as providing sub-slab or crawlspace depressurization are appropriate strategies for control.

With respect to the exfiltration of interior moisture during heating periods, constructing building assemblies which are forgiving and/or tolerant of interior moisture, as well as limiting the positive air pressure which can occur during heating periods (and/or providing negative pressures during heating periods) are appropriate strategies for control.

In all cases the maximum pressurization or depressurization relative to exterior (ambient) conditions should be limited to less than 3 Pascals.

Ducted forced air distribution systems are traditionally viewed as interior circulation systems which move air from place to place within a conditioned space, with a neutral effect on the pressure differences between the interior and exterior. However, as a result of installation practices and design/sizing faults ducted forced air distribution systems can have significant effects on air pressure relationships.

Duct leakage can result in either pressurization or depressurization of entire conditioned spaces or specific rooms. Duct leakage can significantly increase space conditioning energy requirements. Incorrect duct sizing, distribution layout or lack of adequate returns can lead to pressurization and depressurization of rooms and interstitial spaces. These effects should be limited to less than 3 Pascals positive or negative relative to the exterior or between rooms and/or interstitial (between two surfaces) cavities within building enclosures.

II

Exhaust fans and appliances such as whole house fans, attic ventilation fans, indoor grills, clothes dryers, kitchen exhaust range hoods can also significantly alter air pressure relationships. These effects should also be limited to less than 3 Pascals positive or negative relative to the exterior or between rooms and/or interstitial cavities within building enclosures (except in the case of whole house fans and indoor grills). Where whole house fans and/or indoor grills are operating, no other combustion appliances or heating and/or mechanical cooling systems should be in simultaneous use. Furthermore, windows and/or doors should be opened when whole house fans and/or indoor grills are operating.

Testing Pressure Differentials and Commissioning

Air pressure relationships between conditioned spaces and the exterior, as well as between rooms and between rooms and interstitial spaces should be measured under all operating conditions. Equipment should be cycled on and off at all speed settings. Interior doors should be both opened and closed during all testing. Measurements are typically taken with a digital micromanometer. Where any air pressure differential greater than 3 Pascals is measured, remediation work and/or adjustments to equipment, or the building enclosure will be necessary.

Combustion Safety

If combustion appliances are selected, they should not interact aerodynamically with the building. In other words, changing interior air pressure differentials should not be able to influence the operation of combustion appliances. In order to meet this requirement only sealed combustion, power vented, induced draft or direct vented combustion appliances should be used for space conditioning and domestic hot water.

Gas cook tops and ovens should be only installed in conjunction with direct vented (to the exterior) exhaust range hoods. Recirculating range hoods should be avoided even in the absence of combustion appliances as they become breeding grounds for biological growth and a source of odors.

Fireplaces and wood stoves should only be installed with their own correctly sized air supply from the exterior. Fireplaces should also be provided with tight-fitting glass doors.

High interior negative air pressures can lead to the spillage and backdrafting of combustion appliances and significant depressurization can lead to flame roll out and fire. In all enclosures containing combustion appliances, the maximum depressurization relative to the exterior should be limited to less than 3 Pascals.

All combustion appliances (except fireplaces and wood stoves) should be tested for carbon monoxide production prior to occupancy and on a yearly basis thereafter. Carbon monoxide production of any appliance

II

should not exceed 50 ppm. All measurements should be taken in the draft hood or vent before exhaust gases are mixed with dilution air. The installation of household carbon monoxide detectors is recommended.

Air Leakage — Determining Leakage Ratios and Leakage Coefficients

Using a blower door, measure the flow rate necessary to depressurize the building 50 Pascals. This flow rate is defined as CFM50. Alternatively, determine the Equivalent Leakage Area (EqLA) in square inches at 10 Pascals using the procedure outlined by the Canadian General Standards Board (or, alternatively, ASTM calculated at 4 Pascals). When determining these values, intentional openings (design openings) should be closed or blocked. These openings include fireplace dampers and fireplace glass doors, dryer vents, bathroom fans, exhaust fans, heat recovery ventilators (HRV's), wood stove flues, water heater flues, furnaces flues and combustion air openings.

Calculate the leakage ratio or the leakage coefficient using the entire surface area of the building enclosure. When determining the surface area of the building enclosure, below grade surface areas such as basement perimeter walls and basement floor slabs are included.

For example, a 2,550 square foot (777.2 m^2) house constructed in Grayslake, Ill., has a building enclosure surface areas of 6,732 square feet (2,051.9 m^2) and a conditioned space volume of 33,750 cubic feet (10,287 m^3) (including the basement). The measure Equivalent Leakage Area (EqLA) using a blower door is 128 square inches (325.1 cm^2). This also corresponds to a blower door measure CFM50 value of 1,320 cfm and a blower door measure 2.3 airchanges per hour at 50 Pascals.

Surface Area	EqLA	CFM50	ach@50 Pa	Volume
6,723 ft^2	128 i^{n2}	1,320 cfm	2.3	33,750 ft^3
(2,049.2 m^2)	(325.1 cm^2)	(402.3 cmm)		(10,287 m^3)

To determine the Leakage Ratio, divide the surface area of the building enclosure by 100 square feet and take this interim value and divide it into the EqLA.

$$\textbf{6,732 } ft^2 \div \textbf{100 } ft^2 = \textbf{67.32 (20.5 m}^2)$$
$$\textbf{128 } in^2 \div \textbf{67.32} = \textbf{1.9 } in^2/100 \ ft^2 \ (15.8 \ cm^2/m^2)$$
$$\text{(Leakage Ratio)}$$

II

To determine the Leakage Coefficient, divide the CFM50 value by the surface area of the building enclosure.

$$1,320 \text{ CFM50} \div 6,732 \text{ ft}^2 = 0.20 \text{ cfm/ft}^2$$
$$(402.3 \div 2,049.2 = 0.2 \text{ cmm/m}^2)$$
(Leakage Coefficient)

Many airtightness measurements are recorded as air changes per hour at a pressure differential of 50 Pascals (ach @ 50 Pa). To convert ach @ 50 Pa to CFM50, multiply the volume of the building enclosure (including the basement) by the ach @ 50 Pa and divide by 60 min/hour.

For example, 2.3 ach @ 50 Pa across the building enclosure of volume 33,750 ft^3 (10,287 m^3) is equivalent to a CFM50 value of 1,320 cfm.

$$33,750 \text{ ft}^3 \times 2.3 \text{ ach @ } 50 \text{ Pa} \div 60 \text{ min/hour} = 1,320 \text{ CFM50}$$

Ductwork Leakage

To determine the allowable limit for ductwork leakage, determine the rated air flow rate of the air handler, furnace, air conditioner, etc., at high speed from the manufacturer's literature. For example, a Carrier or Lennox or York heat pump system may have a high speed flow rate of 1,200 cfm across the blower according to the literature supplied with the unit. Ten percent of this value is 120 cfm. This 10 percent value becomes the ductwork leakage limit when the total air handling system is depressurized to 25 Pascals with a duct blaster.

II

Appendix III
Best Practices for High Performance Homes in All Climates

High performance homes must deal with the environmental loads imposed on them. That means controlling rain, groundwater, airflow, water vapor and heat flow.

The following Best Practices are recommended:

1. Process

Building Design, Systems Engineering, and Commissioning

- *Design for Energy Performance*
  Energy performance 40% better than the 2003 International Energy Conservation Code™ (IECC) base case house.

- *Systems Engineering*
  - Design structure using advanced framing methods.

  - Design structure to accommodate efficient duct distribution that locates all ducts and air handling equipment within conditioned space (see Part I: Design and Chapter 11: HVAC).

  - Design and detail structure for durability: exclude rain, control air, promote drying.

- *Commissioning – Performance Testing*
  - Air leakage (determined by blower door depressurization testing)

III

should be less than 2.5 square inches/100 square feet surface area leakage ratio (CGSB, calculated at a 10 Pa pressure differential); or 1.25 square inches/100 square feet leakage ratio (ASTM, calculated at a 4 Pa pressure differential); or 0.25 CFM/square foot of building enclosure surface area at a 50 Pa air pressure differential. If the house is divided into multiple conditioned zones, such as a conditioned attic or conditioned crawlspace, the blower door requirement must be met with the access to the space open, connecting the zones.

- Ductwork leakage to the exterior for ducts distributing conditioned air should be limited to 5.0 percent of the total air handling system rated airflow at high speed (nominal 400 CFM per ton) determined by pressurization testing at 25 Pa. Two acceptable compliance mechanisms are (1) test duct leakage to outside at finish stage, or (2) test total duct leakage at duct rough-in stage.

- Forced air systems that distribute air for heating and cooling should be designed to supply airflow to all conditioned spaces and zones (bedrooms, hallways, basements) as well as to provide a return path from all conditioned spaces or zones. Interzonal air pressure differences, when doors are closed, should be limited to 3 Pa. This can be achieved by installing properly sized transfer grilles or jump ducts (see also Chapter 11: HVAC).

- Mechanical ventilation system airflow should be tested during commissioning of the building.

- Testing of the house should be completed as part of the commissioning process. Unique or custom house plans should each be tested. In a production setting, each model type (i.e., floor plan) should be tested until two consecutive houses of this model type meet testing requirements. At this point, testing on this model type can be reduced to a sampling rate of 1 in 7 (i.e., 1 test, with 6 "referenced" houses). Small additions to a floor plan (e.g., bay window, conversion of den to bedroom) should be considered the same model type; major changes (e.g., bonus room over the garage, conversion of garage into a hobby room, etc.) should be considered a separate model type.

III

2. Site

Drainage, Pest Control, and Landscaping

- *Drainage* – Grading and landscaping shall be planned for movement of building run-off away from the home and its foundation, with roof drainage directed at least 3 feet beyond the building, and a surface grade of at least 5% maintained for at least 10 feet around and away from the entire structure.

- *Pest Control* – Based on local code and Termite Infestation Probability (TIP) maps, use environmentally-appropriate termite treatments, bait systems, and treated building materials that are near or have ground contact.

- *Landscaping* – Plantings should be held back as much as 3 feet and no less than 18 inches from the finished structure, with any supporting irrigation directed away from the finished structure. Decorative ground cover—mulch or pea stone, for example—should be thinned to no more than 2 inches for the first 18 inches from the finished structure.

3. Foundation

Moisture Control and Energy Performance

- *Moisture Control* - The building foundation should be designed and constructed to prevent the entry of moisture and other soil gases.
  - Semi-permeable rigid insulation should be used for both thermal control and vapor control beneath the slab—a 6-mil polyethylene vapor barrier is required if rigid insulation is not used here. Use either rigid insulation or poly, or both.

  - Sub-slab drainage should be enhanced with a granular drainage layer beneath the slab vapor barrier and thermal insulation.

  - Perimeter drainage should be used (see Chapter 6: Foundation Design)

  - Radon resistant construction practices as referenced in the ASTM Standard "Radon Resistant Design and Construction of New Low Rise Residential Buildings are recommended.

- *Energy Performance* – A foundation insulation system (type of insulation, location, thermal/air sealing/vapor permeability properties/fire rating) that controls the flow of heat **and** moisture is required for this climate (see Chapter 6: Foundation Design).

4. Enclosure

Moisture Control and Energy Performance

- *Moisture Control*
  - Water management - Roof and wall assemblies should contain ele-

ments that provide drainage in a continuous manner over the entire surface area of the building enclosure, including lapped flashing systems at penetrations.

- Vapor management – Roof and wall assemblies should contain elements that, individually and in combination, permit drying of interstitial spaces. Control of the first condensing surface by boosting the thermal resistance of exterior sheathing is recommended.

- *Energy Performance*
  - Air leakage - An interior air barrier—gypsum board is sealed to the slab and frame walls—is recommended (Airtight Drywall Approach) (see Chapter 3: Air Barriers).

  - Windows:
    - U-factor 0.35 or lower and SHGC (solar heat gain coefficient) 0.35 or less.

5. Mechanicals/Electrical/Plumbing

Systems Engineering, Energy Performance, Occupant Health and Safety, and Enclosure/Mechanicals Management

- *Systems Engineering*
  - HVAC system design, both equipment and duct, should be done as an integral part of the architectural design process.

  - HVAC system sizing should follow ACCA Manual J and duct sizing should follow Manual D (see Chapter 11: HVAC).

  - Mechanical ventilation should be an integral part of the HVAC system design; see Chapter 11: HVAC).

- *Energy Performance*
  - Air conditioner or heat pump of SEER 15 and HSPF of 9 or higher are recommended.

  - Energy Star rated appliances should be selected.

- *Occupant health and safety*
  - Base rate ventilation: controlled mechanical ventilation at a minimum base rate of 15 CFM per master bedroom and 7.5 CFM for each additional bedroom should be provided when the building is occupied.

  - Spot ventilation: intermittent spot ventilation of 100 CFM should be provided for each kitchen; all kitchen range hoods should be vented to the outside (no recirculating hoods). Intermittent spot ventilation of 50 CFM, or continuous ventilation of 20 CFM when

III

the building is occupied, should be provided for each washroom/bathroom.

- All combustion appliances in the conditioned space should be sealed combustion or power vented. Specifically, any furnace inside conditioned space should be a sealed-combustion 90%+ AFUE unit. Any water heater inside conditioned space should be power vented or power-direct vented. Designs that incorporate passive combustion air supply openings or outdoor supply air ducts not directly connected to the appliance should be avoided.

- Filtration systems for forced air systems at a MERV rating of 10 or higher are recommended.

- Indoor humidity should be maintained in the range of 25 to 60% by controlled mechanical ventilation, mechanical cooling, or dehumidification.

- Carbon monoxide detectors (hard-wired units) should be installed per code or at one per every approximate 1000 square feet in any house containing combustion appliances and/or an attached garage.

- Information relating to the safe, healthy, comfortable, energy efficient operation and maintenance of the building and systems that provide control over space conditioning, hot water, or lighting energy use should be provided to occupants.

- *Enclosure/Mechanicals Management*
  - Plumbing - No plumbing in exterior walls. Air seal around plumbing penetrations in pressure boundary (air barrier) such as rim (band) joist or ceiling (see Chapter 12: Plumbing).

  - Electrical - Seal around wires penetrating air barrier or pressure boundary (see Chapter 13: Electrical).

  - HVAC - Seal around penetrations in air barrier or pressure boundary (see Chapter 11: HVAC).

III

III

Appendix IV
SIPs for Severe Exposures

SIP assemblies by virtue of their unique properties such as air tightness, strength, portability, and assembly characteristics are often employed in somewhat unique applications such as pool enclosures, spa enclosures and in severe exposures such as the high Arctic and Antarctic regions.

In almost all of these "severe exposure applications" the vapor drive is from the interior to the exterior. Consider the worst possible exposure scenario – an indoor swimming pool at the North or South Pole. Yes, I know, that is pretty dumb, but if you wanted to do it you would do it using SIPs. Indoor swimming pool and spa enclosures anywhere else are pretty easy to construct by comparison. So, the following approach is based on a North or the South Pole indoor swimming pool exposure, and as such it will pretty much work anywhere for mixed climates and up (Climate Zones 4 and higher). Do not use this enclosure for refrigerated warehouses in hot-humid climates – or for that matter any refrigerated space anywhere.

The key to addressing extreme outward vapor drives is air tightness and vapor tightness at interior SIP surfaces coupled with exterior SIP surface vapor permeability and ventilated wall and roof claddings.

IV

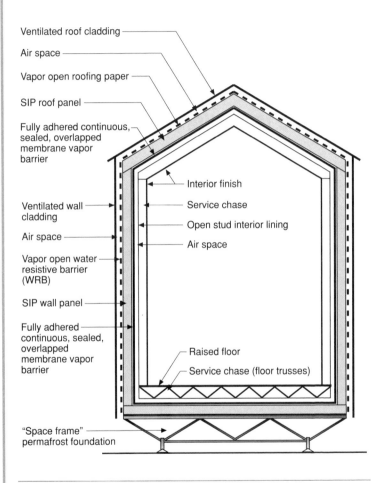

Ventilated roof cladding

Air space

Vapor open roofing paper

SIP roof panel

Fully adhered continuous, sealed, overlapped membrane vapor barrier

Interior finish

Service chase

Open stud interior lining

Ventilated wall cladding

Air space

Air space

Vapor open water resistive barrier (WRB)

SIP wall panel

Fully adhered continuous, sealed, overlapped membrane vapor barrier

Raised floor

Service chase (floor trusses)

"Space frame" permafrost foundation

Figure A.1
Severe Exposure Enclosure
- Arctic or antarctic locations
- Note the "inner" building constructed within the SIP enclosure; the "inner" building provides the spaces for services without penetrating the membrane vapor barrier

IV

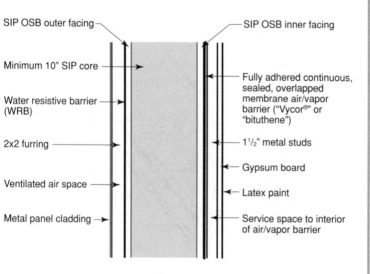

SIP OSB outer facing

SIP OSB inner facing

Minimum 10" SIP core

Fully adhered continuous, sealed, overlapped membrane air/vapor barrier ("Vycor®" or "bituthene")

Water resistive barrier (WRB)

2x2 furring

$1^1/_2$" metal studs

Gypsum board

Ventilated air space

Latex paint

Metal panel cladding

Service space to interior of air/vapor barrier

Figure A.2
Severe Exposure Wall
- Air barrier on interior wall
- Vapor barrier on interior wall
- Vapor open WRB on exterior
- Ventilated exterior cladding
- Service space to interior of air/vapor barrier

IV

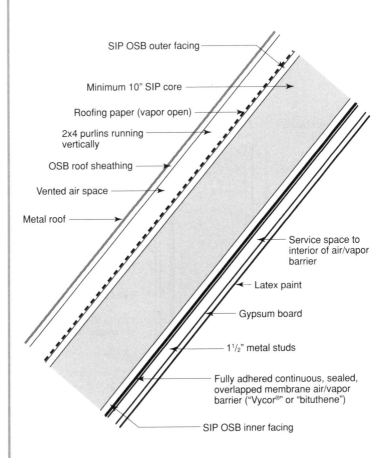

SIP OSB outer facing

Minimum 10" SIP core

Roofing paper (vapor open)

2x4 purlins running vertically

OSB roof sheathing

Vented air space

Metal roof

Service space to interior of air/vapor barrier

Latex paint

Gypsum board

1¹/₂" metal studs

Fully adhered continuous, sealed, overlapped membrane air/vapor barrier ("Vycor®" or "bituthene")

SIP OSB inner facing

IV

Figure A.3
Severe Exposure Roof
- Air barrier on interior roof
- Vapor barrier on interior roof
- Vapor open WRB on exterior
- Ventilated exterior roofing cladding
- Service space to interior of air/vapor barrier

Appendix V
Transfer Grille Sizing Charts

- Goal is to prevent pressurization of individual bedrooms when door is closed
- Maximum pressurization of 3 Pa (0.012 WIC) is recommended
- Transfer grille size is based on supply flow to room
- At master bedroom suite (or any other multi-room suite), supply flows must be totaled, and transfer grille sized based on that total

Given:

Door width: 32 inch (81.3 cm)

Door undercut: 0.5 inch (1.3 cm)

Transfer grille width: 10, 12, or 14 inches (25.4, 30.5 or 35.6 cm)

Net free area: 0.75 fraction of total grille area

Find: How high does the return air transfer grille have to be to meet the 3 Pa criteria?

Based on $Q = 1.07 \times A \times \Delta P^{1/2}$ for square edged orifice flow

where: Q = room supply flow (CFM)

    1.07 = constant, including unit conversions

    A = free area (in^2)

    ΔP = pressure difference between room and central area (Pa)

V

Transfer Grille Sizing Table (Imperial)

Room supply air flow	Net free area required	Area required after door undercut	Transfer grille height required for listed width in inches			Jump duct diameter required
			10	12	14	
(CFM)	(in²)	(in²)	(in)	(in)	(in)	(in)
50	27.0	11.0	1.5	1.2	1.0	3.7
75	40.5	24.5	3.3	2.7	2.3	5.6
100	54	38	5.1	4.2	3.6	7.0
125	67.4	51.4	6.9	5.7	4.9	8.1
150	80.9	64.9	8.7	7.2	6.2	9.1
175	94.4	78.4	10.5	8.7	7.5	10.0
200	107.9	91.9	12.3	10.2	8.8	10.8
225	121.4	105.4	14.1	11.7	10.0	11.6
250	134.9	118.9	15.9	13.2	11.3	12.3
275	148.4	132.4	17.7	14.7	12.6	13.0
300	161.9	145.9	19.4	16.2	13.9	13.6
325	175.4	159.4	21.2	17.7	15.2	14.2
350	188.9	172.9	23.0	19.2	16.5	14.8

V

Typical Free Area Measurements of Return Air Grilles (Imperial)

- Ameri-Flow Return Air Grilles
- Data from Grainger Catalog (2001)

Width (in)	Nominal Height (in)	Width (in)	Overall size Height (in)	Free area (in²)
10	6	11.5	7.5	51
12	6	13.5	7.5	61
12	12	13.5	13.5	121
14	6	15.5	7.5	71
14	14	15.5	15.5	163
20	20	21.5	21.5	336
30	6	31.5	7.5	153

V

Transfer Grille Sizing Table (Metric)

Room supply air flow	Net free area required	Area required after door undercut	Transfer grille height required for listed width in centimeters			Jump duct diameter required
			25.4	30.5	35.6	
(CFM)	(cm²)	(cm²)	(cm)	(cm)	(cm)	(cm)
50	68.6	22.9	3.8	3.0	2.5	9.4
75	102.9	62.2	8.4	6.9	5.8	14.2
100	137.2	96.5	13.0	10.7	9.1	17.8
125	171.2	130.6	17.5	14.5	12.4	20.6
150	205.5	164.8	22.1	18.3	15.7	23.1
175	239.8	199.1	26.7	22.1	19.0	23.1
200	274.1	233.4	31.2	26.0	22.3	25.4
225	308.4	267.7	35.8	29.7	25.4	29.5
250	342.6	302.0	40.4	33.5	28.7	31.2
275	376.9	336.3	45.0	37.3	32.0	33.0
300	411.2	370.6	49.3	41.1	35.3	34.5
325	445.5	404.9	53.8	45.0	36.6	36.1
350	479.8	439.2	58.4	48.8	41.9	37.6

V

Typical Free Area Measurements of Return Air Grilles (Metric)

- Ameri-Flow Return Air Grilles
- Data from Grainger Catalog (2001)

Width (cm)	Nominal Height (cm)	Width (cm)	Overall size Height (cm)	Free area (cm^2)
25.4	15.2	29.2	19.1	129.5
30.5	15.2	34.3	19.1	154.9
30.5	30.5	34.3	34.3	307.3
35.6	15.2	39.4	19.1	180.3
35.6	35.6	39.4	39.4	414.0
50.8	50.8	54.6	54.6	853.4
76.2	15.2	80.0	19.1	388.6

V

Appendix VI
Additional Resources

Organizations

Advanced Energy Corporation
909 Capability Drive
Suite 2100
Raleigh, NC 27606-3870
(919) 857-9000
www.advancedenergy.org

American Council for an Energy-Efficient Economy
1001 Connecticut Avenue, NW
Suite 801
Washington, DC 20036
Research and Conferences (202) 429-8873
Publications (202) 429-0063
www.aceee.org

American Society of Heating, Refrigeration and Air Conditioning
Engineers
1792 Tullie Circle, NE
Atlanta, GA 30329-2305
(404) 636-8400
www.ashrae.org

APA–The Engineered Wood Association
7011 South 19th Street
Tacoma, WA 98466
(253) 565-6600
help@apawood.org

Building Science Press
3 Lan Drive, Suite 102
Westford, MA 01886
(978) 589-5100
buildingscience.com

Energy and Environmental Building Association
6520 Edenvale Boulevard, Suite 112
Eden Prairie, MN 55346
(952) 881-1098
www.eeba.org

Florida Solar Energy Center
A Research Institute of the University of Central Florida
1679 Clearlake Road
Cocoa, FL 32992
(321) 638-1000
www.fsec.ucf.edu

Residential Energy Services Network
P.O. Box 4561
Oceanside, CA 92052-4561
(760) 806-3448
www.natresnet.org

Rocky Mountain Institute
1739 Snowmass Creek Road
Snowmass, CO 81654-9199
(303) 927-3851
www.rmi.org
www.natcap.org

Structural Insulated Panel Association
P.O. Box 39848
Fort Lauderdale, FL 33339
(253) 858-7472
www.sips.org

Southface Energy Institute
241 Pine Street
Atlanta, GA 30308
(404) 872-3549
www.southface.org

VI

U.S. EPA ENERGY STAR Buildings Program
U.S. EPA Atmospheric Pollution Prevention Division
401 M Street, SW (6202J)
Washington, DC 20460
(888) STAR-YES
www.epa.gov/energystar.html

Publications - Books

Building Air Quality
U.S. Environmental Protection Agency
Indoor Air Division
Office of Air and Radiation
Washington, DC 20460
(202) 564-7400

Building with Structural Insulated Panels (SIPs)
Morley, Michael
The Taunton Press
P.O. Box 5506
Newton, CT 06470

Canadian Home Builders' Association Builders Manual
Canadian Home Builders' Association
150 Laurier Avenue West
Suite 500
Ottawa, Ontario, Canada K1P 5J4
(613) 230-3060

Energy Source Directory: A Guide to Products Used in Energy Efficient
Construction
Iris Communications, Inc.
P.O. Box 5920
Eugene, OR 97405
(541) 484-9353

Understanding Ventilation: How to Design, Select and Install
Residential Ventilation Systems
Bower, J.
The Healthy House Institute
430 N. Sewell Road
Bloomington, IN 47408
(812) 332-5073

VI

Publications - Periodicals and Catalogs

Energy Design Update
> Cutter Information Corporation
> 37 Broadway
> Arlington, MA 02174
> (800) 964-5118

Environmental Building News
> R.R. 1
> Box 161
> Brattleboro, VT 05301
> (802) 257-7300

Fine Homebuilding
> The Taunton Press
> 63 S. Main Street, P.O. Box 5506
> Newtown, CT 04670-5506
> (203) 426-8171

Home Energy Magazine
> 2124 Kittredge Street
> No. 95
> Berkeley, CA 94704
> (510) 524-5405

Journal of Light Construction
> R.R. 2
> Box 146
> Richmond, VT 05477
> (800) 375-5981

Solplan Review
> Box 86627
> North Vancouver, British Columbia, Canada V7L 4L2
> (604) 689-1841

VI

Appendix VII
Glossary

Air Barrier Air barriers are systems of materials designed and constructed to control airflow between a conditioned space and an unconditioned space. The air barrier system is the primary air enclosure boundary that separates indoor (conditioned) air and outdoor (unconditioned) air. In multi-unit/townhouse/apartment construction the air barrier system also separates the conditioned air from any given unit and adjacent units. Air barrier systems also typically define the location of the pressure boundary of the building location. In multi-unit/townhouse/apartment construction the air barrier system is also the fire barrier and smoke barrier in inter-unit separations. In such assemblies the air barrier system must also meet the specific fire resi8tance rating requirement for the given separation.

Air barrier systems are assembled from "materials" incorporated in "assemblies" that are interconnected to create "enclosures." Each of these three elements has measurable resistance to airflow. The minimum resistance or air permeances for the three components are:

- Material $0.02 \ l/(s\text{-}m^2)@75 \ Pa$
- Assembly $0.20 \ l/(s\text{-}m^2)@75 \ Pa$
- Enclosure $2.00 \ l/(s\text{-}m^2)@75 \ Pa$

Materials and assemblies that meet these performance requirements are said to be air barrier materials and air barrier assemblies. Air barrier materials incorporated in air barrier assemblies that in turn are interconnected to create enclosures are called air barrier systems.

Air Barrier System An air barrier system is an assembly of materials that together are designed, installed, or act to control the flow of air across the building enclosure. The pressure boundary of the enclosure should, by definition, be coincident with the plane of the air barrier system. The complete air barrier system is comprised of materials and assemblies, each with their own performance requirements.

Air-impermeable A material or assembly having an air permeance equal to or less than 0.02 l/(s-m^2) @ 75 Pa tested according to ASTM E 2178 or E 283.

Air Retarder Materials and assemblies that do not meet the performance requirements of air barrier materials and air barrier assemblies and air barrier systems, but are nevertheless designed and constructed to control air flow are said to be air retarders.

Building Enclosure A building enclosure is an environmental separator. It separates the interior environment from the exterior environment. A building enclosure controls heat flow, air flow, water vapor flow, rain, groundwater, light and solar radiation, noise and vibrations, contaminants, environmental hazards and odors, insects, rodents and vermin, and fire. A building enclosure provides strength and rigidity and must be durable, aesthetically pleasing and economical.

Note: The enclosure is a special type of environmental separator. Environmental separators also exist within buildings as dividers between spaces with different environmental conditions.

Cold Roof A vented roof in any hygro-thermal zone.

Conditioned Space* The part of the building that is designed to be thermally conditioned for the comfort of occupants or for other occupancies or for other reasons.

Diffusion The movement of individual molecules through a material. The movement occurs because of concentration gradients and thermal gradients, independent of airflow.

Drainage Plane Drainage planes are water repellent materials (building papers, housewraps, foam insulations), which are designed and constructed to drain water. They are interconnected with flashings, window and door openings, and other penetrations of the building enclosures to provide drainage of water to the exterior of the building. The materials that form the drainage plane overlap each other shingle fashion or are sealed so that water flow is downward and outward.

Equivalent Leakage Area of a building (EqLA or ELA) Quantitative expression of the airtightness of a building enclosure. EqLA is the method set by the Canadian General Standards Board in which a blower door depressurizes the building enclosure to 10 Pascals and the leakiness of the enclosure is expressed as a summary hole in square inches. ELA is set by the ASTM equivalent procedure at a pressure differential of 4 Pascals. *See also* Builder's Guides Appendix II: Air Leakage Testing,

Pressure Balancing, and Combustion Safety for a complete discussion of these and other expressions of air leakage.

Expanded Polystyrene (EPS) Rigid foam insulation material commonly used as the core in structural insulated panels. EPS is a petroleum-based byproduct molded into large blocks for a variety of insulating purposes.

Foundation, Water-managed Systems for at or below-grade enclosure assemblies where gravity (drainage) is used to move liquid water away from the structure, relieving hydrostatic water forces. *See* Chapter 9: Foundations — Water Managed Foundations.

Grade Beam A foundation wall that is cast at or just below the grade of the earth, most often associated with the deepened perimeter concrete section in slab-on-grade foundations.

Habitable Space* Building space intended for continual human occupancy. Such space generally includes areas used for living, sleeping, dining, and cooking, but does not generally include bathrooms, toilets, hallways, storage areas, closets, or utility rooms.

Hot Roof An unvented roof in any hygro-thermal zone.

Housewrap Any of the numerous spun-fiber polyolefin rolled sheet goods, or perforated plastic films designed to function as drainage planes.

Indoor Air* Air in a conditioned space.

Jump Duct A flexible, short, U-shaped duct (typically 10-inch diameter) that connects a room to a common space as a pressure balancing mechanism. Jump ducts serve the same function as transfer grilles. Used when return ducts are not located in every room. *See also* Chapter 11: HVAC.

Kiln-dried Lumber Any lumber placed in a heated chamber or "shed" to reduce its moisture content to a specified range or average under controlled conditions. For softwood framing lumber, the moisture content of KD lumber is somewhat based on regional conventions but is most often an average of 12% by weight. In comparison, the moisture content of thoroughly air-dried softwood framing lumber is 15% to 20%.

Low-E Most often used in reference to a coating for high-performance windows, the "e" stands for emissivity or re-radiated heat flow. The thin metallic oxide coating increases the U-value of the window by reducing heat flow from a warm(er) air space to a cold(er) glazing surface. The best location for the coating is based on whether the primary heat flow you want to control is from the inside out (heating climates) or the outside in (cooling climates).

VII

Mechanical Ventilation Controlled, purposeful introduction of outdoor air to the conditioned space. *See also* Chapter 11: HVAC.

Occupiable Space* Any enclosed space inside the pressure boundary and intended for human activities, including but not limited to, all habitable spaces, toilets, closets, halls, storage and utility areas, and laundry areas.

Outdoor Air* Air outside the building.

Oriented Strand Board (OSB) is manufactured from waterproof heat-cured adhesives and rectangularly shaped wood strands that are arranged in cross-oriented layers, similar to plywood. This results in a structural engineered wood panel that shares many of the strength and performance characteristics of plywood.

Ozone O_3 instead of O_2. This 3-atom molecule is an even more active oxidizing agent than its more common 2-atom relative. At ground level, ozone is a pollutant and in the upper atmosphere it is a solar shield (location, location, location). Touted for its ability to "clean" air in room or household ozone generators, this application actually does more harm than good—ozone's highly reactive nature tends to accelerate the breakdown of synthetic materials in homes such as paints, plastics, and ever-available volatile organic compounds, often with less-than-desirable results. All told, we look to protect ozone in the heavens and shun it here at home, inside and out.

Permeance The physical property that defines the ease at which water molecules diffuse through a material. It is to vapor diffusion what conductance is to heat transfer. The unit of measurement is typically the "perm."

Pressure Boundary* The primary air enclosure boundary separating conditioned air and unconditioned air. Typically defined by the air barrier system. *See also* Air Barrier.

R-value Quantitative measure of resistance to heat flow or conductivity, the reciprocal of U-factor. The units for R-value are ft^2 °F hr/Btu (English) or m2 °K hr/W (SI or metric). While many in the building community consider R-value to be the primary or paramount indicator of energy efficiency, it only deals conduction, one of three modes of heat flow, (the other two being convection and radiation). As an example of the context in to which R-value should be placed, 25% to 40% of a typical home's energy use can be attributed to air infiltration.

VII

SIP Core Rigid insulation material that is sandwiched between structural skins to form a structural insulated panel (SIP). Core thicknesses and materials can vary based on application and insulation requirements.

SIP Spline Connection system used to connect two panels together at vertical, in-plane, joints. Many different spline systems are available, including surface spline, block spline, I-joist spline, dimensional lumber spline, and engineered lumber spline. The type of spline specified will depend on structural considerations and manufacturer preference.

Structural Insulated Panel (SIP) Structural Insulated Panels (SIPs) are sandwich panels and/or stress skin panels that contain a structural foam core insulation bonded to structural panel exterior and interior skins. The foam core in a SIP performs a structural, insulating and air-sealing function in wall, roof, and floor systems.

Thermal Boundary The layer in a building enclosure that controls the transfer of energy (heat) between the interior and the exterior. It is a component of the building enclosure and it may, but does not have to align with the pressure boundary.

U-factor Quantitative measure of heat flow or conductivity, the re-ciprocal of R-value. While building scientists will use R-values for measures of the resistance to heat flow for individual building materials, U-factor is always used as a summary measure for the conductive ener-gy measure of building enclosures.

Vapor Barrier A vapor barrier is a material that has a permeance of 0.1 perm or less. A vapor barrier is a material that is vapor imperme-able. A vapor barrier is a Class I vapor control layer. The test procedure for classifying vapor barriers is ASTM E-96 Test Method A—desiccant or dry-cup method.

Vapor Control Layer (or Layers) The element (or elements) that is (or are) designed and installed in an assembly to control the movement of water by vapor diffusion.

Language use example: "A Class III vapor control layer is used to man-age vapor flow in this assembly."

Vapor Impermeable Materials with a permeance of 0.1 perm or less (rubber membranes, polyethylene film, glass, aluminum foil)

Vapor Permeable Materials with a permeance of greater than 10 perms (housewraps, building papers)

Vapor Permeance Classes Test procedure for determining vapor permeance class is ASTM E-96 Test Method A—the desiccant or dry-cup method.

VII

Class I: Materials that have a permeance of 0.1 perm or less (**Note:** this is the definition of a "vapor barrier.")

Class II: Materials that have a permeance of 1.0 perm or less and greater than 0.1 perm (**Note:** This is the definition of a "vapor retarder.")

Class III: Materials that have a permeance of 10 perms or less and greater than 1.0 perm

Class IV: Materials that have a permeance greater than 10 perms

Vapor Retarder A vapor retarder is a material that has a permeance of 1.0 perm or less and greater than 0.1 perm. A vapor retarder is a material that is vapor semi-impermeable. A vapor retarder is a Class II vapor control layer. The test procedure for classifying vapor retarders is ASTM E-96 Test Method A — the desiccant or dry-cup method.

Vapor Semi-Impermeable Materials with a permeance of 1.0 perm or less and greater than 0.1 perm (oil-based paints, most vinyl coverings)

Vapor Semi-Permeable Materials with a permeance of 10 perms or less and greater than 1.0 perm (plywood, OSB, most latex-based paints)

Water Resistive Barrier A water resistive barrier (WRB) is also referred to as a drainage plane.

Wind-Washing The phenomenon of air movement that occurs due to wind entering building enclosures typically at the outside corners and roof eaves of buildings. Wind-washing can have significant impact on thermal and moisture movement and hence thermal and moisture performance of exterior wall assemblies.

Xeriscaping Climate-tuned landscaping that minimizes outdoor water use while maintaining soil integrity and building aesthetics. Typically includes emphasis on native plantings, mulching, and no or limited drip/subsurface irrigation.

Zero Energy House Any house that averages out to net zero energy consumption. A zero energy home can supply more than its needs during peak demand, typically using one or more solar energy strategies, energy storage and/or net metering. In a zero energy home, efficiencies in the building enclosure and HVAC are great enough that plug loads tend to dominate and so these homes must have the added focus of high efficiency appliances and lighting.

* ASHRAE Standard 62.2

Index